BETWEEN TWO CULTURES

BETWEEN TWO CULTURES

MIGRANTS AND MINORITIES IN BRITAIN

EDITED BY
James L. Watson

BASIL BLACKWELL · OXFORD

© Basil Blackwell 1977

First published 1977

Reprinted 1978
Reprinted 1979
Reprinted 1984

Basil Blackwell Publisher Ltd,
108 Cowley Road, Oxford OX4 1JF, UK

Basil Blackwell Inc.
432 Park Avenue South, Suite 1505,
New York, NY 10016, USA

British Library Cataloguing in Publication Data

Between two cultures.
  1. Minorities—Great Britain
  I. Watson, James Lee
  301.45′1′0941   DA125.A1

  ISBN 0-631-18300-0
  ISBN 0-631-18710-3 Pbk

Printed in Great Britain by
Billing & Sons Limited, Worcester

Contents

Editor's Preface

Anthropologists who work in complex societies have to be attuned to the wider political implications of their research. The essays in this volume deal with a number of sensitive and highly emotive social issues, including the effects of immigration on employment, housing, education, social services, and racial discrimination. The reader should be warned in advance, however, that anthropologists are not social workers or 'community relations' specialists. Few would presume to pass judgement on social policies or to make recommendations for the future of Britain as a 'multi-racial society'. Rather, the primary duty of the anthropologist, in my own opinion, is to publish and—whenever possible—to make his or her findings available to the wider public. This volume was conceived with that end in mind.

The current debates regarding immigration quotas, repatriation, and the entry of dependants constitute an integral part of the social environment in Britain. Accordingly, these issues are discussed in several of the following essays. But the book is not, and is not intended to be, about the politics of race relations in Britain. We hope that by treating the subject with the dispassionateness proper to academic inquiry we shall have contributed to fuller and more informed discussion of these issues. Only thus can we understand the actual processes of immigration and the real meaning of ethnic identity.

The title of this book, *Between Two Cultures*, was suggested by the work of Nancy Foner and Verity Saifullah Khan. Two of the papers (chapters two and seven) were presented, in much abbreviated form, at a conference on ethnicity sponsored by the Royal Anthropological Institute.

Chapters three and eleven were discussed at research seminars held in London at the School of Oriental and African Studies. The editor wishes to thank various friends and colleagues for the help and encouragement they offered during the preparation of this volume: Abner Cohen, Gaynor Cohen, Mark Hobart, Igor Kopytoff, Adrian Mayer, David Parkin, and Rubie Watson. They, of course, bear no responsibility for the views and interpretations expressed in the Introduction or in any of the chapters. Expert secretarial assistance was provided by Yvonne Turnbull.

J. L. Watson
SOAS, London, March 1977

CHAPTER 1

JAMES L. WATSON

Introduction: Immigration, Ethnicity, and Class in Britain

This volume represents the work of twelve anthropologists who have studied ethnic minorities in Britain. It contains original essays on the following people: Sikhs, Pakistanis, Montserratians, Jamaicans, West Africans, Chinese, Italians, Poles, Greek Cypriots, and Turkish Cypriots. The selection is largely arbitrary. Our purpose is not to present an exhaustive catalogue of British minorities; had this been true, it would have been necessary to include studies of Jews, Arabs, Maltese, Irish, East African Asians, Gypsies, and many others (see e.g., Dahya 1965; Dench 1975; Freedman 1955; Jeffery 1976; Michaelson 1976; Swinerton 1975). Instead, we have tried to illustrate—with appropriate case studies—the range and diversity of peoples now settled in Britain. This book is aimed at a general audience; readers with specialised interests should consult the bibliographies for more detailed analyses.

Some of these studies focus on migrants who conceive of themselves as temporary sojourners, working only for the day when they can retire in comfort to their home villages. Others deal with settlers who have no intention of returning to their country of origin, either because of political circumstances at home (Poles and Greek Cypriots) or financial commitments in Britain (Turkish Cypriots). Besides making the volume more representative, the inclusion of several European minorities provides a comparative perspective so often missing from surveys of ethnic relations in Britain. Many observers automatically equate 'immigrants' with 'coloured' peoples who trace their origins to South Asia or the Caribbean. Skin-colour is obviously of great significance in determining how migrants are treated in England, Scotland, and Wales; but, as many contributors demonstrate, it must not be assumed that White minorities are 'absorbed' or 'assimilated' without a trace—even after several generations. For non-Europeans on the otherhand, assimilation is rarely a matter of choice. Racism is the single most important fact of life for large numbers of South Asian and Caribbean peoples in Britain. One cannot understand the history and character of these minorities without analysing their differing reactions to White racism (see especially chapters two and five).

Each of the following essays constitutes a separate study; the projects were all conducted on an independent basis. This volume is not, therefore, the result of team research. Anthropologists are notorious mavericks and, even if they agree to focus on a specific problem in advance, the research situation itself invariably dictates a flexible approach. Unlike other social scientists, therefore, fieldworking anthropologists cannot plan their research strategies with great precision until *after* they have begun. In this context, 'fieldwork' means an intensive, long-term (usually 12 months or more) study of a specific group in its own setting—be it a traditional village, an isolated atoll, or the London Borough of Hackney. There are special problems involved when one's 'field' is located in modern cities (see Foster and Kemper 1974), but first-hand research is still the primary technique employed by urban anthropologists.

A unique feature of this collection is that all contributors have had field experience at *both* ends of the migration chain, in the migrants' own country of origin and in Britain. This was a major criterion for recruitment into the project. Although some might disagree, my own experience leads me to conclude that it is impossible to gain a true picture of immigration as a *process* without investigating the people and their families on both sides (Watson 1974). Half of the contributors started their research in Britain and soon realised that they would have to visit the migrants' home society before their studies could really be considered complete. Conversely, the other half began their projects as conventional village studies in widely scattered parts of the world. Only after following some of the villagers abroad did they end up in Britain. For some of us, therefore, our interest in British society is a secondary development from other research. No matter which side of the migration chain is emphasised, the dual perspective gives the essays a depth often lacking in studies of British migrants. Much of the earlier literature in this field is based on surveys undertaken by social scientists who had little, if any, knowledge of the migrants' backgrounds. It is still possible, even in 1977, to read of social surveys that proceed, with breathtaking naïveté, from the assumption that Pakistanis, Indians, and West Indians share the same basic 'black family system'. One of the purposes of the present volume is to provide reliable information on the backgrounds of various minorities in Britain. This information is presented, insofar as possible, in a nontechnical manner—free of unnecessary jargon.

Even though the contributors pursue their own arguments, a number of central themes emerge. Perhaps the most important is indicated by the book's title: 'Between Two Cultures'. Many of the people discussed, especially those who were born in Britain, are caught between the cultural expectations of their parents (the first-generation migrants) and the social demands of the wider society. Young Sikhs and Jamaicans, for instance, often feel that they do not 'fit' in either culture (see chapters two and five). Largely in response to racism, these two minorities have begun a process of ethnic redefinition—or 'creolisation' to borrow a term from the Caribbean specialists—which entails the active recreation of a new cultural tradition that only has meaning in the British context. Other people, notably the Italians and the Turkish Cypriots, have not been subjected to the same degree of racism or xenophobia as the Sikhs and Jamaicans but, nonetheless, a separate cultural tradition has emerged in each case. Turkish Cypriots in London are not English, nor are they like Mainland Turks or Turks in Cyprus; similarly London's Italians are distinct from their relatives in Italy and from their English friends (see chapters nine and eleven).

Effects of Emigration: The Other Side

Another theme covered in this volume is the effect of emigration on the migrants' home societies. Many of Britain's minority peoples originated in specialised villages with economies which are dependent on money from abroad. These are 'emigrant communities', a term used by anthropologists to designate any village or town that relies on remittances for at least half of its regular income (see Chen 1939, Watson 1975). In order to avoid confusion, this label is usually reserved for villages with high rates of international emigration as opposed to internal, or rural-to-urban, migration. Migrants from these settlements retain close ties to the kinsmen they leave behind, even after years of residence abroad.

A comparison of the essays in this volume, along with other studies available (e.g. Chen 1939; Dahya 1974; Gonzales 1969; Lewis 1968), reveals that certain uniform features emerge as a consequence of emigration. Emigrant communities almost invariably experience a housing boom as returnees invest their savings in new dwellings. In Hong Kong they are known as 'sterling houses' (after the remittances that pay for their construction) and in India, they are called '*pakka* houses' ('brick-built' or 'good'). Other acts of conspicuous consumption, notably those relating to wedding ceremonies and public philanthropy, are commonly undertaken by successful migrants in their home communities. However, as several contributors illustrate, it is wrong to assume that emigrants always act like agents of 'modernisation' or 'westernisation'. Philpott (see chapter four) has argued that 'returned migrants produce very little social or economic innovation' in Montserrat (1973:190). In my own study (Watson 1975:213–18) I discovered that Chinese emigrants are often the most outspoken proponents of traditional values and that their experiences abroad sometimes reinforce conservative attitudes.

By focusing on both sides of the migration chain, anthropologists are able to highlight the inherent fragility of emigrant communities. A dependence on remittances means that the village economy is particularly susceptible to economic fluctuations in Britain. Furthermore, many emigrant communities have become so specialised that residents are no longer able to compete in the local society (see chapter seven). The ever-increasing restrictions against Commonwealth immigration in Britain threatens the very survival of these villages.

Settlers, Sojourners, and Refugees

As noted earlier, the term 'immigrant' now carries a pejorative connotation in British English (foreign visitors learn very quickly that, in colloquial usage, 'immigrant' means 'coloured newcomer'). White workers who have emigrated from Europe are particularly sensitive about being called 'immigrants' since, in their view, this is tantamount to slander (see chapter eleven). Not surprisingly, British citizens who came originally from South Asia and the Caribbean object strenuously to being categorised as 'immigrants', especially those who have settled here. In order to avoid confusion, therefore, many of the contributors use the term 'migrant' to describe the people they studied. Even that designation must be used with care, however, because it obviously does not apply to the British-born second generation. As might be imagined, the selection of an appropriate title for this volume was a difficult task indeed. 'Migrants and Minorities' is a compromise that emerged only after months of debate.

In all studies of migration, one must distinguish between 'settlers' who intend to remain permanently abroad and 'sojourners' who plan to return to their home society upon retirement (cf. Dayha 1973). It is not always possible to sort out the sojourners from the settlers, however, because they commonly share a 'myth of return' (see chapters two through five). Another factor to consider is choice: many people who have settled in Britain, such as the Poles described in chapter eight, came originally as refugees, or 'exiles' to use Sheila Patterson's term (1961).

The classic example of the sojourner is the Chinese merchant who retires in his home village after spending most of his life working abroad. Rose Lee captures the essence of this life style in her study of the American Chinese: 'a sojourner is a person whose mental orientation is towards the home country. [He] spends a major portion of his lifetime striving ... for economic betterment and higher status, but the full enjoyment and final achievement of his objective is to be in his place of origin' (Lee 1960:69). To a large extent, the Chinese restaurant workers in Britain maintain a similar orientation (see chapter seven). The West African migrants, described by Goody and Groothues constitute a special category of sojourners—often referred to in official circles as 'educational transients'. African students come to Britain with the express purpose of acquiring credentials which they can use to great advantage at home. Although they may not intend to stay more than a few years, the high cost of education inevitably prolongs the sojourn. In the meantime, many choose to have their children fostered by White English families. The problems that arise from this traditional custom are detailed in chapter six. Some of the children are quite literally caught 'in between' as their parents and their English guardians fight custody battles in the courts.

Before moving on to other issues, it might be noted that the migrant categories discussed above all relate to international emigration. Migration within a single society, usually referred to as internal migration, has different consequences (see chapter seven). It is often assumed that internal migration is a necessary prelude, or stepping stone, to international emigration. According to this view, villagers must first move to a nearby city before acquiring the expertise and sophistication necessary for emigration. In fact, most of Britain's first-generation migrants came directly from rural areas; Kingston, Karachi, and Kowloon are often less familiar to them than London, Leeds, or Liverpool. The rural-urban dichotomy so prevalent in third world countries is reflected in the politics of Britain's minorities. With few exceptions, the self-proclaimed 'immigrant spokesmen' or 'community leaders' are highly-educated, middle-class migrants from larger cities; the mass of ordinary workers are preoccupied with their own affairs and usually have little in common with these leaders (see chapters on the Sikhs, Pakistanis, Chinese, Greek Cypriots, and Turkish Cypriots).

The Causes of Migration

Although their writings sometimes obscure this fact, social scientists have found it very difficult to explain the causes of migration movements. One of the most popular methods of explanation is to use a 'push-pull' model which distinguishes between the 'push' of economic necessity in the migrants home society and the 'pull' of opportunity from abroad (see e.g., Jansen 1970; Wrong 1961). The difficulty with this approach is that it obscures the inherent complexity of population movements and, as some critics have pointed out (Douglass 1970), it often treats the subjects as if they were automatons reacting to forces beyond their control. Ceri Peach, in his study of West Indian migration to Britain (1968), warns against relying too much on 'push' determinism. The movements he describes did not take place during periods of economic depression in the Caribbean and they were not correlated to high rates of population growth. Peach concludes that there is 'strong evidence for the view that [West Indian] migration was reacting not to internal conditions, but to a single external stimulus'—namely the demand for labour in Britain (1968:93). This conclusion might be satisfactory if one wishes to leave the analysis at the highest levels of abstraction, but generalisations of this nature are rarely accepted by the migrants themselves. Furthermore, anthropologists who have reconstructed the history of various emigrant communities demonstrate clearly that it is impossible to categorise all of the relevant factors as either 'push' or 'pull' (Philpott 1973; Watson 1975; Foner and Palmer, Chapters in this volume).

After the initial movement has begun and the local economies have readjusted, emigration often becomes routinised. The village of San Tin, located in rural Hong Kong, is a good case in point. In the late 1950s, San Tin's agricultural economy collapsed as a result of a change in Hong Kong's rice market. The local farmers were forced to seek employment elsewhere but they would not accept the low status, and poorly paid, jobs available in the cities nearby. Instead, they chose to emigrate and take advantage of a restaurant boom that was beginning in Britain at this time. By 1962, the village had made the transition to a remittance economy; eighty-five to ninety per cent of the male residents now work abroad, primarily in Britain and Holland. Emigration soon became a way of life for residents of San Tin and the contemporary restaurant workers are less influenced by the 'push' or 'pull' factors that affected their predecessors. One migrant summed it up accordingly: 'In some villages everyone grows rice for a living, but in San Tin we are all emigrants. That's what we do best' (Watson 1975).

What is Ethnicity?

Ethnicity is a term that reappears in many contexts throughout this volume. Limitations of space permit only a brief exposition on the meaning of this term and its use in the social sciences (for more thorough coverage see Barth 1969; Cohen 1974a; Glazer and Moynihan 1975; Morris 1968). The views expressed here are my own—I do not claim to speak for the other contributors. First of all, 'ethnicity' is not, as some critics have suggested, simply a euphemism for 'race'. Physical appearance is only one of many possible criteria that can serve as the basis for ethnic divisions. In any case, definitions of 'race', like 'colour', vary widely according to the perceptions and social expectations of the beholder. American visitors find it strange that the English categorise South Asians as 'coloured peoples'; in the United States, the same individuals would be classified as 'caucasians'. Anthropologists are concerned with *social* divisions that may or may not be based on physical differences. In Northern Ireland, for instance, religion is the primary source of friction. The Chinese, on the other hand, are basically indifferent to religious affiliation, but they are acutely aware of subtle differences in dialect and draw ethnic boundaries accordingly ('ethnic wars' between speakers of Cantonese and Hakka were once common in South China).

Some scholars have argued that ethnicity is a reflection of 'primordial loyalties' (e.g., Isaacs 1975). This view has been severely criticised because it assumes that people have primal and unchanging attachments to a particular social category—however that category is defined. The primordial loyalty approach is ultimately as much of a dead end as earlier theories based on racial determinism. Anthropologists have demonstrated repeatedly that people tend to create alliances and change loyalties according to their own best interests (Cohen 1974b; Parkin 1974; O. Patterson 1975).

A more fruitful line of analysis is what might be called the 'political approach' to ethnicity. The best example of this is found in the work of Abner Cohen, a specialist on West African societies. His classic study, *Custom and Politics in Urban Africa* (1969), is one of the clearest expositions on ethnicity available in the anthropological literature. Briefly summarised, Cohen argues that alliances based on ethnicity function like 'informal interest groups' and are therefore best seen as political entities; they operate through the idiom of shared 'custom', or what other anthropologists might call 'culture' (1969:5). In the Nigerian city of Ibadan, Hausa migrants have manipulated their cultural distinctiveness 'in order to develop an informal political organisation which [they use] as a weapon in [their] struggle for power with other groups' (Cohen 1969:ix). The vocabulary of struggle and competition recurs in all of the subsequent work inspired by Cohen's approach.

Ethnicity in this context only has meaning when two or more groups are interacting and competing for control over scarce resources (Parkin 1974:119). A good illustration is the scramble for political and economic power that followed the Black Power movement in the United States (Glazer and Moynihan 1975). White Americans, most of whom were thought to have disappeared into the melting pot, began to stress their immigrant heritage and an 'ethnic revival' spread rapidly throughout the country. One can see evidence of this in the most unlikely places: People in a small midwestern town began to call themselves 'Belgian-Americans' and the local merchants now display 'Being Belgian is Beautiful' posters in their shops. Until recently, the European origins of this town had been a matter of complete indifference to local residents; they had not even retained an ethnic church or a distinctive cuisine like the Swedish-Americans in a neighbouring town.

This revival was inspired primarily by the federal government's campaign to elevate, through affirmative action, disadvantaged minorities in other parts of the country—Blacks, Puerto Ricans, Chicanos, and Amerindians. The farmers in question are careful to explain that they have nothing against these minorities, but they deeply resent the fact that 'Belgian-Americans' do not benefit from this redistribution of wealth. In response, many White midwesterners have formed ethnic associations and they are now applying for federal funds to support their activities.

The political manoeuvres of American farmers may seem rather remote from the problems of Jamaican bus drivers in

London or Sikh factory workers in Leeds. British readers are likely to find the next example to be of more immediate relevance. Following is an excerpt from the Letters To The Editor section of the *Sunday New York Times* (29 August 1976):

To my surprise I found the other day the Association for Indians in America Inc., a New York based non-profit organization claiming to represent immigrants from India, loudly protesting against the categorization of Indians as Caucasians by the Federal Interagency Commission. The principal thrust of the protest was that if classified as Caucasians or whites, Indians would be ineligible for consideration in affirmative action programs which assist members of other minority groups like Asian-Americans, blacks, Hispanics, American Indians, etc. In its drive to seek minority status for Asian-Indians, the organization is ready to deny the racial heritage of the people it is supposed to represent, and to my mind, it is the height of political opportunism.

I happen to be an Indian resident of the United States for almost two decades... It is time Indians abroad, especially in the United States, merged with the mainstream ... [we should] not walk with the motley crowd of the minorities motivated by economic and material interests. The diversified cultural heritage that Indians possess will always set them apart as a distinctive ethnic group from their other Caucasian brothers.

Although the potential for conflict is always present, it is clear that ethnic divisions vary greatly in terms of intensity and hostility. As Cohen observes, 'there is ethnicity and ethnicity'; it cannot be measured, yet there is an obvious difference between the ethnic consciousness generated by a group of Latvians who meet periodically to dance in London and the ethnic allegiance manifested by Northern Ireland Catholics (1974a:xiv). Another factor to bear in mind is that ethnicity can change or be modified according to political and economic circumstances. Sarah Ladbury provides an excellent illustration of this in her essay on the Turkish Cypriots (chapter eleven). Turks in London are economically dependent on Greek Cypriot employers and, hence, they go out of their way to dampen ethnic hostilities that could aggravate relations between the two communities. The recent Cyprus conflict has made this task more difficult but Turks and Greeks in Britain remain on speaking terms.

There is also a fundamental distinction to be drawn between ethnic *groups* and ethnic *categories* (see Morris 1968). Welsh in England and Scots in Canada may represent identifiable categories but, unless they interact on a regular basis or form an association, it is unlikely they will ever constitute a group. Some manifestations of ethnicity actively militate against the formation of groups. Geoff Dench shows in his book, *The Maltese in London* (1975), how an entire ethnic category can be stigmatised by the criminal activities of a few people. Rather than uniting as a group to combat this image, the Maltese have denied their cultural heritage and opted for total assimilation. Dench's study is appropriately subtitled 'A Case Study in the Erosion of Ethnic Consciousness'. Similar reactions to unfavourable publicity have occurred in North America (e.g., among Italian immigrants who resent being identified with the mafia); however, if these examples are any guide, it would be premature to enter the London Maltese in a register of extinct ethnic categories. Should it ever prove to be in their own interests, we might expect to see a revival of Maltese ethnicity.

Immigration and Class: The Marxist Approach

During the 1960s, 'race relations' was a subject that received a great deal of attention in British academic circles. The results can be found in an impressive monograph series published through the auspices of the Institute of Race Relations in London. Many of these studies were inspired by the pioneering work of Kenneth Little (1948), Michael Banton (1955), and Sheila Patterson (1963). Banton and Patterson argued that Black migrants from Africa and the Caribbean would eventually be absorbed into the indigenous working class, much like the Irish and Jews before them. The 'assimilation approach' dominated the field of ethnic studies until the late 1960s and, even today, its influence can be seen in government policy (the May, 1976 issue of *Race Today: The Voice of the Black Community in Britain* contains an advertisement for an 'Immigrant Assimilation Officer', placed by the London Borough of Hackney).

The excessive optimism of the 'race relations industry', as

it is called by detractors, soon generated a wave of critical literature. It is perhaps ironic that the most outspoken of these critiques is published in the same IRR monograph series, now under different management. This book, *Immigrant Workers and Class Struggle in Western Europe* (Castles and Kosack 1973), warrants close inspection because it is widely heralded as the Marxist answer to the assimilationists. Castles and Kosack argue that one must start by analysing the economic position of migrant workers; they expressly reject ethnicity and racism as determining factors (1973:2). Furthermore, they are critical of studies that accept the migrants' own definition of their position:

Immigrants [in Europe] should be looked at not in the light of their specific group characteristics—ethnic, social, and cultural—but in terms of their actual social position. Immigrant workers have come to form part of the class structure of the [host] countries (p. 5)...In objective terms [they] belong to the working class. But within this class they form a bottom stratum, due to the subordinate status of their occupations (p. 6–7).

Emigration must be understood, according to the authors, in the context of international capitalism: it nurtures the European elite but does nothing to alleviate the backwardness of the sending societies. In their view, 'labour migration is a form of development aid given by poor countries to rich countries' (*Ibid.*:8). The presence of a 'bottom stratum' also gives the indigenous working class the illusion of social mobility and material advancement, thus eroding class consciousness. Castles and Kosack conclude on the orthodox Marxian note that the ruling classes in Europe actively manipulate the concept of race in order to divide the working class (*Ibid.*: 450–6).

There are some compelling insights here but, in my own view, Castles and Kosack's main thesis is seriously flawed. Their approach completely ignores the differences between groups and it treats 'the immigrants' as if they were a uniform, faceless mass of new proletarians. Ethnicity is conveniently dismissed as a manifestation of 'false consciousness'. In this model, nefarious ruling classes (never defined) take the place of 'push' and 'pull' forces; migrants are thus the pawns in a game they neither control nor understand. Castles and

Kosack make the same error that characterised the work of many assimilationists: South Asians, West Indians, Turks, Greeks, Italians, Chinese, and Arabs are all thought to have only one goal—to join the British working class. The fact that thousands of migrants treat their working-class jobs as stepping stones to self employment is never considered. Furthermore, it is a fallacy to argue that the migrants' own cultural predispositions and personal attitudes are irrelevant. Ethnicity cannot be reduced to excess baggage that will somehow disappear on the road to a 'rational' or classless society.

The polemical tone of Castles and Kosack's book may lead some to dismiss their entire argument without a fair hearing. Lest I be accused of throwing the baby out with the bath water, I would like to make my position clear. There *is* evidence in Britain that migrants sometimes suppress differences and align themselves on the basis of class, particularly in voting behaviour (Anwar 1975). Anthropologists are not irrevocably attached to ethnicity as the motivating factor in all group interactions; many have worked in cities where class takes precedence over ethnic ties even though migrants make up the bulk of the population (see e.g., Robins 1975).

Castles and Kosack are most convincing when they discuss the economic impact of migration on the sending societies. They argue, rightly in my opinion, that remittances never really improve the balance of payments between the countries involved and that the money is seldom reinvested in productive activities (1973:416–9; see also Bellini 1974–5:9). Remittances generally improve the living standards of dependants left at home but, as noted earlier, the net result is a local economy highly susceptible to recessions in Europe. Labour recruitment is another topic that the authors treat with considerable insight. They argue that migrants are admitted because they are willing to take the jobs indigenous workers refuse to accept (1973:6). London Transport (buses and underground railways) set up a recruiting office in Barbados during the mid-1950s to attract and assist prospective employees. The Island thus became a reliable source of labour through the boom years of the 1960s (Brooks 1975: 257). A subsequent rise of unemployment in Britain has solved London Transport's labour problems and the office is now closed. French authorities also encourage and facilitate emigration from their West Indian *départements*, in part to relieve the welfare burden of these dependent territories but primarily to build up labour reserves. West Indian women are always in demand as domestics in France (Goossen 1976: 48–9).

And finally, it cannot be denied that Castles and Kosack have some basis for arguing that management benefits when workers divide their loyalties on ethnic rather than class lines. In Bradford, for instance, Asian factory workers often find themselves in all-Pakistani night shifts (see chapter three); inevitably this makes union activities more difficult to coordinate. However, the problem is not as clear-cut as Castles and Kosack would have it. Whether or not the managers are to blame for manipulating 'false consciousness', White union leaders are often the focus of minority hostility during industrial disputes. In 1974, South Asian workers at the Imperial Typewriter Company in Leicester went on strike. The dispute soon took on the characteristics of an ethnic drama, played out in full view of television cameras. The factory employed 1650 workers, 1100 of whom were Asian women recently expelled from East Africa. Their White-dominated union refused to intervene and the dispute lasted for months (see Runnymede Trust 1974–5: 32–4). Cases like this occur often enough in Britain to warrant a more thorough investigation.

Many critics have argued that if social anthropology is to survive as a separate discipline it must adapt itself to the study of modern, complex societies (see e.g., Cohen 1974b: 10). This is a rather pessimistic view and not everyone would agree. Yet, for those who do, there can be no better place to start than the factories of Leicester and Bradford. Only then can we begin to sort out the interconnections between class and ethnicity in a convincing manner. To date, most anthropologists—including the contributors to this volume—have not really come to grips with the problem of class in complex societies.

Research Problems and Prospects

Anthropologists who choose to work in their own societies face a special set of problems. Instead of making the research easier, quite the opposite is often true. The greatest difficulty is maintaining one's perspective as an outside observer. Few can claim to be 'detached' or 'dispassionate' no matter where they work; anthropologists are, after all, only human. However the outsider's perspective is essential because, without it, fieldworkers may ignore certain problems as being too obvious or commonplace to warrant attention. The English perception of ethnic categories is a good example. As noted earlier, foreigners sometimes have difficulty understanding the colloquial usage of 'coloured', 'Black', and 'Asian'. Yet, few anthropologists who have worked in Britain have bothered to delve into this classificatory system and map out its organising principles. Why, for instance, are the Chinese not categorised as 'coloured' or 'Asian' (see chapter seven)? Under what circumstances, if any, do Sikhs, Mirpuri Muslims, Gujarati Hindus, Sinhalese Buddhists, and Goan Christians who live in this country define themselves as 'Asian'? The Ballards show that a pan-Asian consciousness appeared in the wake of an ethnically-inspired murder, but this lasted for only a short time (see chapter two). Michael Banton found that many English could not distinguish between South Asians and African Blacks during the early years of mass immigration. To illustrate, he cites a case in which a Nigerian was asked by his English foreman to interpret for Pakistani work mates (Banton 1967:374). The English are not unique in this regard: most Chinese restaurant workers in Britain do not bother to make fine distinctions between their customers, except to pigeonhole them as 'Black' (good tippers), 'European-White' (medium tippers), and 'Indian' (bad tippers). The point is that the Chinese waiters, and some English foremen, do not always *need* to be aware of subtle distinctions. Ethnic classification systems are like social barometers; they reflect the dominant mode of interaction between people and groups.

Another topic that anthropologists have almost completely ignored is the organisation and maintenance of professional elites within (or outside?) the minority communities in Britain. Several contributors discuss the intermediary role of leaders (see chapters two, three, seven, and ten) but no one, to my knowledge, has yet undertaken a full-scale study of minority professionals. This category includes doctors, solicitors, lecturers, teachers, and corporate executives among others; sociologists would probably classify them all as 'middle-class' on the basis of their occupations. Until we have detailed ethnographic accounts focusing on the life styles of these professionals it would be unwise to generalise. However, studies of this nature may give us new insights into the British class system.

And finally, it may seem obvious to many readers that a major dimension—some would say the most important of all —is missing from this collection of essays. We have not included studies that examine the attitudes, beliefs, and ethnic identities of the British *majority*. Anthropologists are clearly guilty of overspecialisation; their energies are directed almost exclusively to the problems of ethnic minorities in Britain. It is time to look at the other side of the picture. A number of younger fieldworkers are already engaged in studies of the 'White backlash', including at least one survey of the National Front. These investigations are important and I, for one, await publication of the results with great anticipation. Of course, the National Front and other organised 'anti-immigration' movements are only one aspect of a larger problem. The real challenge is to determine how the ethnic minorities have sparked a reaction in the general society (Ballard 1976:200). We do not know, for instance, whether the recent success of the Scottish nationalists and the Plaid Cymru movement (Welsh nationalists) is in any way related to the appearance of organised lobbies for 'coloured' minorities in Britain.

Maurice Freedman, the late Professor of Social Anthropology at Oxford, once observed that the English do not have much respect for anglicised outsiders, but they appreciate foreigners who adhere to their indigenous culture. He suggests that this may be a consequence of Britain's colonial heritage (Freedman 1955:242). On the face of it, many would probably agree with Freedman's observation. It strikes a responsive chord. And yet, if this is true, how does one account for the obvious hostility that some English have shown toward minority workers who have experienced an 'ethnic revival' and readopted the cultural symbols of their forefathers (see e.g., Beetham 1970)? On a related issue, Michael Banton ventures some interesting views about the way Britons treat new arrivals who wish to assimilate. According to Banton (1967:371–2), migrants are socialised to become 'British' by implicit norms and tacit modes of instruction. This is quite distinct from the American approach which turns 'foreigners' into 'Yanks' by explicit, on-the-surface corrective socialisation ('Don't dress like that, it looks stupid. Don't hold your knife and fork that way, watch me.') The use of an 'unspoken code', Banton suggests, is particularly true of the middle and upper classes in Britain; and, hence, it may be easier for migrants to gain entrance into the working class (1967:372).

Assuming that Banton is correct, what are the implications? Does this mean that, in order to be middle-class *and* 'British', an immigrant has to shed all vestiges of his cultural heritage? Why are there no 'hyphenated subcultures' in Britain, like those one finds in the United States (e.g., Swedish-American, Japanese-American, etc.)?

The work presented in this volume, therefore, is only the starting point for broader studies of British society. The people under scrutiny represent a significant proportion of Britain's population, but they are still *minorities* in the strict demographic sense of the term. Many, like the Chinese, have managed to keep themselves remarkably insulated from contacts with the British majority. One cannot assume, however, that Hong Kong villagers react to British society in this way 'because they are Chinese'; this particular adaptation is largely a reflection of opportunities in Britain. Similarly, the reappearance of turbans among British-born Sikhs and the attraction of reggae music to West Indian youths cannot be understood by looking for internal causes. Both are quite obviously consequences of *inter*ethnic relations: turbans and reggae are symbols of separatism designed to distinguish 'us' from 'them'. By implication, therefore, the essays that follow tell us as much about Britain as a 'host society' as they do about the minority peoples themselves.

REFERENCES CITED

Anwar, Muhammad, 1975, 'Asian Participation in the October, 1974 General Election'. *New Community* 4(3): 376–83.

Ballard, Roger, 1976, 'Ethnicity: Theory and Experience'. *New Community* 5(3): 196–202.

Banton, Michael, 1955, *The Coloured Quarter*. London: Cape.

Banton, Michael, 1967, *Race Relations*. London: Tavistock Publications.

Barth, Fredrick, 1969, Introduction. In *Ethnic Groups and Boundaries* (ed.) F. Barth. London: George Allen and Unwin.

Beetham, David, 1970, *Transport and Turbans*. London: Oxford University Press for the Institute of Race Relations.

Bellini, James, 1974–5, European Migrant Labour: Present and Future Conditional. *New Community* 4(1): 5–18.

Brooks, Dennis, 1975, *Race and Labour in London Transport*. London: Oxford University Press for the Institute of Race Relations.

Castles, Stephen and Godula Kosack, 1973, *Immigrant Workers and Class Structure in Western Europe*. London: Oxford University Press for the Institute of Race Relations.

Chen, Ta, 1939, *Emigrant Communities in South China*. Shanghai: Kelly and Walsh, Ltd.

Cohen, Abner, 1969, *Custom and Politics in Urban Africa: A Study of Hausa Migrants in Yoruba Towns*. London: Routledge and Kegan Paul.

Cohen, Abner, 1974a, 'The Lesson of Ethnicity'. In *Urban Ethnicity* (ed.) A. Cohen. London: Tavistock Publications.

Cohen, Abner, 1974b, *Two-Dimensional Man: An Essay on the Anthropology of Power and Symbolism in Complex Society*. London: Routledge and Kegan Paul.

Dahya, Badr, 1965, 'Yemenis in Britain: An Arab Migrant Community'. *Race* 6(3): 177–90.

Dahya, Badr, 1973, 'Pakistanis in Britain: Transients or Settlers'. *Race* 14(3): 242–77.

Dahya, Badr, 1974, 'The Nature of Pakistani Ethnicity in Industrial Cities in Britain'. In *Urban Ethnicity* (ed.) Cohen. London: Tavistock Publications.

Dench, Geoff, 1975, *Maltese in London: A Case Study in the Erosion of Ethnic Consciousness*. London: Routledge and Kegan Paul.

Douglass, William A., 1970, 'Peasant Emigrants: Reactors or Actors?' In *Migration and Anthropology*. Proceedings of the

1970 Annual Meeting of the American Ethnological Society. Seattle: University of Washington Press.

Foster, George M. and Robert V. Kemper (eds.), 1974, *Anthropologists in Cities*. Boston: Little, Brown and Co.

Freedman, Maurice, 1955, 'Jews in the Society of Britain'. In *A Minority in Britain: Social Studies of the Anglo-Jewish Community* (ed.) M. Freedman. London: Vallentine, Mitchell and Co.

Glazer, Nathan and Daniel P. Moynihan, 1975, 'Introduction'. In *Ethnicity: Theory and Experience* (ed.) N. Glazier and D. Moynihan. Cambridge: Harvard University Press.

Goossen, Jean, 1976, 'The Migration of French West Indian Women to Metropolitan France'. *Anthropological Quarterly* 49(1): 45–52.

Gonzalez, Nancie L. Solien, 1969, *Black Carib Household Structure: A Study of Migration and Modernization*. Seattle: University of Washington Press.

Isaacs, Harold R., 1975, 'Basic Group Identity'. In *Ethnicity: Theory and Experience* (ed.) N. Glazer and D. Moynihan. Cambridge: Harvard University Press.

Jansen, Clifford J., 1970, 'Migration: A Sociological Problem'. In *Readings in the Sociology of Migration* (ed.) C. J. Jansen. Oxford: Pergamon Press.

Jeffery, Patricia, 1976, *Migrants and Refugees: Muslim and Christian Pakistani Families in Bristol*. Cambridge: Cambridge University Press.

Lee, Rose Hum, 1960, *The Chinese in the United States of America*. Hong Kong: Hong Kong University Press.

Lewis, Ralph K., 1968, 'Hadchite: A Study of Emigration in a Lebanese Village'. Ph.D. thesis, Columbia University, New York.

Little, Kenneth, 1948, *Negroes in Britain*. London: Routledge and Kegan Paul.

Michaelson, Maureen, 1976, 'East African Gujarati Castes in the United Kingdom'. Paper Presented at the Anthropology Research Seminar, School of Oriental and African Studies, University of London.

Morris, H. S., 1968, 'Ethnic Groups'. In *International Encyclopedia of the Social Sciences*, Vol. 5., (ed.) David L. Sills. New York: Macmillan.

Parkin, David, 1974, 'Congregational and Interpersonal Ideologies in Political Ethnicity'. In *Urban Ethnicity* (ed.) A. Cohen. London: Tavistock Publications.

Patterson, Orlando, 1975, 'Context and Choice in Ethnic

Allegiance: A Theoretical Framework and Caribbean Case Study'. In *Ethnicity: Theory and Experience* (ed.) N. Glazer and D. Moynihan. Cambridge: Harvard University Press.

Patterson, Sheila, 1961, 'The Polish Exile Community in Britain'. *The Polish Review* 6(3): 69–97.

Patterson, Sheila, 1963, *Dark Strangers: A Sociological Study of a Recent West Indian Migrant Group in Brixton, South London.* London: Tavistock Publications.

Peach, Ceri, 1968, *West Indian Migration to Britain: A Social Geography.* London: Oxford University Press for Institute of Race Relations.

Philpott, Stuart B., 1973, *West Indian Migration: The Montserrat Case.* London: Athlone Press.

Robbins, Edward, 1975, 'Ethnicity or Class? Social Relations in a Small Canadian Industrial Community'. In *The New Ethnicity: Perspectives from Ethnology* (ed.) John W. Bennett. *1973 Proceedings of the American Ethnological Society.* St. Paul: West Publishing Co.

Runnymede Trust, 1974–5, 'Trade Unions and Immigrant Workers'. *New Community* 4(1): 19–36.

Swinerton, E. N., et al., 1975, *Ugandan Asians in Great Britain.* London: Croom Helm.

Watson, James L., 1974, 'Restaurants and Remittances: Chinese Emigrant Workers in London'. In *Anthropologists in Cities* (ed.) G. Foster and R. Kemper. Boston: Little, Brown and Co.

Watson, James L., 1975, *Emigration and the Chinese Lineage: The Mans in Hong Kong and London.* Berkeley: University of California Press.

Wrong, Dennis H., 1961, *Population and Society.* New York: Random House.

CHAPTER 2

ROGER BALLARD and CATHERINE BALLARD

The Sikhs: The Development of South Asian Settlements in Britain

Although large numbers of settlers from the Indian sub-continent have been resident in Britain for only a relatively short time, the Asian settlement has a long history, and its internal structure is now complex and diverse. Not only are there variations between the settlements in different British cities, but also migrants of different backgrounds and from different areas have coalesced separately. However, despite this diversity, there are strong indications that all the settlements composed of South Asians of rural origin have passed through several distinct phases of development. Evidence from the available literature, as well as from our own material collected during the course of fieldwork among the Sikhs in Leeds, shows that it is possible to isolate a chronological sequence of four phases in the development of South Asian settlements in Britain. The timing and duration of each phase, as well as its particular characteristics varies considerably from one group to another, but such a framework provides a useful basis for comparative analysis.

The first phase was that of individual pioneers, who were initially almost all ex-seamen, and slightly later, pedlars. Men from the sub-continent have been present in Britain for at least a century, but only in the period between the two World Wars did some of them begin to put down permanent roots. This led to the establishment of small nuclei of South Asians, mostly working as pedlars, in almost all of the major British cities. The second phase developed after the end of the last war, when there was a huge demand for unskilled labour in British industry. Mass migration from the sub-continent took place during this period and most of the workers lived in densely packed all-male households in inner-city areas. The third phase, which began in about 1960 for the Sikhs, was marked by the large-scale entry of wives and children, a move to less crowded housing conditions and a general consolidation of the ethnic settlement. The fourth and final phase to date is marked by a move away from the most unsalubrious ghettoes and the emergence into adulthood of a British-educated, if not yet British-born, second generation. For the Sikhs in Leeds, the final phase began in about 1970. Other groups, particularly those from Pakistan and Bangladesh, have moved through these phases more slowly. Although seamen from Mirpur District first arrived in Bradford at least 30 years ago (Dahya 1974:85) and now constitute the largest South Asian group in the city, comparatively few of their wives and children have yet joined them, and those that have arrived recently. Thus the Mirpuris are only now entering the third phase of settlement, some 15 years after the Sikhs.

Our central purpose in writing this paper is to give a diachronic perspective to the study of South Asian ethnic minorities in Britain. Although there is a certain amount of literature now available on various settlements, most studies are rather limited in scope and take little account of possible changes over time. However, although it is our thesis that common structural patterns can be detected in all South Asian groups, it is evident that there are many differences between them and this makes a detailed discussion of every group impossible within the confines of a short paper. We shall, therefore, restrict ourselves here to a description of the development of Sikh settlement in Leeds, but at the same time we shall try, briefly, to indicate the similarities and differences between the Sikhs and the other main groups of migrants from South Asia.

The Early Settlers: The Nineteenth Century

Information about the earliest Asian residents in Britain is scanty, but a book published in 1873 by Joseph Salter, 'Missionary to Asiatics in England' is a valuable, if somewhat biased source. There was evidently a well-established settle-

ment of Asian seamen in the East End of London at that
time: most were of Indian origin, but Salter also mentions
Arabs, Chinese, and Malays. Many had come ashore as the
only escape from particularly brutal officers, but there was
also an economic incentive: a man who signed on in London
got higher European rates of pay, as opposed to the Asiatic
rate he would have earned if he had taken the same job in
Bombay. Asian seamen could, however, only sign on in
London when the supply of European seamen was exhausted.

Although all Asians in London were ex-seamen, they did
not sit back passively waiting for a ship. They took up a
variety of shore-based occupations: some ran lodging houses,
others worked for circuses and many, according to Salter,
were professional beggars. Salter has nothing good to say
about those Asians who chose to reside in Britain, but it
seems likely that their activities were more sophisticated
than simple begging. For instance, although the Indian
jugglers in Wilkie Collins' novel 'The Moonstone', written at
about this time, are 'strangers', their role as peripatetic enter-
tainers needs no explanation to Collins' readers. Meanwhile
Salter (1873:221) maintains that:

At this period about 250 Asiatics ... were constantly visiting the
provincial towns, and especially the autumn retreats at the seaside, to come into contact with the English *sahib*, and extract a
backsish ... These disciples of the prophet of Mecca wander from
Plymouth to Ben Lomond and from Aberdeen to Hastings ...

Moreover,

The Asiatics residing in London, as well as those residing in all
provincial towns are like the links in a long chain; if one link is
found, the others soon come into view. (Ibid:24)

These settlers had developed a specialised economic niche
for themselves as well as a social network of their own, both
to sustain themselves and to exploit that niche. In Salter's
time, most Indian seamen were recruited by shipping companies from Surat District, on the coast north of Bombay,
and from Sylhet District, in the north-east of what is now
Bangladesh. Nearer to the turn of the century, they also
began to recruit in Mirpur and Campbellpur, in the north of
what is now Pakistan. These three areas, together with the
Punjab—from which migration has rather different historical

origins—have provided the overwhelming majority of South Asian migrants to Britain. The specialised development of the Sylheti settlement is worth mentioning here. It seems that Sylhetis gained something of a monopoly of work as cooks and galley-hands aboard British ships and many of them continued in this speciality when they came ashore, establishing tea-houses and cafes along the waterfront. These businesses slowly grew in size and popularity, and relatives of those already established came ashore to help them, or to start new businesses. Expansion and proliferation has continued over the years and now the majority of 'Indian' restaurants in British towns are run by Sylhetis.

Overseas Migration from the Punjab

British rule over the Punjab was finally consolidated in 1850 and due largely to the Sikhs' loyalty during the Mutiny in 1857, they came to be regarded as ideal recruits for the Indian army. Those recruited were, for the most part, drawn from the numerous and politically dominant Jat caste of peasant farmers. At first they served mainly in India, but from the 1880s onwards, Sikh regiments were regularly posted overseas. Emigration proper seems to have begun when soldiers in Sikh regiments stationed in Singapore and Hong Kong realised the opportunities to earn money there, and returned when they left the army to become guards and night-watchmen. They then began to establish small businesses and migrated outwards to Indonesia and the Philippines, and by the turn of the century had reached Australia, Fiji, California, and Canada. However, this Asiatic presence was generally regarded as unfair competition by the European settlers who were also moving into these frontier regions. As a result, they were all closed to further Asian immigration by racist immigration legislation passed during the first decade of this century.

For the first half of the twentieth century, Punjabi migrants went mostly to Southeast Asia and East Africa. Those who went to Southeast Asia were largely Jats, following the occupations described above, but migration to East Africa followed a rather different pattern. The Sikh village craftsmen, Ramgarhia by caste, had a high standard of skill, and they were soon recruited in large numbers to work on various civil engineering projects in the expanding *raj*: railways, canals, dams and so forth. When construction of a railway in East Africa began, large numbers of Punjabi craftsmen, including Sikhs, were brought over to build it and many stayed on to run it. Punjabi craftsmen continued to be recruited by the railways and other government bodies in East Africa until the 1950s when, with the approach of independence, the process of Africanisation began. From then on, the position of all South Asians in East Africa became increasingly uneasy. Their overall position can perhaps best be described as 'filling in the colonial sandwich', superior in status to the indigenous population but inferior to the Europeans. With the advent of independence, Africans began pressing to move into precisely those positions which Asians were occupying and it was soon clear that for many there was no alternative but remigration. Some South Asians returned to India and Pakistan; a considerable number, often the most highly qualified, went to Canada, but the majority came to Britain.

Large-scale migration to the metropolitan heartlands only became possible during the 1950s. The reasons for this are clear. After the last war, Britain's economy began to boom and its traditional sources of unskilled labour—the countryside and Ireland—were almost exhausted. As a result, large numbers of South Asian and West Indian workers were recruited and have now come to form a permanent underclass, carrying out those jobs which indigenous white workers are unwilling to do. The emergence of such an underclass is not, of course, unique to Britain. Similar groups of migrant workers can be found in almost every advanced industrial economy. The migration of adult Asian males, as opposed to their dependant wives and children, has been reduced to a trickle in recent years, due to the passage of restrictive immigration laws and also to the end of the British economic boom. Overseas migration from the Punjab has, however, continued to Canada, Germany, and Scandinavia and more recently to the Persian Gulf.

Although migrants have always left the Punjab for economic reasons it would be quite wrong to conclude that either this area, or other parts of the sub-continent from which there has been substantial migration, is necessarily poverty-stricken. The Punjab has, in fact, been moderately prosperous and in the last decade it has become one of the richest areas in India. It is a region of peasant farmers where large estates under the control of a single landlord are virtually unknown. In most villages at least half of the population are owner-cultivators, typically of the Jat caste, and they are normally members of a single patrilineage, the *bhaiachara*, or brotherhood. The families which make up the lineage are, in principle, equal, although in practice family landholdings normally vary between two and thirty acres. It has been these variations in size of landholding within the fiercely egalitarian, but strongly competitive, Jat caste which has been one of the most important spurs to migration. Most of the earliest migrants were from Jat families which had grown rapidly over several generations, with the result that the family land could no longer support them. The great majority of Sikh migrants have come from the Jullundur Doab, one of the most densely populated parts of the region. Emigration began, then, not just as a straightforward response to rural poverty but also as a result of status competition and the differential distribution of land among families of the same caste within a single village. If land was short or misfortune of some kind struck, one or more members of the family would be sent abroad to recoup its fortunes. Such emigration was by its very nature temporary, for the aim was always to earn money to buy land and hence to maintain the family's honour.

Apart from the Jats, who make up 50 per cent of the rural population of the Punjab and who predominate among Sikh migrants to Britain, the rural population of the Punjab can be divided into three main categories. Firstly, there are the high ranking Brahmins and Khatris, comprising about 10 per cent of the population, who were traditionally priests and businessmen. Few of them have emigrated to Britain, although Ursula Sharma's rather isolated 'Rampal' (Sharma 1971) is of this group. Secondly, there are the medium ranking craftsmen and service castes, about 15 per cent of the population, of whom the largest group are the Ramgarhias. They have had both the skills and the resources to make significant economic advances in recent years, as small-scale industrial entrepreneurs in the Punjab or as businessmen and craftsmen overseas. Lacking any particular ties to the land, a higher proportion of the craftsman castes than of any other have probably emigrated. The third major category of the population, comprising about 25 per cent of the total, are the members of the ritually unclean castes, the so-called untouchables. Their main traditional occupation was that of landless labourers for Jat farmers. Relatively few untouchables have been able to raise the necessary funds to send emigrants abroad.

The question of caste complicates discussion of emigration from the Punjab, but nevertheless some fairly regular patterns can be discerned. The bulk of emigrants have been drawn from families of medium wealth in the rural areas: the wealthy have no reason to go and the poorest are unable to finance the journey. Until very recently, emigration has been regarded as a temporary move, an episode before a final return to the village. Those who do emigrate are in no sense out of touch but continue to be regarded, and regard themselves, as members of their families. Although many emigrants are now more firmly based abroad than their predecessors, cheap air travel has made frequent return trips much more feasible. During such visits, the migrant not only reaffirms his loyalty to, and concern for, his kinsmen but he also displays his new wealth. Such demonstrations have further fuelled migration fever, so much so that wealthy families who disdained migration in the past are now willing to pay enormous sums to get one of their sons well placed abroad.

As far as can be discerned, the causes and patterns of emigration from other rural areas of the sub-continent are very similar. Almost all the migrants have been drawn from families of middling wealth and status, and none of them regarded their departure as permanent and final. Their aim, almost always, was to earn money to restore or to improve the prestige and status of the family.

The Pioneers: Punjabi Pedlars

Most of the earliest Sikh migrants to Britain were members of the very small Bhatra caste, whose traditional occupation was hawking and peddling. When pioneers of the caste came to Britain in the early 1920s, they began to make a living by hawking suitcases of clothing from door to door, mostly in rural areas. Word about the opportunities available in Britain began gradually to circulate in the Punjab, so that many non-Bhatra adventurers also set out for Britain. Most of them were Sikhs, but there were also a substantial number of Moslems who at that time lived alongside the Sikhs in an undivided Punjab. By the end of the 1930s, small colonies of Punjabi pedlars, among which the Bhatras had already become a minority, could be found in almost every British city. The secret of the success of these pedlars seems to have lain in their skilful manipulation of prices and credit. An ex-pedlar said,

We were always ready to knock a few pennies off the price, because we always put it up beforehand. We always sold on credit too, 'a bob now, love, and the rest next month'. That way we had a chance to come back and sell something else.

Instant credit was obviously attractive to the hard-pressed housewife, and an essential part of the pedlar's technique. The successful manipulation of such relationships required considerable judgement—without credit it was impossible to sell, but too much credit could turn the customer into a bad risk. The itinerant Punjabi had few sanctions which he could exercise over non-payers. However, a continuous but well managed small debt kept the pedlar's foot in the door and the customer under an obligation to keep buying (see Taylor 1976:47–8).

As the colony of Punjabi settlers in each city grew in size, specialisation developed within it. For example, one man might regularly make the round of factories and warehouses to collect stock. While this was at first simply a convenient sharing of labour among co-operating equals, the sub-wholesaler usually began to gain a dominant position with respect to the others. He was himself in a position to advance goods on credit to them as well as to newcomers to the trade. As time went on, such a man would begin to spend the greater part of his time in sub-wholesaling activities, slowly building up financial capital and a network of clients and followers. This was the course taken by Darshan Singh, a man who has been extremely influential in the growth of the Sikh settlement in Leeds. He is a Ramgarhia (craftsman) by caste and he had intended to migrate to East Africa, but changed his mind at the last minute and came to Britain instead. In 1938, he joined a small group of pedlars working out of Bradford, and was sufficiently successful to be able to open a small shop-cum-warehouse of his own in Leeds immediately after the war. As time went on, he developed a powerful position with respect to all newcomers, and he was also able to sponsor the passage of his kinsmen to Britain and to help them to establish themselves on their arrival. South Asian settlements in British cities each have their own particular composition depending very often upon the identity of the earliest settlers. Due largely to Darshan Singh's influence, Leeds has become, for the Sikhs, a community dominated by the Ramgarhias.

Most members of the small Sikh colonies which could be found at the end of the war were men who had financed their own passages to Britain and had begun work as pedlars. The Moslem and Gujerati settlements at the same period were, however, largely composed of ex-seamen (see, for instance, Dahya 1974:84), many of whom had left their ships during the war to take jobs in munitions factories and the like. Although their mode of arrival and their occupations may have been different, they organised themselves in much the same way as did the Sikhs. Each of these settlements provided a bridgehead for the rush of migrants who came to Britain during the post-war economic boom.

The 1950s: Mass Migration

Wherever their origins in the sub-continent, migrants from rural backgrounds came to Britain in the 1950s with very similar intentions. They sought high wages and were prepared to do tedious and unpleasant jobs for very long hours

—often twelve hour shifts, six days a week. They also sought to minimise their living expenses in order to maximise their savings, and this could most easily be achieved by communal residence in an all-male household. Life during this period was tough: all the niceties of normal social life were abandoned and all gratification deferred in the expectation of a rapid return home. The migrants regarded their villages of origin as the only meaningful arena of social interaction and tended to view Britain as a social vacuum, a cultural no-man's land. Nevertheless, it is clear that very distinctive patterns of social relations were being established. In the early days, Britain was a hard and hostile environment in which to live, and the pioneers used the skills and assumptions which they had brought with them both in the pursuit of income and in the organisation of institutions of mutual support. It was upon these social foundations that the newly arrived migrants built. At the outset, they had two immediate needs: to find shelter and employment. Usually a new migrant had a contact (perhaps only an address) but if not he would soon discover the location of established South Asian households in the city. In the 1950s, a particular pub was patronised by the Sikhs who lived in Leeds and all new arrivals would find their way there. The obligation of hospitality is deeply engrained and newcomers were not turned away: they were given food and lodging, and efforts were made to find them jobs. However, it was clearly understood that all this was taking place within a framework of Punjabi moral norms governing reciprocity: the provision of assistance put the recipient under an obligation to his sponsors.

With an increasing flow of new migrants, these arrangements soon became more clearly structured. Specialist brokers, who had contacts with either established workers or the personnel departments of local factories (see, e.g., Aurora 1967:35), were able to place new arrivals in jobs very quickly, on the understanding that the client was then under an obligation to render some appropriate service to the patron when called upon to do so. By manipulating the obligations due to him so that clients in fact provided services for each other, many broker/patrons built up powerful positions for themselves. They established inter-locking networks in the spheres of housing, shopkeeping, and politics as well as in the provision of jobs. Careful reading of Aurora, Dahya, Desai, James, and John (see bibliography) provides ample, if disjointed, evidence of the existence of such networks. As the settlements grew in size, these social networks began to be confined to migrants from a particular area or even, as numbers grew, from a particular caste or group of villages. The closer the prior relationship, the greater was the sense of obligation between migrants and the wider the area of shared understandings and assumptions. Moreover, before long chain migration began in earnest so that instead of arriving in a random scatter migrants increasingly came to, or were called to join, kinsmen who had already established themselves. All this hastened the re-establishment of regional, caste, and village groups in British cities, together with the genesis of meaningful and self-sufficient networks of relationships insulated from the external British world.

The All-Male Household

The characteristic institution of this period was the all-male household, which was essentially a supportive and co-operative venture whose members regarded themselves as being linked by ties of quasi-brotherhood. Sometimes the house was jointly owned by its members, or at least by a group of them, but more usually it had a single landlord who assumed a kind of patriarchal authority over its members. The all-male household was ordered in terms of an adaptation of well-understood norms of kinship, and it also facilitated the achievement of the migrant's primary goal—saving money. In the early days, most men sent money home almost as soon as they had earned it. Remittances were spent, first, to pay off the loan that had often financed the passage to Britain, secondly, to cover the family's accumulated debts (which were often the reason for emigration) and, finally, to buy land and agricultural implements. However, as time passed, migrants began to retain more and more of their savings so that they could send or take it home as an impressive lump sum. As a result, they began to look for profitable investments in Britain to increase their capital, and one obvious area for investment was housing. There was a constant stream of new arrivals looking for shelter, but established migrants disliked paying rent and being obligated to a landlord. As one of Badr Dahya's informants told him (1974:97):

What is the status of a fifteen shilling tenant? Does anyone respect him? He is always at the mercy of his landlord and his *'party'*, and dare not express himself openly lest he offend them ... and he can be kicked out at a week's notice.

In contrast, buying a house with savings eliminated rent payments and brought additional income from lodgers who would be brought in to fill the house. These lodgers were, of course, expected to become their landlord's political supporters in factional disputes. Most migrants were peasant farmers by origin: not only did they value the idea of independence, but being an owner of property in itself brought prestige.

The houses that were purchased during this period were both cheap and large, for these brought most profit. They were invariably decaying Victorian and Edwardian terrace houses which could be found in the inner areas of most British cities. Building Societies were generally reluctant to lend on such property, and in addition most South Asian migrants were unhappy about the idea of long-term indebtedness where several times the principal might eventually have to be paid over in interest. These houses were often bought for cash, either from the savings of a single migrant or from loans arranged through fellow migrants, usually kinsmen. Sometimes short-term bank loans were negotiated, which the entrepreneur endeavoured to pay off as quickly as possible by filling his house (or houses) with tenants who were prepared to live in austere and over-crowded conditions. Those who bought houses did not usually see themselves as putting down roots in Britain, but rather as making a temporary investment which could be sold whenever necessary in order to buy land back in the village.

Although migrants had started with the assumption that the village of origin was the only social arena which really counted, they began to find that they were becoming involved in social obligations in Britain which they were bound to fulfil if they were not to lose face in the eyes of their fellows. To the South Asian villager, the maintenance and enhancement of his family honour, *izzat*, is perhaps the most important of all goals and it is the quest for greater *izzat* that often lies at the root of the decision to migrate. The most significant transformation in overseas settlements came about when these, too, became arenas within which *izzat* could be gained or lost. Once this occurred, all migrants had to compete or else lose face: this was the point at which the transition to the third phase of settlement, consolidation, took place.

A good deal of the literature on South Asians in Britain refers to settlements which were in the phase of development characterised by the all-male household. The structure of this institution seems to have been very similar whether it was made up of Sikhs, Gujeratis, Pakistanis or Bangladeshis, but the duration of this phase of settlement has varied considerably between the different groups.

The Reunion of Families

As the various ethnic colonies took on a self-sustaining life of their own and became arenas for status competition, so there was a gradual move away from absolute austerity in life style. Although saving continued, more was spent on visiting the cinema, clothes, and entertaining guests. But the most significant indicator of change came with the decision to bring over their wives and children. Despite its obvious drawbacks, the lengthy separation of husband and wife is not regarded as particularly anomalous in most parts of the sub-continent. Marriage is set within the context of the joint family and there is no great emphasis on the exclusive relationship of married couples. Wives and children who are left in the migrants' home villages are in no sense abandoned or alone. They are still part of the joint household, under the care of the father or brother of the absent husband: for them daily life will continue to be much the same. There is a long-established tradition in South Asia of husbands leaving the village for long periods, on army service for example, but frequent as such absences may have been, they were obviously not pleasant for either husband or wife. Male migrants were constantly homesick for their families and despite the quasi-familial ties of the all-male household, life for the settler was ascetic.

As the migrants' social relationships in Britain intensified, and as viable ethnic colonies emerged, it became increasingly attractive for a man to consider bringing over his wife and children. There were, however, several disadvantages in doing so. Firstly, the original purpose of migration would begin to be undermined, for the rate of saving would be reduced, and secondly, wives and daughters would be exposed to the influence of British culture, which most migrants regarded as morally degenerate. The situation was further complicated by changes in British immigration legis-lation which prompted a range of migratory strategies among those already settled in Britain who wished to bring their kinsmen over. As a result, there have been considerable differences in the speed with which different groups have reunited their families. The Sikhs and Hindu Gujaratis have done so most rapidly. Before 1960 few women had arrived but in the years following, their numbers began to rise sharply (see Aurora 1967 and Desai 1963). Moslems have generally been slow to reunite their families and those from Sylhet in Bangladesh and from Mirpur in Pakistan are the slowest of all. When we began fieldwork in 1971, we hardly met a Sikh family in Leeds that was not reunited, with the exception of a few elderly grandparents who were still awaiting entry. In contrast, Sylheti and Mirpuri all-male households are still common.

There are a number of reasons for these differences. Moslems put greater emphasis on *purdah*, the seclusion of women, than do Hindus and Sikhs, so they have tended to be more concerned about bringing their wives and daughters to Britain. Secondly, unlike Sikhs and Hindus, the Moslems generally prefer marriage with close kin, thus allowing the head of the family to exercise a great deal of control over his sons and their spouses (see Dahya 1972:29). This also leads to more frequent marriages between people of the same village. As a result, all Moslems, and particularly Mirpuris and Sylhetis, have tended to keep closer contacts with their home village than have other groups, so delaying the emergence of a more autonomous social arena in Britain. However, this is rapidly changing and large numbers of Mirpuri and Sylheti women and children are joining, or trying to join, their husbands. The reunion of these families is proceeding slowly because of administrative obstacles to the entry of dependants, despite their legal right to come (see Akram 1974). It is now much more difficult for a migrant to reunite his family than it was a decade ago.

The 1960s: Consolidation of the Sikh Settlement

For the Sikhs, the 1960s were very much a period of consolidation in which the all-male household, previously the most common form of residence, virtually disappeared. Once wives and children arrived, each family needed a house of its own; but since the settlers still regarded themselves as essentially transient they only bought the cheapest houses which would satisfy their basic requirements. These were usually close to the rapidly decaying areas in which the all-male households had previously been established. Migrants were able to live cheaply, but the overcrowding and squalor of the earlier days disappeared.

With families reunited, guests could at last be entertained in proper style, for women were available to prepare the food. The presence of a wife and children meant that living expenses became higher and as time passed patterns of expenditure rapidly changed. In particular the competition for status and prestige with other settlers began in earnest and instead of virtually camping out, migrants began to spend more on furnishing and equipping their houses. Perhaps most important of all was the fact that it became possible to celebrate life-cycle rituals in Britain. Whole families and major parts of their kin networks had been reconstituted and all the traditional expectations and obligations could now be fulfilled. The prestige of each family ultimately depends upon the elaborateness of gift exchanges with affines and the arrival of women made the appropriate conspicuous consumption possible in Britain. This was a complete reversal of the situation prior to 1960: in the days of the all-male household, elaborate spending in the search for prestige had been restricted to the village and had been matched by conspicuous non-consumption in Britain. At the core of the prestige-generating rituals of the family life-cycle is a series of ceremonies which begins with marriage and continues through the birth and marriage of every child; each occasion demands elaborate gift-giving. In the earlier part of the decade, it was the rituals of childbirth that were celebrated most often, but towards the end, marriages became more frequent. At first marriages were arranged largely through intermediaries in the Punjab, but as time passed more and more of the arrangements were made in Britain. While the traditional rules of caste endogamy and *gotra* (clan) exogamy continued to be followed, the audience before whom prestige was sought was increasingly British-based, and local criteria became of greater importance in arranging matches. The family's educational and occupational standing in Britain began to outweigh the question of exactly how many acres they owned in India, and a strong preference for city exogamy has emerged in Britain, for the wholly traditional reason of wishing to distance oneself from one's affines. Sikh marriages in Britain have become increasingly elaborate affairs, and currently a father can hardly avoid spending at least £2000 on each daughter to keep up with the standard that is expected. Much larger amounts are spent, especially on the dowry, at some marriages.

Throughout the 1960s, the Sikhs set about recreating as many of the institutions of Punjabi society as possible. This was a strong contrast to the earlier period where they merely utilised those cultural values which eased their survival. Liaisons with white girls had been common in the earlier phase, as Aurora (1967) describes, but these are now increasingly condemned. The reconstitution of the family, ideally in its joint form, became the over-riding goal. As networks tightened, gossip and scandal became an even more effective sanction in securing conformity to the ideal, traditional norms. As one man explained it to us:

In the early days, we were all bachelors together. We worked very hard and we lived very rough, but when we enjoyed ourselves we really had a good time. We had plenty of beer and girls too. . . . Now our families have arrived, everyone has turned very strict. Many people have put their turbans on again and some won't even drink now.

In the pioneer period, migrants rarely practised religious rituals and, if anything, they scorned the idea of doing so. However, in Leeds a group of men (who were, incidentally, mostly from East Africa) began holding a *diwan* (religious service) in their own homes in 1957, and by 1958 the first regular *Gurdwara* (Sikh Temple) in Yorkshire had been established. By the mid-1960s, regular Sunday attendance at the temple was the rule. The reasons for this were varied. Partly it reflected a deepening interest in religion and, more generally, in the maintenance of the fundamental values of Sikh society. But the *diwan* was also a social event which provided an opportunity to meet all the other Sikh residents in the city, to exchange news, and to join together as a community in a familiar corporate activity. The *diwan* is also intrinsically entertaining. It consists largely of singing compositions based on the Sikh scriptures by skilled musicians, *ragi*, and lectures by preachers, *gyani*, whose principal task is to interpret and transmit, in popular terms, the moral and theological fundamentals of the faith. It is both striking and significant that temple attendance abroad has become much more frequent than it is in the Punjab.

The 1960s also saw an increasingly overt expression of cultural differences by the settlers: when the women arrived there was no thought of them dressing in anything other than *salwar kamiz* (trousers and tunic), even if these were of the tighter 'modern' style. At the same time many Sikh men became rather embarrassed by their rapid abandonment of the turban in the early days. Some men began to grow their hair and beard again, feeling confident enough to make a public statement of their ethnic identity. The leaders of this trend were the increasing number of arrivals from East Africa. In some ways these new migrants were much more 'westernised' than those who had come directly from India, for they were usually better educated, spoke better English, and had expectations of a high material standard of living. Nevertheless, they had established a tradition, as a minority group in East Africa, of maintaining separate moral and religious standards and of preserving their ethnic identity. The turban has always been quite as much a social as a religious symbol and its retention by East Africans, along with its readoption by established residents, was a public assertion of their pride in themselves. Caste factors were also involved because, while the majority of those who came direct from India were Jats, almost all of those who came from East Africa were Ramgarhias. Since they traditionally ranked lower than the Jats, the Ramgarhias have long sought to improve their status by following the rules of religious orthodoxy more closely, and they have continued this strategy both in East Africa and in Britain. Ramgarhias in Britain are often scornful of the Jats' lack of sophistication, their deviation from religious orthodoxy and their attachment to their villages in Punjab, which leads them to adopt a rather lower standard of living in Britain. Jats, on the other hand, tend to regard Ramgarhias as behaving like *nouveaux riches* and to see their devotion to religious orthodoxy as mere ostentation. One corollary of this is that Ramgarhias, and indeed the members of every other caste, tend to move in separate circles even when they live in the same city. It is only in overarching institutions such as the temple that there is much social interaction between different castes, at least as far as the older generation is concerned.

Finally, although there had been Sikh business enterprises since the very earliest period, they only began to proliferate in the 1960s. The pedlars expanded their businesses and moved on through market stalls and shops to warehouses and then manufacturing. The final customers were English, but the internal market chain through wholesaler to retailer was organised in ethnic terms. This was particularly important with respect to advancing credit to new or expanding entrepreneurs: the sanctions of the network provided the security for the loan.

With the rapid growth of the Punjabi population during the 1960s, there was also an expansion of the specialist ethnic market, and within a short period an elaborate infra-structure of services and businesses emerged. Cinemas, grocers, cloth shops, sweet shops, goldsmiths, and travel agents all grew up to serve an Asian clientele. Beyond these, garages, driving schools, taxi services, insurance brokers, and television repair shops were also established. A few businesses have an almost exclusively Asian clientele but most service English clients as well. A garage owner told us that although he started off by doing jobs mainly for other Asians, now that he had moved to proper premises roughly half his trade came from non-Asians and the other half through the ethnic network. The attraction of going into business was, and remains, twofold. Not only does it bring the possibility of greater financial rewards and the fulfilment of the peasant ideal of being one's own master, but it also offers a means of circumventing the discrimination which increasing numbers of men became aware of at work.

The 1960s also saw the growth of complex factional disputes within each settlement. We have already outlined how patrons recruited followers in the early days and how they began to compete for power and prestige among themselves. These men called on elaborate networks of kinsmen and clients, whom they led in constantly shifting patterns of allegiance. But as time passed new men came forward to challenge their dominance, often in the context of disputes about slights to honour, dishonesty, or alleged failure to fulfil social obligations. Very often these disputes were a continuation of long-standing feuds in the homeland. The growth of the settlements also meant that new arenas for status competition emerged and control of the temple committee and other such institutions became a major concern of factional leaders.

Such manoeuvring was carried out almost entirely within the ethnic colony but, as settlements grew in size and significance, a whole range of British institutions, from political parties and local authorities to the various 'international friendship' associations, began seeking out the leaders which it was assumed the South Asian settlements must possess. Those who stepped forward and presented themselves as leaders were almost always accepted at face value, and indeed their positions as representatives of their communities has now been institutionalised in the Community Relations Councils which have been established in major cities. However, most such 'leaders' find themselves in a very difficult position. Only those with a reasonable command of English can make much progress as 'leaders' and such men by no means always play an important role in the internal politics of their own ethnic colony, particularly as they are often of the professional, urban middle class. But, even if they are truly representative, leaders find it virtually impossible, and certainly unprofitable, to try to explain to their British sponsors what these disputes are really all about or what their fellow migrants really believed. Instead it was much easier to try to please their sponsors, many of whom had strong ideas of their own about what 'immigrants' ought to be doing, by saying what they want to hear. It was soon discovered that the 'leaders' who were most acceptable to the British were those who followed these tactics, and so a whole new class of intermediaries arose. They could be very successful as long as those whom they 'represented' did not speak good English and as long as those that did played the same game. 'Leaders' of this type are still to be found operating in most British cities, often having acted as buffers between their own community and the British authorities over a considerable period. Increasingly, however, they are now being challenged by younger people.

'Leaders' of this kind could only emerge because the majority of migrants had rather limited social contact with English people. Few Punjabis, at least from rural backgrounds, had great expectations of establishing close social relationships with the indigenous population, and many felt that those friendly overtures which they did make were rebuffed. They were often not sure whether this was because of misunderstanding or racial hostility. Nevertheless, some friendships were established across the ethnic boundary, especially at work, but these often took the form of elaborate joking relationships, so containing the underlying tension.

Despite the fact that the migrants were establishing an increasingly complex and autonomous social world in Britain almost all continued, and indeed continue until the present day, to maintain that they will return to the Punjab 'in a few years' time'. From its original status as a realistic short-term goal, the idea of return has gradually become a myth which, although increasingly unrealistic, has important social consequences. The myth can be used to explain and justify the settlers' commitment to saving, albeit on a reduced scale compared to the earliest phases; it can be used as a vehicle for the expression of unease about prospects in Britain as racial tensions sharpen; but above all, the myth of return is used to legitimise continued adherence to the values of their homeland and to condemn the assimilation of English cultural values as irrelevant and destructive. The importance of return as a real goal has gradually faded and instead it has become a central charter for the maintenance of Sikh ethnicity in Britain.

Why have the migrants not returned as they originally intended? Although returning home to be a businessman or farmer offered the attraction of a familiar and much more autonomous life, there was always the temptation of staying on a little longer to accumulate more savings. Secondly, most migrants had very mixed feelings about bringing up their children in Britain for, while they appreciated the quality of the educational opportunities available, they were most concerned about the possibility of their children's anglicisation. However, most parents decided that the socialisation they could give their children at home outweighed the dangers of school. Once their children began climbing the educational ladder it made little sense to disturb them by returning home. Finally, those who did return found unexpected difficulties. They complained universally of corruption. While corruption is certainly widespread, what probably hindered returnees most was the fact that long absence had removed them from the network of political and economic contacts without which it is difficult to run a farm or business successfully. Nevertheless, a small number of people have overcome these difficulties and returned, although for many of them ill health in Britain's damp climate has been an important motivating factor.

The 1970s: The Emergence of a Second Generation

To talk of a new phase beginning in 1970 is a good deal more artificial than drawing a boundary at 1960, but some significant changes are discernible. For this phase we are only able to call on our own fieldwork in Leeds and the often unpublished fieldwork of colleagues. The changes are rather more subtle than those which have demarcated previous phases, where comparisons can easily be made between reports on various groups in different cities.

In the sphere of employment there has been a strong attempt to move away from the bottom of the hierarchy. Members of the older generation have not met with much success unless they managed to set up business on their own account, very often starting with a stall in one of the local markets. Even those in highly skilled occupations have begun to do the same, usually because they feel that promotion to staff and managerial grades will almost certainly be blocked for them. Among Sikhs, although much less among Moslems, it is now quite common for women to go out to work, both before marriage and when their children have started school. Instead of leaving school at the earliest possible opportunity in order to start work, most Sikh children, and especially the boys, are now encouraged to continue their education. Educational ambition is so great that it is considered rather shaming if a son is not able to achieve some kind of professional or technical qualification. Asian graduates of the second generation are beginning to emerge in numbers from the universities although they frequently experience extreme difficulty in finding appropriate employment (Ballard and Holden 1975).

There is also a growing tendency to move away from the cheap terraced housing of inner-city Leeds, which are now often sold to Mirpuris and Sylhetis. More and more Sikhs are buying semi-detached houses in the northern suburbs of the city—which, incidentally, is an area noted for its high proportion of Jewish residents. This shift to the suburbs, which almost all Sikhs in Leeds would now like to make, is revealing a considerable income differential within the community. The distinction is particularly obvious between those families which have a large number of small children and those which contain several earning members and can therefore afford the move to a new house with ease. With this has come a greater interest in birth control and an even stronger appreciation of the advantages of an extended family. If sons and daughters-in-law are contributing to family income and the multiple purchase of consumer durables is avoided by joint residence, a high standard of living can be maintained. Although Sikhs in Leeds may be moving out to live in more salubrious areas, this does not mean that their ethnic organisation is weakening, any more than it did for the Jews when they made similar moves twenty or thirty years ago. Those who do make the move usually attempt to establish friendly relations with their non-Asian neighbours, although they often meet, at least initially, with hostility. However, they are still so tightly bound up in Punjabi networks of hospitality that they may have little time left for their neighbours. In any case, their commitment to Punjabi social and moral values remains intense even if they are rapidly adopting 'western' material standards with the purchase of fitted carpets, colour televisions, and large cars.

Members of the first generation who are putting down stronger material roots in Britain nevertheless often have very mixed feelings about their continued residence in Britain. We have stressed already the contradictions between their high estimation of economic opportunities and their negative feelings about British moral and social practices, but additional important factors are now beginning to enter the equation. Every time that Enoch Powell makes a speech advocating repatriation, people begin, once again, to think about whether they should consider returning home quickly. Incidents involving assaults on Asians, such as the recent murder of a Sikh boy in Southall, redouble these fears. Several Mirpuri families whom we visited shortly after this murder referred to the dead Sikh as 'our boy' (a significant indicator of their feelings since Moslems and Sikhs are normally hostile to one another) and they were talking bitterly about the necessity of returning home for the sake of their children's safety.

The Second Generation

The most important change in the character of Sikh settlement in the 1970s has been the emergence of a second generation: the British born, or at least British educated, children of immigrant parents. These young people have been exposed to socialisation in two very different cultures, at home and at school. The crucial questions are, firstly, how successfully are they managing to resolve the contradictions between these two cultures and, secondly, whether and in what form are they sustaining their Punjabi ethnicity. It is widely assumed by outsiders that there will inevitably be major problems of 'culture conflict' between 'traditional' repressive parents and their freedom-seeking, 'anglicised' children. However, it is our experience that although many young Asians go through a period of rebellion against their parents' values (as do most adolescents in Britain), for the time being at least, almost all of them are returning to follow a modified version of Punjabi cultural norms in their late teens and early twenties.

Although the second generation is preserving a separate Punjabi ethnicity, this is not to say that conflicts between parents and children do not arise: they can sometimes become extremely serious and children are faced with some difficult choices. At home it is emphasised that the individual's primary loyalty should always be to the family group, that children should respect the authority of their elders and put obligations to others before personal self-interest. In contrast, at school, children are encouraged to see themselves as independent individuals, taking decisions according to their own personal views and inclinations. Asian parents expect their children to work very hard academically while at the same time dissociating themselves from the ethos of their white peers and playing an increasingly important role in family and communal activities. The adoption of British fashions and resistance to visiting the temple or relatives are often the focus for conflict. Many parents make great efforts to explain their values meaningfully to their children and a good number are able to maintain easy and flexible relations with them. Very often they turn a blind eye to their children's, and particularly their sons', behaviour away from home provided that an appearance of respect and conformity is maintained within the family. Others, however, become increasingly worried by their children's behaviour and misinterpret their wish for a slightly greater degree of independence as the beginning of a headlong rush into total anglicisation. In such circumstances, and especially where daughters are concerned, parents often react by becoming increasingly strict and conservative. Stories of Asian girls running away with boys circulate rapidly and are frequently featured in the vernacular press, thus reinforcing parents' fears. The result is that girls may not be allowed to go to college but instead are sent out to work while a marriage is arranged for them. When a girl is so confined, and especially if her engagement has not taken place, she is very likely to look for every oppor-

tunity to escape and meet boys, which leads to violent repercussions should she be discovered.

When young Asians run into major difficulties with their
families they often seek help from an English friend, teacher,
or doctor. They will be able to explain their feelings in
English terms and it will be easy for them to gain support
against their parents who will almost always be assumed to
be repressive and authoritarian. So they are often advised to
move out altogether, abandoning their family and culture.
Taking such a step will in fact often precipitate a realisation
of just how strong the feelings of obligation and loyalty to
the family actually are and how different this makes them
from other British people. As one Sikh girl told us:

Things got so bad at home after they found out about my boy-
friend that I thought I was going to have a breakdown and went
to my doctor for some pills. He's a nice man and really kind to
me. He told me that leaving home was the best thing I could do
and he lent me £5 so that I could move to a hostel straight away.
I had three sleepless nights there and then I went back home. I
couldn't stand being alone. I missed my family terribly in spite of
all the rows. And I knew that by sleeping away from home I
might be getting myself into real trouble for the future. Who's
going to want to marry a girl who has run away? When I tried to
explain to my doctor why I'd gone back he thought that I was
barmy, or that my parents had threatened me. He's never been
quite the same to me since. He just didn't get it.

Because their chastity is of such great importance to the
family honour, girls tend to get into greater difficulties with
their parents than do boys. But in our experience, almost all
young Sikhs, as well as members of other South Asian groups,
do eventually return to seek solutions within the context of
their families. They have been socialised into deep-rooted
loyalty to the family and they find the outside world alien
and unsympathetic in comparison. Many British people,
when they discover that all is finally resolved by the celebra-
tion of an arranged marriage lament the cost to the young
person's personality of being, as they see it, 'blackmailed'
into conformity. Such a view is sustained by the ethnocentric
assumption that the loyalties and obligations on which the
South Asian family is based are reactionary and authoritarian,
and it obscures the fact that teenage rebellion is probably a

universal phenomenon in industrial societies. As young
people seek self-definition and self-discovery, they almost
inevitably go through a phase of rejecting their parents and
all that they stand for which may well mislead the outsider
into concluding that they are finally 'liberating' themselves
from the traditions of their parents.

In fact, the second generation of young Sikhs in Leeds,
some of whom are now in their mid-twenties, are exploring
and evolving a wide variety of behaviour patterns. There is
general agreement that they should reform and modify their
parents' values, rather than abandon them completely. The
idea of 'becoming English' in a cultural sense is almost
universally rejected. Young people are, of course, thoroughly
conversant with British cultural norms and are quite capable
of presenting themselves as British whenever necessary.
Nevertheless, they still feel that British self to be rather un-
real. One of our informants told us,

I've learned to be two different people. I'm quite different when
I'm away at college with English people than when I'm here with
my family and my Punjabi friends. I'm so used to switching over
that I don't even notice. I don't have any trouble getting along
with English people, but I suppose though that I'm really Punjabi
at heart. Sometimes I get very depressed when I'm at college.
I long to go home and be Indian.

Although skilled at making multiple presentations of self, it is
very noticeable that young people of South Asian origin tend
to associate together wherever possible. In Leeds University,
students from all parts of the sub-continent form a loosely
integrated group which includes those who have come
directly from overseas as well as the children of immigrant
parents. At school, Punjabi children tend to have their closest
friendships with members of their own ethnic group. And, in
the covert romances that follow later, South Asian boy or
girlfriends are usually chosen despite the much greater availability and lesser dangers of taking non-Asian partners.

We have already mentioned childhood socialisation as a
very important factor in the ethnic encapsulation of young
people, but there is a further factor which we have not yet
considered in any detail: the effect of racial discrimination.
Young people find that they experience some hostility from
the moment they first enter school and know that they are

always likely to be the target of abuse. They know that, however much they try to conform, they can never really be British because of the colour of their skins. This knowledge of their non-acceptance is a strong and effective counter to complete anglicisation and it is leading them to make some overt expression of a separate ethnicity. For example, a growing number of young Sikhs are readopting the turban, and its abandonment is becoming increasingly rare. This is partly the result of growing pressure towards orthodoxy and conformity from within the ethnic colony, but it is also a reassertion of ethnic pride in the face of white rejection. As one student said to us:

Why shouldn't I wear a turban? I'm a Sikh and proud of it, so why should I pretend that I'm not? Perhaps it will make it more difficult for me to get a job, but it won't make much difference. Everyone can see that I'm an Indian whether I wear a turban or not.

The contemporary situation is changing rapidly, but for some time there has been an undercurrent of resentment towards all white people among young Punjabis. This recently came to the surface during the demonstrations in Southall which followed the murder referred to earlier. This has not yet led to the formation of any organised, explicitly political groups with a broad membership; the anger and militance which was felt in all South Asian settlements throughout the country immediately after the Southall murder faded rapidly away in the following weeks. At present, most young people of the second generation are still either working for their apprenticeships, studying for professional or technical qualifications, or are at an early stage of their careers. Although they are bitterly aware that being coloured is a major disadvantage, they are very conscious that their numbers are small and that militant objections might well produce a backlash which would only increase their difficulties. Resistance, in so far as it exists, has been mainly on a symbolic and cultural, rather than an active and political level.

Marriage and Encapsulation

It is marriage which is very frequently a turning point in the process of self-definition for young people of South Asian origin in Britain. An impending arranged marriage forces them to take stock of their own identities, to assess who they are in relation to others, and to make a firm decision about their future. It is the point at which the conflict between loyalty to the family and personal independence is finally brought into the open. Respect and affection for parents along with guilt about dishonouring the family almost invariably take precedence over the desire for freedom and self-determination. One Sikh boy spoke for many when he told us,

I'm really in love with this girl, but she's a Hindu and from a different caste. My father is a very proud man, and he'd never let me marry her. He might disown me if I did, and I couldn't stand that. The family counts above everything for me. Even if I do have to give in to them in the end and have an arranged marriage to please them, I know I'd do it.

Parents feel that one of their most important obligations is to secure suitable matches for their children. They try to send their daughters off in style, with a large dowry, to a respectable family and to find a daughter-in-law who will fit well into their own family. It is she who will look after them in their old age. Marriage is not normally arranged without the consent of the participants and there is always at least a formal meeting between the prospective spouses, while siblings may bring back long reports and impressions of the girl or boy concerned. On the basis of this rather limited information it is almost always possible for either side to veto any particular match, at least as far as the Sikhs are concerned. The system is gradually becoming more flexible. An established relationship between a boy and girl, such as may grow up when they meet as students, may be presented as if it were a conventionally arranged engagement—provided of course that the complex rules of endogamy and exogamy are fulfilled. Once the engagement ceremony has taken place more contact is generally allowed. Couples often spend a good deal of time on the telephone to one another before their marriage and some may even be allowed to meet un-chaperoned.

The institution of the arranged marriage shows no signs of disappearing. As long as obligations to a wide kinship group are maintained, and marriage remains a contract between two families rather than between two individuals, kinsmen will be deeply involved in approving, if not in making, the choice. Apart from the dishonour that arises from a breach of the established rules, anomalous marriages are objected to because the expected relationships between affines cannot easily be established if a marriage takes place outside the caste. Parents therefore put very great pressure on their children to obey the formal rules, even if the marriage is not directly arranged by them.

The participants in an arranged marriage, especially if they have previously had boy or girl friends, often approach the event with trepidation. Yet in our experience most couples rapidly achieve a satisfactory relationship. It should be remembered that the marriage usually begins within a supportive family structure and that, although they may have mixed feelings about it, the idea of an arranged marriage is very familiar to the participants. This is not to imply, however, that arranged marriages do not fail. Some do, for a variety of reasons. In an era of considerable social change, especially when parents of peasant origin have highly-educated children, it may be very difficult for them to make an appropriate choice of partner for their son or daughter. Furthermore, the sanctions which were traditionally exercised when a relationship broke down, usually a mixture of threats of violence and public shame, may be absent or ineffective in the British context. And finally, the fragmentation of the extended family into smaller and often geographically scattered residential units may sometimes put great strain on individual relationships. For example, the traditionally expected tension between mother-in-law and daughter-in-law may become unbearable without the buffer of other female members in a wider household. On the other hand, the residential fragmentation of families in Britain may provide an escape from such tensions.

If, for parents, marriage is an indication that their children have been properly brought up and launched into adult status, for children it is a formal indication of their loyalty to their family and the community. This does not mean, however, that parental values are accepted wholesale. Having made the necessary bow in the direction of tradition by accepting an arranged marriage, most young couples subsequently begin to behave very differently from their parents. They have a much less formal and more egalitarian relationship with one another, go out together, and place a higher value on their separate identities. They may postpone the birth of their first child in order to give themselves more freedom and time to become better acquainted, despite parents' worries about fertility if a grandchild is not quickly conceived. Most young couples also begin to make friendships on the basis of interest and compatibility and, although these are usually restricted to other similar couples of South Asian origin, they nevertheless begin to move away from the kin-dominated world of their parents. Almost all young couples start their marriage in the boy's parents' household and, provided the house is big enough, many continue to live in such an extended family. However, once the pledge of loyalty implied by an arranged marriage has been given, it is quite easy for the young couple to find an acceptable reason for setting up a separate domestic establishment of their own.

Many of these young couples are now having children and most say that they are very concerned about bringing up their children with a distinctive sense of Punjabi identity. Even though they are fluent in English, they usually try to make sure that their children learn Punjabi in infancy and that they understand something of Punjabi history and culture. Yet most second generation Punjabis have very mixed feelings about their children, the future third generation. They expect that their children will be at least as different from themselves as they are from their own parents, yet they obviously do not know how this will manifest itself. Many young Punjabis whom we met early in the course of fieldwork, and who were then strongly opposed to having an arranged marriage, now ruefully admit that they think arranged marriages, and thus by implication adherence to some form of Punjabi culture, will be best for their children. We cannot speculate about how the third generation might behave, but it is clear that they will be distinctively socialised

by their parents and that they will probably be the targets of
racial hostility, giving rise to yet another ethnic reaction.

Conclusion

Using the Sikhs as our primary example, we have shown how
South Asian settlements in Britain have passed through a
number of phases. In the early pioneering days, ex-seamen
and pedlars utilised the social values and skills which they
had brought with them to sustain themselves, relying heavily
on mutual assistance. This group provided the bridgehead
for mass migration which began in the 1950s when new
arrivals lived in austere conditions, typified by all-male households. The 1960s were characterised, particularly for the
Sikhs, by a process of consolidation: families were reunited
and the ethnic colony in Britain became a significant and
increasingly independent social arena. In the early days, the
activities and attitudes of the indigenous population were of
relatively little interest to South Asian migrants. Discrimination may have forced them to rely upon each other, but it
was only during the 1960s that external white hostility began
to have a really significant effect on internal ethnic consciousness. This process has become much more important
in the current phase, marked by the emergence of the second
generation. Their ethnicity is partly the outcome of childhood socialisation but it would undoubtedly be less strong
were it not for the rejection and hostility to which they are
subject.

Our model would seem to apply generally to all those of
rural and peasant origin in South Asia but not, it should be
emphasised, to those whose educational qualifications have
allowed them to gain professional jobs in Britain. We were
not concerned, during fieldwork, with this relatively small
professional group. It was clear that they were following a
rather different course from the majority of their fellow
countrymen. Most professionals sought to anglicise themselves as rapidly as possible and to assimilate into the British
middle class. Some have succeeded, but most have discovered
that colour is an almost inescapable social indicator in
Britain. Many of them blame those of peasant origin for

their difficulties, claiming that they are mistaken for 'ordinary immigrants'. But it is our impression that an increasing number are now making less of an effort to assimilate. As ethnic consciousness grows stronger in response to growing external hostility, peasants and professionals are coming closer together.

At a more theoretical level, it is important that the effect of external constraints (most importantly of racial discrimination) and of internal preferences (primarily a matter of ethnicity) on the behaviour of South Asian migrants should be analytically separated. A consideration of Dahya's recent criticism of Rex and Moore's widely read book, *Race, Community and Conflict* (1969), based on research in Birmingham during the mid-sixties, can help clarify this problem. One of Rex and Moore's central arguments is that coloured immigrants have no alternative but to seek accommodation in the least attractive sector of the housing market, the lodging house, because racial discrimination prevents them from obtaining either mortgages or council tenancies. Dahya challenges this view, arguing that Pakistani migrants lived in such conditions because they chose to rather than because they were forced to (1974:112):

The immigrants' choice of poorer housing in the inner city wards of industrial cities and their preference for living there is related to their motives and orientations, and is not the outcome of racial discrimination... This is not to deny that there is racial discrimination against Pakistani immigrants, but to point out that during the early stages of their settlement, the immigrants segregated themselves because they realised that their economic goals were more likely to be achieved through conformity to group norms, by means of mutual aid under austere living conditions than through dispersal into the wider society.

The point which Dahya raises is of fundamental importance. On most occasions when sociologists have looked at the question of race, they have tended to assume that the behaviour of coloured people in Britain can be understood solely in terms of the external constraints, such as racial discrimination in jobs and housing, acting upon them. Dahya however, shows very clearly that any analysis which ignores the culturally determined preferences of the group concerned, or of the particular way in which they seek to help themselves or each other, is likely to be seriously distorted. It would, though, be equally erroneous to see the behaviour of the members of an ethnic minority as the outcome of these internal cultural preferences alone, thus ignoring the external constraints on their behaviour. For instance, while Dahya quite correctly insists that his Pakistani informants in Bradford in the mid-1960s were not interested in anything but cheap inner city terraced houses, it is not the case that they would have had no difficulty in gaining access to better housing had they sought to do so. South Asians in Leeds and Bradford are currently moving into more 'desirable' semi-detached houses, although not without meeting discrimination.

It is clear that any understanding of racial and ethnic minorities must rest on a consideration of both the internal preferences and the external constraints which act simultaneously upon them. But at the same time, it should also be recognised that the external constraints, such as the migrant's position in the labour and housing markets or the discrimination he faces, are ultimately prior to the internal preferences of the group. For instance, Dahya's Pakistani informants chose not to look beyond cheap lodging houses, but had they done so they would certainly have met with discrimination. It is the external constraints of discrimination which set the limits within which South Asians and West Indians in Britain may operate. But the particular behaviour of different groups can only be finally explained in terms of the culturally determined choices made within these limits, as well as the various ethnic strategies used to counteract, circumvent, or overthrow those constraints. These internal preferences should not be regarded as fixed or static but rather as positive and dynamic responses to the external constraints. Moreover, the external constraints acting on a minority may, in part, be the outcome of the internal preference of the majority, and these themselves may represent a response to the activities of the minority. The two sides stand in dialectical relationship to one another.

It has been shown that the earliest migrants from South Asia arrived with clear economic goals as well as with assumptions about the proper form of social relationships, which can only be understood in terms of their localities of origin. They arrived, therefore, with a particular set of cultural traits which they proceeded to use in order to achieve their goals. They appealed to, and operated in terms of, the values of their homelands, but it is important to emphasise that they did not necessarily reproduce the structures within which they had lived prior to migration. Rather, the institutions established in Britain are best regarded as emergent, in that a given set of cultural values was drawn upon in order to create new structures which would allow them to respond most effectively to a new environment. It is this utilisation of cultural values in response to a specific challenge which is the basis of ethnicity.

Very few of the first generation of South Asian migrants had any interest, hope, or intention of becoming British in a cultural sense and, thus, it cannot be said that their ethnicity is linked to social rebuff or rejection on the part of white people. For the second generation, however, the fact that they are not accepted—symbolised by the continued public categorisation of them as 'immigrants'—is crucial. If racial discrimination were not a factor, it is likely that family socialisation would have ensured that they continued to maintain a degree of cultural distinctiveness. Racism has precipitated a reactive pride in their separate ethnic identity, but the ethnicity of the second generation is rather different from that of their parents. Young people are, for example, gradually moving towards the establishment of an over-arching South Asian ethnic group, while the first generation have tended to organise themselves in terms of the narrow loyalties of their homelands—based on caste and kinship. Although these divisions remain of some importance to the second generation, not so much because of intellectual conviction but rather because of their commitment to their parents, the fact that all young people are reacting similarly to common external constraints is drawing them together. For them the sub-continent as a whole can provide a unifying cultural heritage, while for their parents the internal divisions of religion, language, region, and caste as well as village-based feuds and alliances are still of overriding importance. The second generation are also competing much more actively with white people for scarce resources in jobs and housing than their parents ever did, and they are reacting more militantly to unequal treatment.

The presence of increasingly vociferous and identifiable ethnic minorities is, in turn, affecting the attitudes of the indigenous population towards them. Many of our informants said that although they were excluded and discriminated against in the early days ('no coloureds' signs in lodging house windows was an example frequently given), they were nevertheless treated with relative tolerance as strange and exotic, but certainly not threatening, newcomers. Today the overt expression of hostility is stronger than it ever was before and physical assaults on coloured people are becoming more common. Over the past ten years, 'immigration' has become a political issue which has generated a great deal of heated argument. Many people now believe that there are too many 'immigrants' in Britain and that their presence constitutes a problem. British society has become polyethnic in the last two decades, and the new ethnic colonies are feared not only because they symbolise material competition by inferiors but also because they appear to pose a threat to the integrity of well-understood cultural patterns and institutions. The more these changes are regarded as unacceptable and, hence, generate open hostility on the part of the white majority, the more strongly will ethnic colonies reinforce themselves.

NOTE

From 1970 until 1975 we were employed by the SSRC Research Unit on Ethnic Relations at the University of Bristol. We carried out the research on which this article is based among the Sikhs in Leeds from 1971 to 1974 and in Phagwara, a town in the Jullundur Doab area of the Punjab, where we lived for six months in the winter of 1972–3.

REFERENCES CITED

Aurora, Gurdip Singh, 1967, *The New Frontiersmen*. Bombay: Popular Prakashan.
Akram, Mohammed and Sara Leigh, 1974, *Where Do You Keep Your String Beds? A Study of Entry Clearance Procedures in Pakistan*. London: Runnymede Trust.

Anwar, Mohammed, 1976, *Between Two Cultures: A Study of Relationships Between the Generations in the Asian Community in Britain*. London: Community Relations Commission Pamphlets.

Ballard, Roger, 1973, 'Family Organization among the Sikhs in Britain'. *New Community* 2:12–24.

Ballard, Roger, 1976, 'Ethnicity: Theory and Experience'. *New Community* 5:196–202.

Ballard, Roger and Bronwen Holden, 1975, 'The Employment of Coloured Graduates in Britain'. *New Community* 4:325–36.

Dahya, Badr, 1972, 'Pakistanis in England'. *New Community* 2:25–33.

Dahya, Badr, 1973, 'Pakistanis in Britain, Transients or Settlers?' *Race* 14:246–77.

Dahya, Badr, 1974, 'The Nature of Pakistani Ethnicity in Industrial Cities in Britain'. In *Urban Ethnicity* (ed.) Abner Cohen. London: Tavistock.

Desai, Rashmi, 1963, *Indian Immigrants in Britain*. London: Oxford University Press for the Institute of Race Relations.

James, Alan, 1974, *Sikh Children in Britain*. London: Oxford University Press for the Institute of Race Relations.

Jeffery, Patricia, 1976, *Migrants and Refugees: Muslim and Christian Pakistani Families in Bristol*. Cambridge: Cambridge University Press.

John, DeWitt, 1969, *Indian Workers Associations in Great Britain*. London: Oxford University Press for the Institute of Race Relations.

Kessinger, Tom, 1975, *Vilayatpur, 1848–1968: Social and Economic Change in a North Indian Village*. Berkeley: University of California Press.

Rex, John and Robert Moore, 1969, *Race, Community and Conflict: A Study of Sparkbrook*. London: Oxford University Press for the Institute of Race Relations.

Salter, Joseph, 1873, *The Asiatic in London*. London: Seeley.

Sharma, Ursula, 1971, *Rampal and His Family*. London: Collins.

Tambs-Lyche, Harold, 1975, 'A Comparison of Gujerati Communities in London and the Midlands'. *New Community* 4:349–355.

Taylor, J. H., 1976, *The Half-way Generation: A Study of Asian Youths in Newcastle Upon Tyne*. Slough: N.F.E.R. Publishing Company.

Thompson, Marcus, 1974, 'The Second Generation—Punjabi or English?' *New Community* 3:242–8.

CHAPTER 3

VERITY SAIFULLAH KHAN

The Pakistanis: Mirpuri Villagers at Home and in Bradford

Contrary to the popular view, Britain's Pakistani population is extremely heterogeneous. The migrants come from different socio-economic and cultural backgrounds, and life-styles of Pakistanis from the same region of origin differ from city to city in Britain. Local housing and employment markets, the history of immigration and composition of other minority populations have produced varying opportunities for, and reactions to, the local Pakistani population. In Bradford there are approximately 30,000 Pakistanis out of a total city population of 300,000. Other Asian, West Indian, and European populations are small in comparison. The majority of Pakistanis in Bradford and in other northern cities in England are from rural areas of the north of Pakistan. About 60 to 70 per cent originate from Mirpur District of the Pakistani part of Kashmir.

The material presented in this paper is based on research carried out in 1972 and 1973 while living with Mirpuri families in Bradford and with their relatives in villages in Mirpur (Saifullah Khan 1974). The dearth of material at that time on Pakistanis in general and the Pakistani family in particular directed my attention to the world of the women and children. This complemented earlier work which had concentrated on male spheres of activity (Dahya 1973 and 1974). The focus of the research, the gender and unmarried status of the researcher, and the marked segregation of the sexes among Pakistanis necessitated living as a family member. This in turn restricted access to other sections of the Pakistani population, 'unrelated' Mirpuri men, and kin with whom the family were temporarily in dispute.

The segmentation of the Pakistani population and the strength of the village-kin network within each section of the population was clear from an early stage of the research. It was also evident that an understanding of Mirpuri life in Bradford necessitated knowledge of the life from which the families had come and to which they still related. Subsequent research in Mirpur prevented serious distortions in the interpretations of the Mirpuri settlement in Bradford.

This paper argues that analysis of the home society, the migration process and the ongoing interrelationship of both with the overseas settlement is essential to an understanding of an ethnic minority in Britain. For the first generation migrant, life in Britain is perceived as an extension of life back home and both must be seen as one system of socio-economic relations. Historical, political, economic and social forces, unbeknown to the migrant have in large part determined the nature of the migration process and settlement patterns in Britain but the migrant's changing perception of his/her situation has had a crucial influence on subsequent behaviour. Understanding the internal dynamics of an ethnic minority in Britain involves studying the process of interaction, or reaction, of these cultural preferences and patterns of behaviour with external determinants. Many of the earlier sociological studies of ethnic minorities and 'race' relations in Britain stressed objective conditions of the host society and discussed the response of various cultures in terms of the ways and degrees to which they 'assimilated' or 'integrated'. The significance of the actor's perception of his situation, his orientation and resources were underplayed. More recent anthropological work incorporating studies of the home society, of which this book is a part, have attempted to balance that perspective without disclaiming its significance. This has not only challenged the ethnocentric tendencies of sociologists but has confronted certain concepts and techniques held sacred by anthropologists.

However 'encapsulated' the minority, an understanding of the structure of the majority society and minority-majority relations at a national and local level are crucial. The anthropologist who ignores these factors by concentrating on the internal and home-bound mechanisms of the minority will, particularly in future generations, distort the picture to the opposite extreme of earlier studies. Furthermore, concentrating on one minority and not on the areas of interaction between different minorities and the majority is bound to over-stress the significance of culture, and for certain minorities, colour.

This paper cannot tackle all of these questions. It aims to illustrate the significance of different levels and perspectives of analysis, with relation to one particular section of an ethnic minority in a city in Britain.

Mirpur District

Mirpur District of Azad Kashmir lies in the North West of the Indian Sub-continent. Azad or 'free' Kashmir is the term given by Pakistan to the Western portion of the old state of Jammu and Kashmir. A cease-fire line demarcates Azad Kashmir from Indian-held Kashmir which holds the old capital Srinagar and the famous and fertile Vale of Kashmir. Mirpur District lies in the foothills bounded by mountains to the north which culminate in the Karakorum range and the more fertile plains of the Punjab to the south. The majority of Azad Kashmiris are Muslims but there are considerable variations in culture and language. The Mirpuri is essentially Punjabi in culture and his language is a dialect of the Punjabi tongue.

Mirpur District is a poor farming area in comparison to many regions of Pakistan and particularly the more fertile parts of southern Punjab. Like other areas in North West Punjab the population has been settled for many centuries and the lack of primogeniture has caused heavy fragmentation of land. Most farms are small and thus unprofitable for cash crop production. The land in these districts is rain fed and fertility differs from area to area according to the type of soil, the height of the water table, and availability of wells.

The topography and climate of Mirpur has hindered the development of a good communication network. There are no rail or air links and asphalt roads only exist between the main towns. Buses are the main method of road transport with the motorised rickshaw in Mirpur city and the *tonga* (horse and buggy) in the countryside. Villages in Mirpur are, as elsewhere in the Sub-continent, compact clusters of houses divided by irregular alleys which open out into one or two main lanes or streets. Most houses consist of two or three rooms leading into a walled courtyard or compound with animal shelters and an open-air kitchen. The courtyard is connected to a village lane by a high door. Much of the daily life of the household takes place in the courtyard, and in the summer the villagers sleep outside or on the flat roof-tops.

Villages vary in size from a few hundred to several thousand and their social structure varies considerably from settlements dominated by large landowners to others with a large number of medium to small landowners. The inhabitants can be divided into those with land and those without land. But landowners may own from two to forty acres and some small landowners work as tenant farmers or labourers to supplement inadequate income from their land. Those who do not own land include hereditary craftsmen, village artisans, and tenant farmers. A further category of people cutting across these divisions are villagers who arrived during or after Partition, *mahajars* or refugees.

Although the caste system is rejected in Islam there are clear vestiges of the pre-Partition social structure. Notions of purity and pollution, restricted commensality and certain other features of the caste system are less evident in Mirpur and Pakistan but there is a general hierarchy of castes (with landowning castes at the top and service castes lower on the scale). Not all sons follow their father's traditional occupation (e.g. *Lohar*—blacksmith, *Nai*—barber, etc.) but the caste (*quom*) name is retained and is thus significant in certain situations.

Village Life

The primary social unit in Mirpuri society is the household. It is frequently a three-generational unit comprising grandparent(s), married son(s) and their wives and children, unmarried sons and daughters, and sometimes an unmarried, divorced or widowed uncle or aunt. Daughters move to their husband's family on marriage. Property is held in common and resources are pooled, whether derived from work on the land or wage-labour. Decisions are made communally but final authority rests with the head of the household, the eldest male. Each position in the family comprises a complex of rights and duties, attitudes, expectations and sentiments which are balanced carefully to ensure the effective functioning of the unit. Roles are precisely and clearly defined into an interlocking pattern of mutual interdependence and individual subordination to the group.

Beyond the household it is the kinship system that regulates and structures relationships. The *biradari* ('brotherhood') is an endogamous group whose members claim descent in the paternal line from a common male ancestor, but in certain contexts the word is used to refer to individuals or groups with whom there is a 'brotherly' and hence loyal relationship. It is convenient to distinguish between a person's *biradari* of participation and *biradari* of recognition and to note that although a *biradari* may traditionally be associated with a particular geographical area, migration and other factors have caused dispersal. The *biradari* tends to be an involuted and compact patrilineage due to the principles of endogamy and preferential cousin marriage. *Biradari* elders are respected and have power to ensure the cohesion of the group by reprimanding deviants and so maintaining the prestige (*izzat*) of the group. The *biradari* functions as a welfare, financial, and advice service. The system of gift exchange gives financial support to *biradari* families in times of considerable expenditure (e.g. rites of passage) and expresses official alignment and solidarity with other households. There are obvious advantages in co-operating with kin in a country without welfare and other basic facilities but interaction between *biradari* members is not always harmonious and can lead to serious and prolonged conflict.

The *biradari* extends beyond the village to other villages in the locality and closely related *biradari* members who live at long distances remain in close touch and attend important family functions. Fellow villagers of the same *quom* (caste), although often unrelated, are another category of villager with whom a household may have close ties.

All men and women are expected to marry and most marriages take place within the *biradari* but beyond the immediate family. Such a marriage is an alliance between two related families and the choice of spouse for one's offspring is determined by relationships between siblings (of the parents' generation), their rights to claim and bestow their children, and the age and personalities of the couple. Marriage within the kin group avoids anguish and worry about the status attributes of the spouse's family, and ensures that land remains within the kin group. The bride does not join an unknown household and is likely to keep in close touch with her natal family.

Relationships in the village are based on personal, face-to-face interaction. Village life is outdoor and gregarious. Everyone knows everyone else and the village forms a moral arena in which reputations are assessed and reassessed, and potential deviants pulled back into line. Child rearing is relaxed and shared, and children learn by observation rather than training. They receive a lot of affection and assume responsibilities toward different kin and villagers at a very early age. The distinct patterns of work and behaviour between the sexes is established by the time of puberty.

All Mirpuri villagers are Muslim and the majority are of the Sunni sect. A major feature of the Islamic religion is strikingly evident in village society; it is a way-of-life and the villagers perceive no clear distinction between the secular and the religious. There is a unanimous belief in God, *Allah*, and submission (the meaning of 'Islam') to God's will which is manifest in the Quran. The Quran covers all spheres of life from the personal to the political. The daily routine of village life is punctuated by obligatory prayers and the yearly calendar by fasting, mourning, and the Islamic festivals.

These all-enveloping Islamic tenets and the villager's shared set of values ensures a relatively uncritical acceptance of the traditional scheme of things. The questioning of tradition and self-awareness comes with contact and experience of alternative life-styles and values. From one point of view this relatively closed and coherent system of thought is a resource, a strength resisting potential disruption in an alien setting. But a sudden change of context or a challenge to the traditional world-view tends to produce anxiety and uncertainty. Similarly the personal interactions of village life do not equip villagers for the move to a more diffuse, bureaucratic and impersonal environment, whether it be a city in Pakistan or abroad.

Social Change in Pakistan

Over the last few centuries village life in the Indian Sub-continent has undergone many changes and the tradition of emigration to Britain should be seen as a more recent stage in this long process. In British India land ownership was reorganised, the education system extended, taxes collected and irrigation schemes were established, enabling the colonisation of new areas. The gradual introduction of a cash crop economy and foreign manufactured goods produced further changes in traditional life-styles. Partition of the Subcontinent caused mass movements of population and left senior posts to be filled by the young and aspiring. The right to vote, the introduction of new laws relating to landownership and female inheritance were further measures which were potential threats to the status quo.

Besides these external factors, rural-urban migration is another precipitant of change which is widespread throughout Pakistan. Out of the total population born and enumerated in West Pakistan in 1961, eight per cent of the total were located outside the districts of their birth. Most districts in Pakistan send out and receive large numbers of migrants but in 1961 there were ten districts where the out-migrants constituted more than ten per cent of the local born population. Such mass migrations have a variety of causes: the poor economic conditions of the district, attractions of prosperous neighbouring districts, population pressures due to waterlogging and salinity, and the attractions of colonising new areas.

Overall, the percentage of rural population has decreased gradually as the urban population has increased. The rural-urban movement now includes a new type of migrant (or his family) who has bought a house, or established a business in the city from the fruits of migration to Britain.

A large percentage of rural-urban migrants within Pakistan are neither structurally nor culturally urbanised. This is particularly true of migrants from relatively poor farming areas (such as Baluchistan and parts of the North West Frontier) who live for many years at a time, often without their families, earning wages as labourers (on building-sites or in factories). For some the migration lasts only a few years to earn money before marriage, for others it involves periodic 'stints' away from the land during lax farming periods or when there are an adequate number of men to maintain the family farm. Many stay longer and their wives and children may join them, but invariably ties with the home locality are maintained and positively valued. Most migrants are orientated toward their home, whether they eventually return there or not. Not only is contact retained with the village but social interactions in the city are largely regulated through existing kinship and locality ties with other city residents.

As social change and closer ties with the West are increasing in Pakistan's cities it is difficult, but important, to distinguish 'modernisation' from 'westernisation'. Although many sectors of the urban middle-classes appear to be adopting western fashions and life-styles they remain distinctly Pakistani in certain crucial respects. As with their counterparts abroad, external indicators and the social skills of altering patterns of behaviour to fit the environment are too often assumed to reflect fundamental values and to produce inevitable confusion. The new generations in Pakistani cities, and abroad, are emerging in a distinctive way. This is due to the increasing rate of industrial employment, higher education for girls, co-education, and the cumulative threat to the system of arranged marriages.

Although Pakistan has a long established tradition of migration, many villagers in Britain are unaware of these changes back home and thus explain their experience in terms of life in the West.

The Tradition of Migration

Each region of Pakistan has a distinct tradition of internal or international migration produced by a complex of historical, economic, political, and social factors. There has always been a movement of population from the northern mountainous areas of the Sub-continent to the more fertile plains and larger urban areas to the South. But politics has been and remains an important factor in the prevailing conditions within Kashmir. Past rulers of Kashmir did little to help, and much to exacerbate, the poor living conditions of the people. It remained a 'backward' area until the introduction of an education and health system in recent years. Most of the population moved or were affected by the disruption during Partition of the Sub-continent. The subsequent Kashmir wars and unstable political situation has also affected decisions at the individual, and government level. Some Kashmiris from the southern borders, or Kashmiris who had migrated to the plains, were involved in the migration of plantation labour from the Indian Sub-continent to Mauritius, South and East Africa, the Caribbean, Guyana, Ceylon and Fiji in the second half of the nineteenth century. The main districts of recruitment were in the South and East of India and parts of the United Provinces, the main ports of embarkation being Calcutta and Madras (Tinker 1974:56). Recruits for the Uganda railway were collected in Karachi in the 1890s.

During the First World War British shipping companies recruited a vast number of Indians into the Merchant Navy, many of whom came from the Punjab and what is now Azad Kashmir. British manpower was being diverted into the armed forces so shipowners had to seek a new source of labour. When the war ended some of the men decided to stay in Britain where they found employment and gradually settled.

During the Second World War many more joined the British Army and Navy. The area that is now Azad Kashmir, and parts of the Punjab were, and have remained, the most important recruiting areas for the Army. Mirpur and Jhelum are particularly well known for their high percentage of men in the Pakistan Army. This is mainly due to the overpopulation and poor quality of land in these areas but a further reason is the tradition of army and navy service. In the Second World War there were also many men recruited from the North West Frontier Province and Baluchistan. From 1941 these former seamen began settling in Britain, leaving the ports and moving inland (Dahya 1974:84). Many men in Mirpur tell of their fathers', or their own decision to stay in Britain in the 1940s. Under the Empire, as British subjects, there were no restrictions but some men 'jumped ship' before their contracts ended.

The earlier settlers in parts of Britain, who had continued in a steady flow during the 1940s and 1950s, sponsored their kinsmen by arranging for their recruitment as seamen hoping that they would eventually arrive in Britain. Men lived in Britain for a few years and replaced themselves with a younger brother or nephew before returning. So particular areas, such as Mirpur, established a tradition of migration, and particular families or villages in each area established a 'chain' between Britain and Mirpur. The numbers leaving for Britain increased markedly at the end of the 1950s and beginning of the 1960s. One-sided success stories reinforced the notion of Britain as a land of promise and news of the intending restriction on further immigration into Britain spurred many to leave. And by this time the institutions of migration (travel agents, banks and airlines) were well-established and facilitated visits to the homeland. A new air route to Islamabad has shortened and eased the journey.

As immigration control in Britain has gradually restricted entrance of male workers, so Mirpuris and other Pakistanis are migrating to the oil producing Arab countries (i.e. Libya, Saudi Arabia, Kuwait, and the Gulf States).

Mangla Dam and Mirpur City

In Mirpur another unique phenomenon caused a large movement of population in the 1960s. Several miles north of the small town Dina (10 miles north west of Jhelum) in the Punjab the northern foothills rise from the plain. This area of Mirpur district harbours a natural cup or 'bowl' of land surrounded by barren hills. Much of the land was relatively fertile compared to other parts of Mirpur. In this bowl of land there were approximately 200 villages and a small town, now called Old Mirpur, of approximately 12,000 inhabitants. In the 1950s a joint international venture (U.K., Canada, Australia, New Zealand, Germany and U.S.A.) started to build the world's largest earth dam here. At the beginning of the 1960s the population near the dam itself was evacuated and from 1963 onwards the whole population of the area was shifted in stages until, in 1967, the water started to fill up behind the dam. About 100,000 people (18,000 families) were moved. Families received compensation in cash for their houses and, those with under half an acre, cash for their land. Farmers with larger plots could exchange land for land in the Punjab.

It is difficult to determine how many people settled on their newly acquired land in the Punjab, how many organised tenants to run it for them, how many moved to work in a city or abroad, and how many stayed and resettled in Mirpur. The number of new villages that have appeared around the lake and the growth of the old villages seems to indicate, as might be expected, that most villagers chose to remain as near as possible to their old home and thus near relatives unaffected by the dam. The new Mirpur City grew rapidly in size and population (in 1972 it was 35 thousand), and large villages like Chak Sawari took in many displaced persons. Many totally new villages arose, often housing the majority of one particular village which, a mile or so away, had been inundated. Some writers have suggested (Deakin 1970:46, Allen 1971:32) that the large numbers of Mirpuris in Britain are a direct result of displacement by Mangla dam, and an arrangement at Governmental level to admit them into Britain. Although the construction of the dam intensified or catalysed migration to the United Kingdom, the movement began long before the dam and the theory that Mirpuris left solely for this reason is incorrect. The answer, Mirpuris say, lies in whether individuals already have relatives or fellow villages there; no villager would go without some established contact.

The forced move of such a large population caused many to consider more satisfactory alternatives. Some men left to join relatives in cities in Pakistan and others used their compensation money to join fellow villagers or relatives in Britain. News of possible restrictive immigration laws in Britain circulated and increasing numbers joined the 'beat-the-ban' rush, but after the 1962 Act special facilities were provided for displaced people who wished to go to England. Previously, Azad Kashmiris had to get their passports from Karachi but in the late 1960s passport offices opened in the cities of Rawalpindi and Mirpur.

New Mirpur City provided an exceptionally beautiful and spacious site for houses built by overseas migrants and the large number of banks and travel agents servicing the migration. The displacement of population by the lake and the move of some migrant families to the city has produced a population with close connections to the villages and, for most families, migrant members in Britain.

Leaving Home

The emigration to Britain, particularly in the last three decades, has widened the villagers contacts. It has also divided villagers into those who have close contact (through family or *biradari* members) with Britain and those without such contacts. The emigration has not only affected the villagers' awareness of new horizons and alternative life-styles, introducing a new perspective to village life, but it has also altered the numbers and type of person experiencing relative deprivation. The distinction between the 'haves' (those who own land) and the 'have-nots' (those without land) is greatly complicated by the emigration of members from both groups. Landowners who have not benefited from emigration experienced a threat to their traditional influence and power. This potentially disrupting influence is modified by the value attached to ancestral landholdings and ascribed (caste) status which remains strong. And yet these traditional values do not prevent the *nouveaux riches* of the villages asserting their new-found independence. They still participate in gift giving, contract traditional marriages and invest their money in traditionally valued effects, but now it can be done in greater style and quantity. They have invested money in the building of larger houses on the edge of their villages.

Many of the conditions which led villagers to emigrate also explain the notable absence of large numbers of permanently returned migrants. Although the majority saw their migration as temporary and still speak of it as such, the conditions in the local area and in the country as a whole do not encourage them to make such a final decision. Changed expectations and awareness of opportunities in Britain also play their part. The opportunities in Mirpur are limited. A villager can build a large house in the city but, unlike in the

Punjab, he will find it hard to rent out. If he does not want to farm there are few jobs available in Mirpur and little sign of change in the future. Living beyond his home locality in the Punjab, for example, he gets less immediate recognition of his status, and does not fit easily into the rigid social strata of the wider society.

Britain, known as *vilayat* (derived from Blighty Englander) is perceived as an advanced land where the people are rich and educated. It is a land of promise, a place to improve one's standard of living and gain greater independence. But the attitudes to *vilayat* and the West are ambivalent. Admiration is coupled with feelings of inferiority which originated in the days of the Raj. Concerned to fulfil his duties to his fellow men, proud of his rights and reputation in his village and believing deeply in Islamic principles, the villager looks upon the West as a land with totally different standards and values. From people returned from *vilayat* and particularly from seeing or hearing of western films shown in Pakistani cities and on the television, the villager has no respect for the morality of the West. In his terms the Western woman is immodest (not covering her body, talking freely with un-related men, travelling alone, etc.) and the Western family is small and appears to have little love and affection (children leave their parents at the age of seventeen or eighteen, and old people live alone).

These basic ideas are fed, modified, and reinforced by the returned migrants from *vilayat* (*vilayati log*, i.e. *vilayati* people). However much they save in Britain, by village standards they return rich, well-dressed, and with knowledge of the outside world. Symbols of success (e.g., clothes, watches, suitcases) and reports of the new life create a half picture, a distorted image. The difficulties encountered in *vilayat* and still to be faced on return are minimised to ensure the delight and pride of family and kin. The fact that the migrant has returned at all, his profuse gift-giving, buying of land or building a brick house, is an obvious declaration of association not with *vilayat* but with his home, kin and village. He may move up the social ladder but he is still positioned on it. When questioned about the British way of life, whether he replies critically or admiringly, he supports the view that people of *vilayat* have different standards of behaviour. The migrant who does not return is painful evidence of the bad influence of that different world. Whether he has married a non-Muslim, stopped sending money home or decided to live in *vilayat* and break links, he loses his reputation. The offender cannot be accepted as a valued member of the village as he has stopped fulfilling his duty as a son, a villager, and a Muslim.

Leaving for *vilayat* is not such a definite move away from traditional life as it may appear. It is a logical step and, as the chain of migration developed, it became a more desirable and accessible alternative. The decision to emigrate, like most big decisions, is made by family and kin and it is those immediately involved who finance the journey. The head of the household, or of the immediate *biradari* grouping, selects the emigrant and makes the preparations. The joint decision reinforces the ties with kin and community, thus cementing feelings of affection and determination. The migrant knows he has support, and he is strongly motivated. The preparations before the departure include a stream of advice, mostly admonitions to profit (financially) from *vilayat* but not to succumb to the bad ways of the West.

Returning Home

By returning home for a visit the migrant demonstrates to himself and his family that he is fulfilling their expectations. He returns to strengthen the tie between them, possibly to create a new tie with home by marrying or by extending his economic and financial stake in the area. During these trips home he may organise the building of a house in the village, buy a plot of land, or establish a small business.

The expense of the return visit and the investment of money in different projects demonstrates where the migrant's loyalties lie. Besides buying the ticket the migrant must, in true village tradition, return with presents for all family members and close relatives. He is expected by the villagers to give money to the poor and to village development projects. Now a rich man, he must demonstrate generosity or be subject to criticism that he is selfish and corrupted. The village expects to be involved in his economic success. Even the *tonga-walla* (driver of the horse and cart) expects to be paid more than the usual fare.

Although the migrant may have been warned in Britain about such aspects of life at home he has invariably idealised it and his expectations are shaken. He is initially delighted to see his relatives and proud of the glamour and status he has brought his family. For some men this is enough. They are happy to accept these limited achievements. Such men are often the older ones (those least westernised) who may stay and invest money for the welfare of their family and the village (e.g., by buying a flour mill, installing a well, or repainting the mosque). The young man who has spent many years in Britain is often more disillusioned and has difficulty in settling. He is upset by the exploitation of his wealth, the corruption and bribery he finds at all levels, and the inefficient bureaucracy. He may find that the bountiful quantities of yoghurt and buttermilk, fresh vegetables and eggs that he expected are in reality limited. He hopes to find improvement in the education, welfare, and housing situation in the country but little is evident. His family may have improved their standard of living to a degree but are still subject to traditional inequalities. However he is likely to fulfil the obligations expected, such as building a house or setting his brother up in business, and may still enjoy visiting all his relatives in different villages, which brings them a lot of attention. The returned villager knows that it is in this land rather than in Britain that he can raise his status. Relative to other villagers he can live in great comfort, gaining status and influence. This, he knows, is far less tangible in Britain where everyone already has so much and other constraints (notably his colour and lack of education) are strong. For those unused to the village or aspiring to other life-styles, the glamour of the first few weeks soon diminishes and more time is spent in the cities, whiling away the hours in hotels or visiting friends.

The New Land

These contemporary and historical processes in the social and political life of the homeland have influenced the emerging patterns of behaviour among Mirpuris in Britain. Except perhaps the early pioneer migrants, Mirpuris in Britain were not exceptional, atypical, or especially entrepreneurial members of their home village. Nor was migration to Britain a dramatic change in the villagers' strategy for improving their standard of living. To many of the first generation, however, the migration has proved to have dramatic and alarming consequences.

When these factors are related to the structure of British society, the local situation in Bradford, and the mechanics of the migration process, it is possible to form a clearer picture of subsequent settlement patterns and emergent institutions. The geographical concentrations and relative social encapsulation of the Mirpuri population is due to simultaneous processes of structured exclusion from the institutions of British society and the reaction of the new arrivals, determined by their perception of the situation.

Compared to the homeland, the Mirpuri finds in Britain a sophisticated and relatively stable welfare state with a complex administration and organised bureaucratic procedures. He finds a society with a marked socio-economic stratification (as in the homeland), a developed industrial urban sector and rapid social change. When the early migrants arrived memories of the Empire, and the related perceptions or misconceptions of its colonised people, were strong among the British population. Whether a sense of duty, paternalism or basic economic self interest prevailed, in the years of labour shortage after the war there were no restrictions on immigration. Mills in Yorkshire sent recruitment officers to the Punjab to ensure a steady flow of workers. Indigenous workers moved out of the dirtier, lower-paid, and shift work and new arrivals slotted into the gaps, frequently obviating the need for plant modernisation. The gaps in the system tended to be the declining industries and sectors with poor conditions (in terms of pay, security, and facilities).

Where such industries were separated physically from others this tended to enforce segregation and facilitated exclusion practices. This in turn encouraged differential treatment and inhibited contact with local workers. Migrants thus had little opportunity to acquire linguistic and other social skills.

In areas of contact, whether in or beyond the work setting, the local indigenous population were not always welcoming. The weight of social history, from the suspicion of the foreigner to the (at times pathological) prejudices felt towards dark-skinned colonials, constrained interaction at a person to person level. The actual rebuffs of prejudice and the perceived rebuffs felt from certain characteristics of British behaviour (e.g., privacy consciousness and personal formality) reinforced the migrants' tendency toward introversion. The mutual stereotyping adjusted accordingly and enhanced segregation.

The majority of Mirpuri men came in the early 1960s, somewhat later than the major Indian flow. The structure and predominant attitudes of the majority society, the experience and attitudes of the Pakistani settlers, and the mechanics of the migration process left the individual arrival with an ever-decreasing series of limited options. The 'permissiveness' of 1960s and the 1970s also affected the migrants. Disgust of its more blatant casualties (invariably exaggerated by the media, for many Mirpuris the main contact with Western culture) coupled with increasing insecurity due to immigration controls reinforced the home-orientation. The economic crisis not only altered the migrants' appreciation of their situation but, as always in times of unemployment and restricted growth, increased resentment against easily identifiable minorities (including their British-born children). But the economic crisis has also demanded of the indigenous population an acknowledgement and difficult psychological readjustment to the realities of the new balance of world power. This has contributed to recent demands for a total restriction on immigration (particularly of West Indians and Asians) to Britain. British immigration control must not only be perceived as a legal mechanism but also as a source of rumours, myths and misunderstandings which encouraged emigration from the homeland and now fosters insecurity in migrant settlements.

Returning home or organising resistance to such pressures in Britain are not easy options. There are many problems of resettlement in the homeland, and resistance is not seen by many as a practical or desired alternative. The Pakistani population in Britain, both at the local and national levels, is fragmented with no 'grass-roots' organisations. The leaders known to British authorities are frequently of the urban middle-class whose values and life-style differ markedly from the majority of their countrymen. Many villagers have no contact with or knowledge of these individuals and their organisations nor of the bodies such as the local Community Relations Councils. But, even if the villagers had representative leaders and channels of communication to the wider society, they (the first generation) would be unlikely to articulate their frustrations and demands with any force. The population tends to be preoccupied with the difficulties of daily life in this country, and maximises effort and time toward specific goals. Involved in loyalties and status acquisition within the home frame of reference, and aware of the predominantly hostile or neutral feelings in the wider society, these first generation migrants maintain an unobtrusive life-style, aimed at minimal disruption of the host society.

Gradual changes in this perspective have been precipitated by recent trends, notably the deterioration of 'race' relations in Britain and the gradual emergence of a second generation. These younger people will not accept the prejudices internal to the Pakistani population and between Asians of different regional or religious origin. Nor will they ignore the external definitions, myths and stereotypes circulating in the majority society.

The English are generally unaware of the internal differentiation of the Pakistani population and through their unquestioned use and reification of the notions regarding the 'Pakistani community' and 'Pakistani leaders' they presuppose a cohesion which rarely exists. Most English people do not question the representativeness of the urban-educated Pakistani speaking on behalf of the majority who profess very different values and priorities (Saifullah Khan 1976c).

The Local Level

The majority of Pakistanis in Bradford, and in the country at large, come from the following areas: Mirpur District of Azad Kashmir; Campbellpur, a District of Punjab Province; other Districts of Punjab Province (e.g., Lyallpur, Sargodha,

Jhelum and Rawalpindi Districts); and the North-West Frontier Province and the cities (e.g., Karachi, Lahore and Rawalpindi). All but the latter two categories are Punjabi in culture and speak some form of Punjabi. Villagers from the North-West Frontier Province, of whom there are relatively few in Britain, are Pathans and speak Pashto. Pakistanis from the cities and some educated villagers speak Urdu, the national language.

When asked 'where are you from?', a Pakistani will reply to an Englishman 'from Pakistan' or he will volunteer the name of the city nearest to his home. To another Pakistani he will reply with his city or district of origin. In any particular context if he thinks that those present know little of his country of origin, or if he feels a strong religious commitment, he will speak of himself as a Pakistani. But the first important distinction between him and other Pakistanis is on the basis of his ethnic identity or region of origin (they frequently coincide). The second distinction is on the basis of socio-economic background. Where his partner in an interaction is from the same area or similar socio-economic background communication is facilitated. There is likely to be a common fund of experiences, values and intentions, and equally essentially a common 'culture'. In the case of region of origin this includes a particular language or dialect, life-style (including dress, food, etc.) and potential kinship or other links. In the case of socio-economic background this includes a similar set of resources (skills, finances, experience of city life) and beliefs (perspective, degree of modernity, attitude to migration). Ethnic animosities and stereotypes retain significance in Britain and, as with the gulf between Pakistani villagers and city-dwellers in Britain, may have increased as a consequence of migration. (Ethnicity among Pakistanis in Britain is discussed in Saifullah Khan 1976c).

Most Mirpuris and the majority of the Asian population live today in the inner-city, some in areas where redevelopment schemes have helped to alleviate the inadequate amenities and facilities of housing and environment. Pakistanis are disproportionately represented in the textile industry, doing unskilled labour and working night-shifts. Bradford's personal income level is lower than the national and regional average, and the percentage of the work-force employed in expanding industries is far below the national average. The population's dependence on declining industries and the Pakistani employment profile as a whole means that economic cut-backs, inflation, and unemployment hit them particularly hard.

The majority of Pakistani men in Bradford have lived abroad for eight to twenty years. Invariably Pakistani women have come to Britain more recently. Most Pakistan-born children have joined their parents and the majority of British-born children are still of primary school age. There are virtually no Pakistani men entering Britain as migrants today. Nearly all new arrivals are wives and children who have a right to enter, subject to obtaining an entry certificate. Many Pakistani adults talk of their eventual return to Pakistan but the passing of the 1971 Immigration Act and the Pakistan Act 1973 has encouraged a large number to apply for UK citizenship.

Mirpuris in Bradford generally have minimal contact with the indigenous population. Men employed in the textile industry, for example, work long hours on all-Pakistani night shifts. The little time for relaxation is invariably spent with friends and *biradari* (kin) in Bradford or other towns. Most Mirpuri women do not go out to work, partly because it is considered to be un-Islamic and partly because there are no close family members with whom they can leave their young children. Women living in a neighbourhood with a high percentage of Pakistanis visit nearby friends or relatives and shop in Pakistani shops. Contact with the local population is limited to visits to the supermarket, post office, clinics, and other relatively impersonal and official settings.

Emergent Institutions

Although strengthened, modified, and altered in significant ways the main institutions of village life remain fundamental principles regulating daily life in Bradford. The smaller household structure and the absence of grandparents gives a young couple greater independence and authority in the socialisation of their children. Most couples appreciate their independence and companionship but often the first years in

Britain, or periods without support of close kin, produce considerable anxiety. Most men, however, came to join kin in Bradford who provided lodgings, found work for them and gave financial and emotional backing. Buffering the initial problems of settlement and facilitating saving, this process also introduced the new arrival to a preexisting life-style which limited the acquisition of the social skills for participation in British society.

As numbers increased, *biradari* members tended to support and trust each other more than unrelated villagers. Although many families have incorporated neighbours from the same region of origin into their social network, *biradari* ties are perceived as stronger and more trustworthy despite intermittent disagreements. In the earlier stages of settlement many distantly related members were incorporated into the *biradari* of participation and families travelled long distances to keep in touch. Now gaps in the traditional network have been filled by the increase in numbers and, as greater security and confidence decreases the need for an extended kin group, there is likely to be a relaxation and modification in *biradari* organisation. Pressures to conform and the economic advantages of cooperation coincide with an increasing desire for disentanglement by some families. However, many *biradari* members may continue to pool resources to buy a house or start a business. Interest is not expected on loans, for example to buy return tickets to visit relatives or to lend assistance during times of crisis. Women receive guidance and emotional support on arrival in Britain and leave children with close *biradari* if they visit the homeland. Many families visit each other regularly, participate in family celebrations, and attend religious festivities.

Like the *biradari*, the *purdah* system is another traditional institution of village life which has assumed new significance in Britain. Contrary to the frequent assumption that traditional forms of behaviour are bound to modify and become more westernised in Britain, Mirpuri women are subject to a stricter form of *purdah* (seclusion) than in the home village. Cultural and religious preference, the improved financial position and urban life have restricted the movement of women who in Mirpur have an active, out-door life. They collect water from the village wells and participate in agricultural and farming activities. The nature of the family unit and village life provide constant companionship and support with domestic chores and child care. As well as caring for the children and household animals, women are responsible for all the cooking and housework. They contribute to the household income and, particularly in a non-monetary economy, have control over the produce of the household. Because of the small-scale, face-to-face nature of village life and the inability of village families to observe strict *purdah*, women have a greater freedom of movement and interaction than their sisters in the city. Interaction with unrelated members of the opposite sex remains restricted, but greetings are exchanged, gatherings are more relaxed and total covering of the body with a shroud (*burqa*) is only expected when women visit distant villages or the local market town. It is only the rich landowners who can afford to seclude their women (Saifullah Khan 1976a).

Women in Britain contribute less to, and have less control over, the household income due to the lack of home-centred economic activity and the independent earnings of their husbands. Besides shopping in local Pakistani shops there are fewer reasons to go outside and greater chance of interacting with unrelated men. Observance of the principle that women should not go out to work is ensured by the size of the population, the close-knit networks, and the fast communication routes among the distinct sub-populations. But it is the nature of Bradford's industries and the age-profile of the Mirpuri population that are other important factors hindering an increase in wage employment of Mirpuri women.

Population Profile

Although there are crucial differences between Mirpuris in Bradford and Sikhs in Leeds, the present Mirpuri population can be slotted into the third phase of development outlined by the Ballards elsewhere in this volume (see chapter two). This phase of consolidation involves the reunion of families, the ability to participate fully in traditional forms of interaction, and a shift of involvement to the British-based arena.

Yet, the Pakistani population in Bradford manifests today the various household forms typical of the different phases of settlement. There are still some all-male houses but these men now have kin or friends living in settled family life nearby. They have access, therefore, to some of the comforts of a home-life and, of particular significance, are aware of the inherent problems as well as pleasures of family reunion in Britain. Many Mirpuri and Pakistani families in Bradford have close kin or lodgers living as part of, or appendages to, the household unit. It often involves more cooking for the women but can provide valued company and help with child care or crisis situations (particularly if the men work different shifts). In the future there will probably be more families living as nuclear units as well as three-generational family households. Some married sons may live permanently with their parents, but others stay only for a short period until they can afford a house of their own. When all the children are married the elder parents are likely to live with one of their sons and his family. The development of this pattern does not only depend on the strength of traditional values and loyalties among the second generation but on the availability of appropriate housing.

The development model outlined by the Ballards is a useful tool for highlighting trends and similarities between the varied categories that constitute the Asian population in Britain. But the internal dynamics of any particular local settlement and its external relations with host and homeland societies are obviously influenced by a variety of factors. By saying that Mirpuris may be ten to fifteen years 'behind' Sikhs in certain aspects of settlement, there is an implication that they will follow and experience the same changes. Although at a very general level this may appear inevitable, there can be no certainty of a corresponding process in any detail.

Arriving in Britain later than many Sikhs meant that the Mirpuris first appeared when public attitudes to immigrants had begun to harden. Restrictive immigration control was increasing and the economic and employment situation was far worse. These factors, coupled with others relating to the culture and conditions of the homeland and the nature of the migration process, encouraged encapsulation.

It is hard to determine whether the later arrival of many

Pakistani women was due mainly to the migrants' intention of return, their negative reaction to the situation in Britain (in terms of 'race' relations, or 'permissiveness'), or the ever-tightening entry procedures at British embassies abroad. What is certain is that this fact, and other distinctive features of the Pakistani settlements in Britain, are not simply explained in terms of religion, which is so often irresponsibly put forward as the explanation. Many Pakistanis, particularly Mirpuris, are people of rural background with little experience of city life even in their homeland. These Mirpuris, like Sylhetis from Bangladesh, have had less education than their countrymen. It is all the more likely therefore that such people would be more conservative of outlook, being unaware of the social changes taking place in urban areas of the homeland and arriving in Britain at a time of greater insecurity for all Asians.

By the time the Mirpuri migration was in full swing there were already ethnic services and facilities established in areas of Asian settlement, which were not available for the earlier migrants. Coupled with the large numbers arriving and the subsequent settlement pattern, an independence from the host society was possible in many spheres of life. As the population grew, pressure to conform increased and dependence on the alternative British system declined. Increasingly encapsulated in their own world, the skills required for communication and participation could not be acquired so easily. The institutions of migration were also well established by the 1960s and facilitated close contact with the homeland.

The population profile of Mirpuris in Bradford is younger than that of many Indian settlements in Britain. There are still families to be reunited and there are many women who have arrived in the last few years. Some of these are new wives of first generation migrants who have returned to Mirpur to marry. This means that most families have young children and the problems and dilemmas relating to arranged marriages have not, as yet, fully appeared. It is possible, however, that for many families such issues may be deferred until the next generation. Similarly Pakistani men and women who retire in Britain may not handle their problems in the same way as their Sikh counterparts.

There are other crucial differences between Pakistani and Sikh populations in Britain which are bound to become more pronounced. It is possible that, over time, marriages will be arranged between British-based families because there will be a greater choice of eligible kin in a few years. There may also be a change in traditional preferences. But marriage within the kin group (which involves a smaller number of possible spouses) and the pressure from kin in the village to marry into *vilayati* families is bound to preserve the trend of arranging marriages with families back home. This could mean that many children will marry a spouse from the homeland, and that some children of future generations will have a parent who is non-English speaking and new to this country. It is likely, however, that such practices will be curtailed when (and if) they produce failures and unhappiness. News of young girls who have been sent back to Pakistan for an unhappy marriage in the village, or young British-educated 'playboys' deceiving wives from the village, circulate fast and are unanimously condemned.

A further difference which may effect the future organisation and communication in local Pakistani settlements is the lack of any community centres. There is no equivalent of the Sikh temple among Pakistanis, and yet there is more need for one, especially for the women. The temple acts as a social centre, where information is exchanged and new contacts and friendships are established. Pakistani women do not attend the local mosque and do not have the additional source of information and companionship from the workplace. Although the lack of support systems has been recognised by some Islamic institutions it is unlikely that their plans to build new mosques (or add to old ones) as community centres will have an immediate impact.

Between Two Worlds

The Mirpuri villager in Britain has partial access to two systems of socio-economic relations. The degree of participation and identification in both differs from family to family and has changed over time. The dynamics of such shifts do not relate simply to the weakening of ties with kin,

religion, and homeland but to the lack of obvious alternative
courses of action and the gradual awareness of hostility in the
host society. At the beginning of mass migration the remittance network developed rapidly and a high percentage of a
man's wages was saved and/or sent home to support the
family. Remittance patterns have changed as families reunited and produced children in Britain. This has coincided
with the rapid rise in the cost of living.

There is no clear correlation between the villagers emotional and financial involvement with the home society and
degree of participation in British society. It is not an either/
or decision; individuals vary in ability and desire to manipulate two cultural systems. Nor is time an obvious factor
influencing one's orientation. It is the movement to and from
the homeland, rather than time in Britain, which makes
villagers more aware of the changes taking place in the village
and their changing perceptions of life at both ends of the
migration chain. Their experience of life in two different
worlds affects their attitudes, which in turn affects their
behaviour. A process which is already apparent is the
dampening of the idealised view of *vilayat* by the villagers
in Mirpur and of village life by migrants in Britain.

The experience of life in two worlds also involves the
migrant's claim to a limited position and economic niche in
both. Thus, his choice between alternative courses of action
is greater than his counterpart in either society, and the
resources gained in one may be used in the other. Lacking in
education, finance, and other skills the migrant to Britain
has, however, the resource of membership in a highly organised and intense kin group. He can use it to overcome initial
problems of life in a new country and to assist his long-term
goals of financial gain. Financial resources earned in Britain
would not markedly alter his status position or power in
British society even if these goals were of consequence to
him. But he can use his new wealth to gain an instant, if
limited, recognition in his home society. Thus, the resources
of one context can be utilised to overcome the constraints of
the other. The majority of returning migrants to Mirpur still
invest their wealth in traditional ways but, even in their
absence, this investment is producing changes in the village
scene.

The migrant's participation in either system is limited by the repercussions or consequences of any particular act in the other system. Constrained by his traditional values and the societal pressures to conform he knows that certain steps toward the dominant British society (for financial reward, the educational advance of his children, etc.) are steps away from his own society. But, having left village life and his home, the migrant becomes dependent on both worlds. In one he achieves economic advancement and in the other he is accorded recognition of his success. Restricted to one world at any one time he lives totally in neither. Life in Britain, and the migration itself is meaningful only in terms of life back home. Having left the village and become associated with *vilayat*, a return to village life as it was originally known is a rejection of opportunities not only beneficial to him personally but also to the family and kin. The changing aspirations and awareness which the migration process involves makes such a return far more difficult than the intending migrant could have foreseen. The migration itself and some specific goals of the migrant have unintended consequences. For example the highest value is placed on education for children in Britain and yet, in its present form, it is the most fundamental threat to all that is valued.

Home and School

Most Mirpuri children in Bradford have limited contact with local English children and, coupled with the strong emotional backing of family and kin, this ensures a relatively coherent and unconfused view of the world. Contact beyond this traditional framework begins for most Mirpuri children at the age of five when schooling starts; few attend any nursery or pre-school group. School is often their first close contact with English adults and certain aspects of British culture (e.g., eating English food).

Mainstream schools in Britain are essentially mono-cultural and mono-lingual. The culture and language of ethnic minority children is not taught and, in most schools, not acknowledged or recognised as an additional skill to be valued. Mirpuri children moving directly into such an environment not only face a new medium of communication but a new perception of self and a new awareness of home (invariably in a negative light). In time they experience a relative decrease in facility with the mother-tongue and gradually increase their command over the second language, English. Schools, therefore, are not fulfilling the educationalists' aim of developing the overall potential of the child but are indirectly causing emotional and psychological stress which is likely to hinder achievement, however efficiently English is taught as a second language.

Few Mirpuri children in Bradford move directly into mainstream schools. A scheme of specialised language centres was developed as a mechanism to ease the child's transition (and no doubt to avoid the re-organisation and re-appraisal of policies in mainstream schools). The advantages of the language centres for Asian children in Bradford are that they are neighbourhood schools. Children do not travel far from home and parents are encouraged to be involved and mothers to attend language classes. They are more likely, therefore, to be able to establish a teacher-parent rapport which has failed miserably in many other schools. Mirpuri children move to the language centres at the age of four and a half to five with no English, stay for one year, and sometimes one and a half years. The centres cannot provide the opportunity for children to use English as a living language nor for Mirpuri children to befriend local English-speaking children.

At the age of five and a half to six and a half these children leave the relatively sheltered atmosphere of the local centre for their 'normal' school which is often several miles away. Small groups of children are seen at bus collection points in the morning and form a visually identifiable group of outsiders at the school where the majority of children live locally. The drastic change in environment, unknown and at times threatening classmates, and the anxiety of performance draw the few children of Asian origin together. Best friends are likely to be Asian and contact with English classmates out of school is rare.

Mirpuri parents often misunderstand the education system in Britain. Their experience of education in the homeland leads them to expect standard books, regular homework, discipline and no involvement on the part of the parents. And yet one of the main reasons for migration to Britain (the education of their children) produces high and unrealistic aspirations for these children. This is a potential source of tension between parents and children.

Another preoccupation of parents which is likely to increase is the maintenance of the mother-tongue and Islamic studies. Many Mirpuri children attend a mosque school several days a week after regular school hours. The additional work and different teaching methods may be detrimental for some children but the schools have supportive functions which help counterbalance the actual and perceived disadvantages of 'normal school'.

Parents are frequently less concerned about their daughters' educational success and possible employment. This causes considerable frustration to some girls who are keen to continue studies or have a career. Parents want to ensure that their daughter's reputation is not blemished by unacceptable behaviour and attitudes which would jeopardise a good marriage. However orthodox a girl's home life, she is influenced by other ideas at school: mixing with friends who discuss boyfriends, the cinema, and fashions. She is also taught to question and develop her individuality. Many Mirpuri parents have not appreciated the strength of these pressures until the effects are noticeable in their own children. Others, who have learned from the experience of friends or relatives, may leave their daughters in Pakistan or send them back to live with grandparents. Some see the answer to be a single-sex or a Muslim school in Bradford. For the truly orthodox, however, this can only be a partial solution because girls will be subject to the 'corrupting' influence of Western society outside the school unless they are completely secluded and banned from watching television.

The New Generation

The difference between Mirpuri parents and children is a generation gap, resulting from time of birth, background and subsequent experience of different cultures and social change. There is also a difference of orientation. Experience of more established and less encapsulated Asian minorities indicates the strength of fundamental Asian values and institutions, plus a tendency for Asian youth to diverge from and then return to the more traditional (Ballard 1976). In abstract, the two cultures appear contradictory. In reality the flexibility of individuals and the separation of social worlds enables the young to maintain consistent pictures of themselves and to avoid the schizophrenia or conflict which might be assumed inevitable. The divergent culture and orientation of British Asians and their parents, particularly for those of rural origin, produce tensions that arise from a mutual inability to appreciate the priorities and preoccupations of the other. The two generations participate in differing degrees in three social arenas; the homeland, the local Pakistani world in Bradford, and the majority society in Britain.

The traditional hierarchy of authority and respect within the family is frequently upset by the migration process and the ability of younger members to use the social skills of the wider society. Although most minors maintain the public authority and respect due to elders, occasions arise when they publicly question and disobey their elders.

Most Mirpuri parents are unprepared for their children's adolescent period. In the village there is a sudden transition from the status of daughter and girl, to that of wife and woman. Such transitions, although supported by customs and socialisation, are not without stress but an extended period of adolescence is of a different nature. In Britain, daughters and sons not only explore themselves but the various social worlds in which they participate. At present, however, many are likely to resign themselves to an arranged marriage. Mirpuri youth of the emerging second generation are likely to remain encapsulated enough to accept arranged marriages or will be aware that the alternatives hold greater problems. To marry against ones parents wishes is, in many cases, to lose ones natal family and to become emotionally (and at times financially) dependent on one individual. Although alien to someone brought up in an Asian family, a relationship of this nature would have greater chance of survival if the pressure of Pakistani public opinion were not so strong and the exclusion and rejection of the alternative British society not so daunting. Marrying traditionally unacceptable partners subjects a couple and their families to criticism and sometimes ostracism. Marrying an English person subjects the Asian partner to sudden loss of a wider supportive system.

The next decade will see an increasing number of Mirpuri youngsters reaching adulthood. It is bound to be a period of tension and anxiety for many families. The new generation is different in certain crucial respects from its elders. But the strength of the home family and culture, coupled with lack of equal treatment in the wider society, will probably ensure the maintenance of a distinctive identity and life-style.

Conclusion

This paper has indicated the main elements in a framework of analysis for a recently established ethnic minority in Britain. The framework will alter for subsequent generations but present trends suggest that ties with the homeland and distinctive cultural patterns will remain crucial for many years. Theoretical and practical limitations, along with personal inclinations, will direct many researchers to focus on one country, locality, or perspective. If such studies are placed firmly in this wider context and acknowledge the migrants' own frame of reference this may help to avoid ethnocentricity in analysis and interpretation. For example, discussions of 'the position' of Asian women in Britain are still phrased essentially in terms of Western values, with emphasis on individuality and the comparability of the sexes (Saifullah Khan 1976b). And sociological studies which slot Asian and West Indian workers into an 'under-class' of the working class tend to interpret the workers subjective allegiances as 'false consciousness'. Such studies attribute greater significance to objective criteria of class membership (income, residence, etc.) and ignore financial commitments or investments in the homeland (as illustrated by Jeffery 1976: 80). Even if ties with the homeland decrease in future generations, growing participation in British mainstream society will not necessarily involve conforming to existing patterns of English behaviour.

While the anthropologist's contribution to the field of ethnic relations gains recognition, we must reorientate ourselves to the new demands of research in highly complex urban settings. We can no longer study cultures in relative isolation or focus on a clearly delimited group of people. An understanding of relations between ethnic groups demands that equal attention be given to the majority culture and the boundaries between various people. The focus on minority cultures has tended to stress differences rather than similarities between ethnic categories and has ignored the significance of the majority society's definition of the minorities (Saifullah Khan 1976c).

As a new generation of British Pakistanis emerges, so future generations of anthropologists will include members of minorities. These scholars will not only contribute to the study of their fellow ethnics but, coming full circle, may also study the indigenous population in Britain. This will help us to gain a more complete picture of British society.

REFERENCES CITED

Alavi, Hamza, 1972, 'Kinship in West Punjab Villages'. In *Contributions to Indian Sociology* (n.s.) 6.

Allen, Sheila, 1971, *New Minorities, Old Conflicts: Asian and West Indian Migrants in Britain*. New York: Random House.

Ballard, Catherine, 1976, 'Culture Conflict and Young Asians in Britain'. Paper presented to the International Congress on Transcultural Psychiatry. Bradford, England.

Dahya, Badr, 1973, 'Pakistanis in Britain, Transients or Settlers'. *Race* 14:246–77.

Dahya, Badr, 1974, 'The Nature of Pakistani Ethnicity in Industrial Cities in Britain'. In *Urban Ethnicity* (ed.) Abner Cohen. London: Tavistock.

Deakin, Nicholas, 1970, *Colour, Citizenship and British Society*. London: Panther.

Eglar, Zekiye, 1960, *A Punjabi Village in Pakistan*. New York: Columbia University Press.

Jeffery, Patricia, 1976, *Migrants and Refugees: Muslim and Christian Pakistani Families in Bristol*. Cambridge: Cambridge University Press.

Korson, J. Henry, 1969, 'Student Attitudes toward Mate Selection in a Muslim Society: Pakistan'. *Journal of Marriage and the Family* 31:153–65.

Saifullah Khan, Verity, 1974, 'Pakistani Villagers in a British City'. Unpublished Ph.D. thesis, University of Bradford.

Saifullah Khan, Verity, 1975, 'Asian Women in Britain: Strategies of Adjustment of Indian and Pakistani Migrants'. In *Women in Contemporary India* (ed.) Alfred de Souza. Delhi: Manohar.

Saifullah Khan, Verity, 1976a, 'Purdah in the British Situation'. In *Dependence and Exploitation in Work and Marriage* (ed.) Diana L. Barker and Sheila Allen. London: Longmans.

Saifullah Khan, Verity, 1976b, 'Pakistani Women in Britain'. *New Community* 5:99–108.

Saifullah Khan, Verity, 1976c, 'Perceptions of a Population: Pakistanis in Britain'. *New Community* 5:222–9.

Tinker, Hugh, 1974, *The New System of Slavery*. London: Oxford University Press.

CHAPTER 4

STUART B. PHILPOTT

The Montserratians: Migration Dependency and the Maintenance of Island Ties in England

Most Britons are probably unaware that a few thousand people from the idyllic West Indian island of Montserrat are living in their midst. Yet this mountainous British colony in the Eastern Caribbean, only 39½ square miles in area, proportionately sent more migrants to Britain in the 1950s and 1960s than any West Indian territory (cf. Davison 1962, Peach 1968). Migration is not a recent phenomenon for Montserrat; in fact, it has been part of the social, economic and cultural fabric of the island for well over a century. A focus on the historical development and effects of its dependency on migration and on the organisation of its migrants abroad sets out, in rather stark fashion, patterns and problems that should illuminate West Indian migration generally.

Early Migration History

Montserrat's social and economic history can be seen as a continuing response to changing overseas demand for a series of agricultural commodities and, ultimately, labour itself. A British colony was first established on the island, apparently uninhabited at the time, in 1632. The earliest settlers were mainly Irish, either dissidents from other colonies or political exiles. Except for two brief periods of French occupation, the island has remained a British possession up to the present day.

The island's first crops were provisions and such export commodities as indigo, tobacco, cotton, and ginger which could be economically produced by white smallholders and indentured servants. As North American tobacco became cheaper and more desirable on the British market, however, agricultural production throughout the Caribbean shifted to sugar. Increased capital outlay for grinding and boiling mills and other equipment required by sugar production concomitantly led to the concentration of land in larger holdings and an increased demand for labour. After various unsuccessful attempts to mobilise an adequate supply of European labour, planters throughout the island purchased African slaves. The first slave arrived in 1664 and by 1678 the number had increased to 992. At this same time, the white population reached a peak of 2,682 from which it progressively declined until the mid-1960s.

When the island's sugar production reached its highest point in 1735, Montserrat was 'esteemed a possession of great importance to England' (Gipson 1960:225). The slave population of the island was then 6,176. In 1772, although the slaves had increased to a maximum of 9,834, the white population had dropped to 1,314 and sugar production had actually declined due to decreasing soil fertility and the lack of new land. Already Montserrat's economy had become marginal to the British colonial market system which had created it.

By the end of the eighteenth century, a characteristic social structure had emerged. The groups of whites, free persons of colour, and black slaves were rigidly structured legally, economically, socially and culturally. Whites were the owners, managers, and overseers, professionals and clergy. Black slaves were the field and mill hands, the domestics and, occasionally, the artisans. Some free coloured persons were land-holding slave owners. Most were hucksters, small shop-keepers, clerks, and artisans (Goveia 1965:228). The local legislature functioned largely to control the behaviour of the slaves.

While sexual liaisons were probably the most prevalent form of inter-group relations, the strict hierarchy was maintained. White men married white women but mated freely with coloured and black women, both free and slave. Mating and family relationships were highly unstable among the slave population largely because the men had no legal rights or obligations with regard to their mates or children and because families could be divided at the will of their owner.

The Post-Emancipation Period

With the end of slavery in 1834, various new modes of attaching labour to the land were attempted and some alteration in the island's pattern of land tenure took place. Most important here is that emancipation initiated Montserrat's development as, what I have elsewhere termed, a 'migration-oriented' society (Philpott 1968, 1970, 1973).

While ex-slaves in larger colonies such as Jamaica and British Guiana took to the uncultivated bush and mountain lands to start their own small-holdings, there was no unalienated land in Montserrat. Instead, as soon as the so-called 'apprenticeship system' which compelled ex-slaves to serve their former owners for 40½ hours a week ended in 1838, newly-free Montserratians began leaving the island by the boatload for richer colonies such as Trinidad (cf. Hall 1971: 41). The estate owners, apprehensive about the disappearance of their labourers, pressured the British government into halting the practice of paying bounties for the removal of workers from one colony to another. While this measure slowed emigration, the exodus has never been halted.

Rather than allow the black labourers their own land, yet faced with mass emigration and a chronic shortage of capital, the estate owners adopted two measures in the 1840s to maintain agricultural production. Both of these measures— tenancy-at-will and sharecropping—were contentious political issues since their inception.

Tenancy-at-will supposedly compensated for pitifully low wages by allowing ex-slaves to occupy a cottage on the estate and cultivate a small provision ground. Share-cropping involved the labourer performing all the sugar cultivation on estate land and receiving one-third or one-half of the resulting crop as his reward. Undoubtedly, the planters had little choice. In addition to the emigration of much of the labour force, a highly destructive earthquake in 1843 destroyed crops and buildings. Furthermore, the British government's reduction of the duty on foreign sugar in 1846 caused a severe depression in the West Indian market and the estate owners were no longer able to obtain the loans from British merchants. The Montserrat planters also failed to introduce new technology. The island's agricultural system continued to be based almost entirely on the hoe and the cutlass until the mass exodus to Britain in the 1950s.

In 1849–50 the island suffered a severe drought and small-pox outbreak. Several of the estates changed hands and some of the most marginally-productive were divided into small-holdings which provided the basis for the development of a local 'peasantry'. Most of the island's arable land, however, remained as undivided estates even in the 1950s. The cultiva-tion of limes began on two of the larger estates. By 1878, lime orchards totalled 120,000 trees and the juice became a very significant export commodity. The spread of lime culti-vation and an improved market for sugar undoubtedly contributed to a reduction of emigration which took effect around 1857. From then until 1890, labour migration was relatively insignificant but by the end of the century it in-creased again. Once more the West Indian sugar industry was severely depressed owing largely to inefficient production and competition from beet sugar (Beachey 1957). Montserrat was particularly hard hit.

Adding to the economic difficulties of the island, the older lime orchards were blighted by insects in 1892 and in 1896 considerable damage and some loss of life was caused by a flood and a series of earthquakes which continued intermit-tently until 1900. Finally, on August 7, 1899, a hurricane struck the island wiping out the lime orchards, killing 100 people, injuring another 1,000 and leaving 9,000 homeless.

Thus Montserrat entered the twentieth century with the prospects for its two main agricultural export commodities—sugar and limes—virtually eliminated. The export of human labour assumed a renewed importance. When the United States government took over the building of the Panama Canal in 1904, British West Indian labour was in great demand. The *Montserrat Herald* reported that 'scores of persons of the labouring and other classes have been leaving our shores by almost every steamer for Panama and Colon' (May 12, 1906). At the same time a new crop, Sea Island cotton, was introduced to revive the island's agricultural export trade. By 1903 some 700 acres were planted in cotton and by the 1930s more than 4,000 acres were cultivated annually. Although production dropped radically in the

1950s, cotton remained the island's most important agricultural export in 1970.

Despite the completion of the canal, large-scale emigration continued into the 1920s. The natural increase in the island's population was more than counterbalanced by emigration to the United States, Canada, Cuba, and San Domingo. This period was marked by the growth of Montserratian 'communities' in New York and Boston which continue to have social and economic significance for the island. But in 1924 the United States government passed the first of a series of acts which restricted West Indian immigration. Once again, as one migratory outlet shrank, another expanded. The development of the oil refineries in the Dutch islands of Curaçao and Aruba in the late 1930s and 1940s created a demand for labour which was met by large numbers of Montserratians and other British West Indians.

In the long series of post-emancipation migrations that have been outlined, patterns of behaviour, values, and expectations developed which have incorporated migration as an integral part of Montserrat's social system. This prepared the islanders for the largest migration of all, that to the United Kingdom.

Migration to Britain

The staggering scale of Montserratian migration to Britain was produced by a unique combination of economic and political events in the early 1950s. The island's cotton industry enjoyed a brief period of post-war prosperity during which the price nearly doubled. However, in 1952, competition from Sudanese cotton on the British market left most of the West Indian crop unsold. Montserrat planters reacted by lowering production.

In the same year, constitutional changes brought about the first election to the island's legislative council based on full adult suffrage. As in other West Indian territories, trade union activity became the pathway to political office. As the election approached, work stoppages on the estates were frequent and class conflict became so explicit and critical that a commission of enquiry was appointed. The union leaders complained to the enquiry about low wages paid to estate labourers and also that 'relics of immediate post-chattel slavery days'—share-cropping and tenancy-at-will—kept the workers in a state of servility and duress.

During this period, many of the Montserratians in Curaçao and Aruba began returning to the island or migrating directly to England. They contributed disproportionately to the exodus both through departing again themselves and financing the passage of others. Although only six Montserratians applied for passports to go to England in 1952, the number increased rapidly the following year when an Italian line began calling at the island on the return run from South America. In 1955 alone, 1,145 Montserratians applied for passports. As the migration mounted, a Spanish line also began picking up passengers. The construction of an airstrip in 1956 also made air connections with Britain possible.

A few months before the election in early 1958, an island-wide strike paralysed the cotton industry. The workers returned only after being promised a second commission of enquiry. The commission attributed the sharp decline in cotton production to an extreme shortage of labour brought about by emigration to the United Kingdom and the reluctance of remaining people to work for low wages when remittances were arriving from migrants abroad. Furthermore, those who were willing to work during this period were less afraid to strike as many had some alternative income from outside the island.

While the commission recommended new wage rates of $1.30 (British West Indian) a day for men and $0.90 for women, compared with $0.90 and $0.60 respectively in 1953, this was not sufficient to stem the emigration of workers which continued at a substantial level until curtailed by the Commonwealth Immigrants Act in 1962. Remittances became increasingly significant during this decade. In 1951, the value of the cotton crop was $620,000 while remittances amounted to $72,400. In 1960, the situation was virtually reversed; remittances totalled $617,000 while income from cotton dropped to $162,000. By 1962, primarily due to the shortage of labour, estate production ceased entirely. Share-cropping had been eliminated three years earlier.

Evidence based on census data, passport applications, and

statistics collected by the Migrant Services Division of the West Indian federal government on arrivals in Britain suggest that between 4,000 to 4,500 Montserratians moved to Britain during the decade. Between the censuses of 1946 and 1960, there was a net emigration of 5,399 people, leaving the island with a resident population of 12,167. Government figures show that between 1955 and 1961 alone 3,835 Montserratians arrived in Britain.

As might be expected, an examination of passport applications for the period indicates the vast majority (84.3 per cent) of Montserratian migrants were between the ages of 15 and 49. More surprising is that female migration was at least equal to male. There is a tendency in most migrations for men to send back for women; more important in the Montserratian case, however, are social and economic factors which stimulate women to leave in order to meet obligations owed to relatives left behind. They do not all migrate simply to join men who precede them.

From 1959, a considerable number of children applying for passports reflected a tendency to bring children to England after the adults became established. Other characteristics such as education, occupational skills, or land ownership, did not act as important selective factors in the migration to Britain. Demographically, the British migration took much of the working-age population out of the island; the old and the young were left behind.

The Social Implications of Migration

While migration had been integrated into Montserrat's social and cultural milieu over the preceding century, the movement to Britain resulted in some major social changes. Following emancipation, a characteristic pattern of social stratification, very similar to the 'colour-class' systems described for other West Indian islands (Braithwaite 1952; Henriques 1953; R. T. Smith 1956), emerged in Montserrat and continues in a modified form today. This system, in turn, drew its main features from the slave society of the late eighteenth century.

The upper class consists of the resident owners or managers

of the larger estates, expatriate colonial officials, professionals, expatriate religious officials, bank managers, and the larger merchants. Most of the people in this small stratum are white or light-skinned. The middle class is primarily made up of the civil servants who staff the post office, the public works department, the hospital, the courts and police, and the education department. Bank employees, small hotel operators, and some shopkeepers are also part of the middle class. There are no whites in this category. While many middle class people are light-skinned ('coloured'), they do not represent a very large group.

The lower class, primarily black, comprises approximately 90 per cent of the island's population. Most do not have a regular job, but tend to work at sporadic wage labour, subsistence or commercial agriculture, and some at commercial fishing. Many are almost entirely dependent on remittances. In short, the lower class is characterised by 'occupational multiplicity' (Comitas 1963) and chronic unemployment.

Lower class black mobility into the middle class seems to be connected with the attrition of the island's coloured population through selective migration, particularly to the United States. Frucht has noted a similar pattern of migration from nearby Nevis (1968:198). This middle class bias was due largely to the high cost of passage and the initial expense of settling in the United States (lacking any kind of state protection, unemployment insurance, sickness and death benefits). These middle-class West Indians, possessing better education and more money than the Black American migrants from the Southern United States were generally incorporated into the higher levels of Negro society in New York and Boston.

The primary requisite for social mobility among lower class Montserratian blacks was the attainment of secondary or higher education. Yet the cost of fees, uniforms, supplies, and incidentals was prohibitive for lower class students; for many years after the secondary school opened it was virtually the preserve of the middle and upper classes. However, remittances from migrants in Curaçao and Aruba, and scholarships established by a Montserratian migrants' organisation in the United States, gradually made such education more accessible. In the late 1950s and early 1960s, most secondary school students were drawn from the lower class and were largely financed by remittances from Britain.

Although the number of middle-class jobs has increased over the past 25 years, these positions have been easily filled by secondary school graduates. The social expectations pertaining to the work an educated person can and should do channel most graduates into the civil service, teaching, banking, and commerce. Thus, while secondary education has permitted upward mobility for some in the island's social hierarchy, for most it is a form of 'anticipatory socialisation' that prepares people for migration and work outside the island.

Migration and Class Structure

In sum, migration has had a significant impact on the socio-economic hierarchies of the island and has promoted a certain degree of upward mobility. At the same time, changes in the political, economic, and educational processes have stimulated further migration.

Statistically, recent migration has been largely a lower class phenomenon; yet class has not acted as an important selective factor. Considerable migration has taken place at all social levels. Consequently, if class distinctions are to be made with regard to migration, they can only be based on *migrant ideology*, defined as 'the cognitive model which the migrant holds [regarding] the nature and goals of his migration' (Philpott 1968:474).

Lower-class workers perceive migration initially as a temporary phase, mainly to gain money and improve their positions *vis a vis* a local island group. Expectations about 'helping the family' with remittances and about the care of migrants' children are also encompassed. In the upper class, migration is more likely to be viewed as permanent, or very long-term, made on the basis of universalistic standards of professional or occupational advancement. No particular expectations about remittances or child care are held. Middle class migrant ideology incorporates elements of both.

Obviously, in any particular case, this polarised abstraction is not meant to apply without qualification. Few upper class Montserratian migrants fail to take some account of their attainment relative to the island society; nor do lower-class migrants totally ignore supra-local standards regarding adequate wage levels or working conditions. The abstraction, however, points up some rather important differences in class conceptions about migration.

There are two potential avenues of social and economic advance for the lower class: education and migration. Secondary education is expensive in Montserrat. Consequently, the most feasible and likely alternative for the lower class islander is to migrate with the hope of ultimately returning to the island a richer person. While some lower class migrants manage to acquire enough skill, education, or money while abroad to gain entrance to the middle class upon their return to the island, this is rare. However, returned migrants are generally accorded higher status in their local communities than they enjoyed prior to migrating.

References to a man's migration—even when referring to middle-aged married men—are often couched in terms which imply the attainment of adulthood: 'He went out to make himself a man' or 'I was only half a man before I went out'. The main reason for the returned migrant's enhanced social standing is his assumed affluence but he (or she) also enjoys greater esteem merely by virtue of having had a socially valued experience; i.e. having 'been out', particularly to England or the United States.

Male returnees frequently recount stories of their travels at rum shops and other places where men gather and obviously relish the prestige which accrues to those who have been abroad. Conversely, the lack of such migration experience is regarded as a form of deprivation. Moreover, the significance of migration is given ceremonial expression at the community level. Aside from the *rites de passage* at birth, marriage and death, the only major ceremonial occasions are those connected with migration—namely feasts when leaving, when returning, or when marrying while away from the island. While such feasts have a religious aspect, they are clearly a form of status validation, sometimes locally referred to as 'signing the progress'. The feast at departure marks a major turning point in the migrant's life.

When a migrant marries while away from the island it is his or her 'duty' to send home money to 'keep up the feeding'.

In cases where both the bride and groom are Montserratian (and this is usually so) the money is sent to both the bride's family and the groom's family for separate feasts. This obligation appears to be generally met. In thus demonstrating that the home community is a group before which the change in status must be validated, the continuing nature of the migrant's ties to the community is also implicitly expressed. The biggest feasts are usually held when a migrant returns from a long period of migration. They mark, as it were, his reintegration into the community, his success and prestige.

While migration experience is valued in itself, a permanent upward alteration of the returned migrant's standing in the community is based largely on the amount of money he brings home. Usually such wealth is manifested in new or improved houses, running water, flush toilets, indoor kitchens, refrigerators, radios, household furnishings and other acquisitions with which returned migrants have consistently altered the material culture of their home areas.

Yet, for the most part, returned migrants produce very little social or economic innovation and, indeed, the potential for such innovation seems very limited. Returned migrants cannot return to the ordinary labouring jobs which they held before migrating without loss of newly-enhanced status. Consequently a suitable capital investment is necessary to maintain a relatively independent position. Such investments tend to be culturally defined; notably rum shops, vans or trucks for use as buses, and cattle. As the demand for rum and bus service has been less than the supply in recent years and pasture land is very scarce, returned migrants, the would-be entrepreneurs, are increasingly forced to remigrate.

Agricultural Production and Remittances

At the community level, the most immediate and obvious economic effects of migration to Britain were the drastic reduction in commercial and subsistence agricultural production and an increased dependence on cash income, notably from remittances. The reduced emphasis on agriculture manifests the general attitude that 'working with the hoe' is hard, unprofitable, unprestigious, and to be avoided

if at all possible. Cotton production is particularly unpredict-
able and, consequently, householders who receive moderate
remittances or other income are reluctant to risk losing it in
expenses for wages, land rental, fertiliser and seed.

The difficulty of obtaining agricultural labour is, of course,
another factor. While property development and government road work created some demand for male labour in the
mid-1960s many men were underemployed. Employment
prospects were worse for women. Yet small producers complained that they could not hire people to help them with
their crops. They contended that, since the migration to
Britain, many of those remaining behind are 'just lazy'. Such
views are exaggerated but intermittent remittances and
sporadic wage labour have made it possible for the younger
men in particular to shun agricultural labour.

As Montserrat's rural settlements have relatively few
'community-based' activities, one of the more crucial consequences of agricultural recession is a related decline in
reciprocal labour exchanges. Prior to the collapse of the
estates, landless men and women earned part of their income
as agricultural wage labourers and part as share-croppers.
While the estate owners and managers obtained labour
through asymmetric cash transactions, the share-croppers
cooperated with fellow villagers in reciprocal labour exchanges called 'maroons'.

In a maroon, groups of five to thirty men or women,
depending on the size and nature of the task to be performed,
gather at the land of the holder to prepare the ground, weed,
or harvest the crop. While the organiser of a maroon is
expected to 'give back the day' in similar labour for each of
those who participated, the maroon also has aspects of a fête.
Most householders were directly involved in share-cropping
approximately equal amounts of land and stood in a relatively equal socio-economic position *vis à vis* each other. As
the men and women of most households were involved in
different, and sometimes two or more, maroon groups, this
institution created a considerable degree of economic interdependence between households within the community.

Since the British migration and the end of estate agriculture, maroons have almost disappeared. Interhousehold
dependence has decreased while migrant dependence has

increased. Many households are no longer involved in agricultural production, depending instead on remittances or
other sources of income. Members of such households are
not interested in participating in maroons. Those who are
willing to undertake agricultural labour usually do not receive
remittances and have no other wage paying employment.
With the increasing emphasis on cash purchases, labourers
now work only for wages.

Social Tension and Conflict

Shared subordination in the agricultural estate hierarchy
seems to have contributed to group cohesiveness and
solidarity, manifested in strikes and other trade union activities, among the landless estate workers. Reciprocal labour
exchange acted as another form of social integration. Consequently, with the decline of both agricultural estates and
maroons, without the development of alternative integrative
institutions within the community, one might expect an
increase in various forms of social tension and conflict (cf.
Frucht 1968:206).

Indeed middle-aged and elderly residents frequently
express the view that there are more quarrels and disputes
in the area than before the migration to Britain and that the
people no longer 'move together' as they should. There was,
in fact, an increase in court cases based on charges of assault,
indecent or threatening language, and disorderly behaviour.
These cases arise out of disagreement over the relative prestige of the parties involved, a situation which is illuminated
by Jayawardena's (1963) analysis of 'eye-pass' disputes on
Guianese plantations. He sees such conflict as emanating
from the incompatibility between the strong egalitarian
ideology of plantation workers, on the one hand, and their
aspirations for social mobility in terms of the values of the
larger society, on the other.

The general harassment of the legal proceedings or, in
those cases that do not reach court, the police investigation
involved, demonstrate that the 'advantaged' party is not to
be trifled with and, further, that the norms which suggest all
villagers are equal in prestige are not to be easily breached.

Apparently in the early phase of the British migration a considerable amount of the 'discretionary' income from remittances was channelled into legal fees, connected with such cases. More recently, the greater need of cash for food and other basic requirements, plus the fact that a number of migrants have reduced their remittances claiming that the money was being wasted in court, has checked this tendency.

Household Organisation and Migration

West Indian family and household organisation is a controversial subject which has spawned a voluminous literature (see R. T. Smith 1963; M. G. Smith 1966). Here I can only touch upon some aspects of Montserratian lower class household or domestic organisation directly impinged upon by migration.

The Montserratians practise three main mating alternatives: extra-residential unions, consensual cohabitation, and legal marriage. These varying unions are normally engaged in sequentially by both sexes. *Extra-residential unions* are those in which both partners are normally resident members of different household groups. Such unions take place most commonly between a single man and a single woman; less frequently, between a married man and a single woman. Unions like this rarely involve a married woman. Fifty to sixty per cent of the children born in any given year originate from extra-residential unions; many are subsequently legitimised by the marriage of their parents.

These children are normally incorporated into the mother's natal household with the mother's mother or her mother-surrogate acting as the 'social mother' while the biological mother is often treated, behaviourally and terminologically, more as an elder sibling or an aunt of the child (cf. R. T. Smith 1956:143–5). This practice contains a latent conflict. The daughter's motherhood is never entirely negated or unrecognised either in the household or the community and, as motherhood is probably the most esteemed social role open to lower-class women, a daughter in this position may increasingly move to perform the role more fully. Furthermore, while both legal and social norms indicate that a father should continue to provide support for his children even after an extra-residential union has terminated, the sanctions are weak and male contributions in such cases are often sporadic or non-existent. Consequently, the need and desire of the biological mother to assume the full parental role, including its economic aspect, underlies the high rate of female migration.

Although *legal marriage* is not regarded as a prerequisite to child-bearing, most lower-class Montserratians eventually marry. The institution of marriage is connected with the attainment of a certain socio-economic standing, a demonstration of 'ambition'. A husband is expected to provide a house and support for his wife and children, and sometimes her children by other men that she may bring to the union with her. In addition, a marriage must be marked by relatively expensive ceremonies in the church and in the community. For most, as already suggested, migration is the main means of achieving the social and economic requisites of marriage. In addition, a considerable number of younger migrants have married in England. Unlike many West Indian societies, *consensual cohabitation* ('common-law marriage') is the least significant form of union in Montserrat.

Mobilisation of Passage Money

Montserratian migration to distant labour centres calls for the use of commercial transport, very costly in terms of lower class earning power. Consequently, accumulation of the necessary fare constitutes an important problem for prospective migrants. For example, the cheapest passage by boat to England in 1954 was $312; in the same year male estate workers in Montserrat were earning only $0.90 a day for a few months of the year.

Although there has been a small amount of seasonal contract labour for Montserratians, employer-financed passages have not contributed significantly to migration from the island. Nor have there been bank or government loans available specifically to finance migration. Shipping agents did not extend credit directly to prospective migrants. In the overwhelming majority of cases, passage money was mobilised on the basis of domestic group or kinship relations.

A quite typical case is that of a migrant who made it possible for twenty-two people—his children, siblings, sibling's children, and their actual or intended spouses—to migrate to London over a 12-year period. The enduring quality of most of the relations involved was rooted in earlier shared membership in the same household group. For example, he brought over his three full sisters who had been reared in the same household with him; he did not help any of his father's 29 'outside' children who had been raised in other households.

The principal sources of passage money, in order of importance, were siblings, parents, parent's siblings, spouses, cousins reared in the same domestic group, intended spouses, and personal income (Philpott 1973:132–3). It has already been suggested that one migration, to some degree, finances the next. A considerable number of initial passages to Britain, for example, were paid for by fathers or siblings absent in Curaçao and Aruba. Furthermore, on the basis of lasting sibling ties, it is not uncommon for Montserratians who migrated to the United States many years earlier to pay the passage and act as legal sponsors for sibling's children whom they have never seen.

Fostering of Children

As many migrants have young children, the care of these dependents during their absence is another important domestic problem. Fostering of children, however, is not unusual anywhere in the West Indies. Due to the variable marriage careers of their parents and changing contingencies of closely related households within communities, children frequently are members of several household groups before they reach adolescence. The fostering of migrants' children, then, is an accentuation of prevailing practice.

During my fieldwork, approximately one-third of the children under 16 lived in household groups in which neither of their parents was a resident member. Two-thirds of these children were left with maternal kin and most of the rest with paternal kin. Grandmothers were the single most important category of fosterers, mother's mothers caring for approximately 47 per cent of the children and father's mothers for 18 per cent.

There is a transactional nature to such fostering arrangements. In the urban labour centres to which most migration
takes place, a child represents an economic liability prevent-
ing the parents from realising their full wage earning potential. Consequently, most migrants leave their children in the
island, believing it is a cheaper and healthier place to raise
children. They do not usually pay their child's passage abroad
until they are old enough to enter the urban work force. Some
migrants even send their foreign-born children back to the
island for similar reasons.

In terms of day-to-day household activities in Montserrat,
on the other hand, children are indispensable. They care for
the goats and sheep, gather firewood, carry water, climb trees
for mangoes and breadfruit, and run numerous errands to the
shops and post office. In addition, girls launder, cook meals
and look after younger children. This fostering process is
infused with the morality which stresses 'helping the family'.
Older people are well aware that freeing a daughter or son to
migrate by caring for their children provides the best assurance of financial security for all concerned. The migrant, in
turn is expected to meet what I term 'remittance obligations'.

Remittance Obligations

The basic principles of these obligations are quite simple.
The migrant is expected to send money ('breaks') and clothing to his mother or mother-substitute. To a much lesser
extent, and depending on the nature and emotional content
of the pre-existing relationship, the migrant is expected to do
the same for his father. A migrant may also send occasional
'breaks' for close kin, mainly siblings reared in the same
household, or attempt to finance their passage should they
wish to migrate. Finally, migrants should send support for
their children left on the island. As a female migrant usually
leaves her children with her mother, she is under dual obligation to remit money to her mother's household. Consequently,
some grandmothers, realising their potential control over the
migrant may be diminished, are reluctant to give up the
grandchildren if and when the mother sends for them.

Rubenstein (1976) found essentially the same remittance obligations operative in a St. Vincent community.

Children are implicitly taught these expectations in the home and the community through the praise of migrants who 'send a good break' and through the condemnation of the 'worthless-minded' kin who do not 'notice their families'. A migrant who reputedly returned from America with 32 trunkloads of gifts for distribution to his family and friends, and a woman who sent her brother a car from America in the days when the only other cars were owned by the wealthiest estate owners, have become near-legendary figures. Furthermore, when children collect the mail at the local post office, the excitement over receiving a registered letter containing money or the disappointment of receiving nothing continually reminds them of the ideal migrant behaviour.

The homeward flow of remittances and clothing is symbolically reciprocated by the people in Montserrat through the periodic sending of parcels of cassava bread, various weeds and bush leaves used to make tea, salt pork and occasionally rum. In sum, the continuing interrelationship between migrant and home community is expressed through the exchange of goods and services.

Montserratians in Britain

For a migration-oriented society such as Montserrat the degree to which migrants meet the expectations of those they have left behind is crucial. Here some incentives and constraints which influence the actions of migrants in Britain are examined.

In treating the social organisation of migrants and their home society as parts of a common analytical framework, I concentrate mainly on those aspects of migrant life which have the most relevance for the maintenance of ties with Montserrat. I have not attempted to deal directly with housing and occupational problems, prejudice, discrimination, or the attitudes of the British towards migrants, which have been a primary concern of much of the work on West Indian and other 'coloured' minorities in Britain (Banton 1959; Glass 1960; Griffith *et al* 1960; Patterson 1963; Rose *et al* 1969). Such works, the media, and recent events in

Britain have made it obvious that there are substantial social barriers impeding the assimilation of Black migrants in Britain which undoubtedly contribute to the maintenance of such social networks as discussed here.

Of the 4,000–4,500 Montserratians resident in Britain, I estimate (Philpott 1973:167–9) that well over 3,000 have settled in London while possibly 500 live in Birmingham. The remainder are scattered in small numbers in such cities as Leicester, Preston, and Ipswich. Their distribution in London is not simply a reflection of the general distribution of West Indians. Some districts with high concentrations of Montserratians, in fact, contain rather small proportions of the overall West Indian migrant population. On the other hand, areas which contain very high percentages of the total West Indian population, such as Brixton and other areas south of the Thames, contain few Montserratians. The heaviest concentration of Montserratians, roughly 2,500 islanders, is found in North and East London, particularly Stoke Newington, Hackney, and Finsbury Park.

Such residential concentration is obviously related to the organisation of migration. The initial migrants send back for kin and friends from the same village or area of the island. These new arrivals might stay temporarily in the same house and later find accommodation nearby. Consequently, not only do Montserratians tend to live in certain urban neighbourhoods but kin and friends from the particular parts of the island often cluster in the same houses and streets within these areas. For example, migrants from a village in eastern Montserrat who are mostly settled in Stoke Newington, often refer to Birmingham as 'Long Ground' because that is where most of the migrants from a nearby village of that name in Montserrat live. Such residential concentration facilitates continuing social contact between fellow islanders.

Montserratian migrants are employed in much the same range of unskilled or semi-skilled labouring, transport, or factory work described for other West Indians (Davison 1966; Patterson 1963; Rose *et al* 1969; Wright 1968). Obviously in the economic sphere social relations cannot be based solely on island ties. However it is not unusual for a Montserratian to work with one or more fellow islanders. This follows from the efforts of Montserratians who get jobs in a particular place to obtain employment for their friends and relatives, or inform them of possible openings.

In non-work contexts, however, island bonds are much stronger. I have already suggested that kin and friendship ties with other Montserratians are continued through residential proximity. These ties are further reinforced by a strong tendency towards island endogamy among migrants marrying abroad. Many younger migrants have married in England; the greater ease of attaining the material requisites of marriage, the desire to conform to British social norms, and the tax relief associated with legal marriage encourage this tendency (cf. Davison 1966:31–2). Eighty per cent (44 out of 55) of the marriages I recorded in Britain in which at least one partner was Montserratian were contracted with other Montserratians.

There is still a lingering distrust of other islanders, a feeling that they are somehow different and that Montserratians cannot understand them as well as their 'own countrymen'. This suspicion is bolstered by stories about men from other islands who have married Montserratian women, taken their money, and then run off with women from their own islands.

Probably more important is the recognition of potential disagreement—which again reflects the commitment to Montserrat—over which partner's island they would settle in if and when they return to the Caribbean. In the West Indies the ideal residence principle is that the 'wife follows the husband' but there is a considerable variability in practice. Within a single island, the choice of residence does not disrupt either partner's kinship or friendship ties unduly. This is not the case when the residential choice is between islands and Montserratians are often reluctant to subject themselves to such a dilemma. This feeling is clear in the statement of a Montserratian who had married in London:

My wife comes from Montserrat too. That way there are no headaches. We can go back to Montserrat—or move anywhere—at any time and we won't be quarrelling. I am not looking to go back to Montserrat just yet. The English are a tolerant people for now. But it might go the other way.

There is sometimes opposition to inter-island marriages from the home community. Kin at home feel that such marriages reduce the possibility of seeing the migrant again and that his commitment to his own island and family will be diminished. There is considerable distrust of other islanders —largely formed by letters from migrants. When one mother in Montserrat received ten pounds through the mail from a Jamaican who sought her permission to court her daughter in London, the woman sent a letter to her daughter telling her to have nothing to do with Jamaicans, 'the wickedest people on earth', although she had never met one. Finally, the Jamaican contempt for 'small islanders', negative British attitudes towards racial intermarriage, and the fact that the majority of Montserratian migrants' social contacts are with fellow islanders further constrain marriage choices.

The Churches and Credit Associations

Church attendance has declined among Montserratian migrants as with other West Indians in Britain (cf. Calley 1965:116; Hill 1963:Chapter 3; Patterson 1963:252–5). However, two Pentecostal churches in the Stoke Newington–Hackney area are led by Montserratians and most of the members are Montserratians. These two churches provide a basis for continuing interaction between islanders, although their membership (approximately 100–150) represents a relatively small percentage of the Montserratian population in London. In addition to their weekly services, both ministers and congregations of these churches visit at regular intervals the Montserratian-based Pentecostal churches in Birmingham and Ipswich. In the services and the social gatherings which follow, ties between Montserratians in different British cities are renewed. The more formal churches, such as the Anglican and the Methodist, have not provided so firm a basis for the continuity of island ties.

Rotating credit associations, called 'boxes' by Montserratians, also reinforce links between migrants. The features of such associations are fairly well known (Ardener 1964). Members contribute a set amount each week to the organiser or 'banker' who distributes the total sum (the 'hand') weekly to the participants in a pre-arranged order. The number of members in the various boxes ranges from eight to twenty-five, the largest ones enabling an individual to amass £250–

£300 in a two-week period if he has the last hand in one box and the first hand in the next.

Migrants who 'throw a box' together are well aware that it is a form of compulsory saving. There is also the notion that by 'keeping the money working', rather than putting it in the bank, 'Montserratians help each other. That is how we get through.' The first migrants to London often used boxes to mobilise passage money for family members, enabling other Montserratians to be brought over more quickly than if the migrants had saved individually for such passages.

Recruitment is almost always on the basis of island ties. The reason is not simply that Montserratians know and trust other Montserratians. More important is the nature of the sanctions. Firstly, a member of a box who fails to keep up his or her payments is traceable. Unless he severs ties with all Montserratians he will be readily found by other members of the box. Secondly, an implicit sanction lies in the fact that the news of such a misdemeanour would be quickly communicated among Montserratians in London and also back to the home island. The offender would be given a bad name which could adversely affect his future relations with other islanders.

There are no formally-constituted voluntary associations such as clubs or mutual aid societies in London recruited on the basis of island ties. Earlier Montserratian migrants to the United States formed a mutual aid society, The Montserrat Progressive Society, which has operated in New York and Boston since 1904. It originally provided for funeral costs and helped with sickness and unemployment insurance. The fact that the British 'welfare state' covers many of these functions undoubtedly impeded the development of voluntary associations.

Social Activities

Montserratians in England are brought together roughly once a month in numbers varying from 25 to 150 for weddings, christenings, and house parties. The renewal of island ties is particularly prevalent during the Christmas season. In a three-day period at Christmas 1965, I accompanied Montserratian friends in 'passing' (i.e. visiting accompanied by

eating, drinking and gossiping) 22 Montserratian households
in North and West London and Birmingham. In almost all of
these households other Montserratians were visiting at the
same time.

Islanders often meet in the markets which carry West
Indian food, and a number of pubs in the Stoke Newington
area are regular gathering places for Montserratian men.
Some Montserratians perform services for fellow islanders
either reciprocally or for reduced rates. Women, for example,
often dress each other's hair; some men repair cars or do
carpentry and household improvements.

Such ties link migrants in social networks within which the
individual's actions are evaluated and which, consequently,
form a basis for social control. In this respect, the following
extract from a letter sent by a girl in London to her father in
Montserrat is revealing. The girl is chastising her father, who
had returned to Montserrat after some years in England, for
having an affair with a young woman:

I am sorry to have to say this but from what I've been *hearing
over here* if that's the life you take X (his wife) home for it's better
you did stay over here. You should remember Y is my age and
you are friendly [i.e. having sexual intercourse] with your
daughter. You know *everyone was looking out* for how you and
X live when you take her home and you know what Montserratians
give. For whether things are true or not you know them and you
make me *feel shame. It's a lot of talking over here* and I am not
very pleased with what I hear because you should remember you
are a married man and I am sure you wouldn't like no man to do
any daughter of yours like that. (Emphasis added.)

Here we see a somewhat diffuse communicative network
within which the actions of an individual Montserratian are
gossiped about and, in relation to which, the girl feels her
standing has suffered. The collective opinion is what matters
because she feels shame whether or not the rumours are true.

Social Sanctions and Remittance Obligations

What induces migrants to meet their remittance obligations?
Although some have already been suggested, I will consider
the various sanctions which may prevail. There are a number

of legal and quasi-official sanctions available. Income tax relief acts as a positive sanction for migrants to support various dependents in Montserrat. But in most cases this relief is simply an added incentive to continue something that would be done anyway for other reasons. Apparently no legal procedure exists by which the judgments of the magistrate's court in Montserrat regarding non-support of dependent children or spouses can be effectively enforced in England. People who have court orders, or other legal claims for support from a migrant, sometimes put their cases before the social services department of the Montserrat Government or go to a lawyer who then attempts to locate the migrant and imply the possibility of formal legal action if the claim is not met. Lawyers also occasionally contact an employer, endeavouring to get him to put some pressure on the migrant. Such measures, however, are rarely employed.

Some sanctions are related to future possibilities. Virtually all migrants believe they will someday return to Montserrat if only for a holiday or for retirement. Migrants anticipate the general community approval of a man or woman who 'never sent an empty letter all the time (s)he was out'. And they fear the displeasure of their family members should they return without having met their obligations: 'I'd be ashamed to face my people, if I hadn't done my best'. There is the notion of insurance, of holding their place with their families in Montserrat, because of the possibility of sickness, declining employment or restrictive legislation compelling them to go home.

In some cases, migrants have the potential of a more tangible future reward such as the inheritance of land or a house. However, there appears to be little difference in remittance patterns between areas of small landholders and those where the people are landless. The reasons should already be apparent. The migrants are anxious to escape from agriculture, so land is not sought as a productive resource. Furthermore it is not easily saleable because peasant land often has no clear title. Most migrants are interested in land mainly for housing sites on which to build if they return to Montserrat. There is a reluctance to build on undivided family land and returned migrants prefer to buy a separate site with a legal title. Finally, houses are normally left to whoever is actually on the spot looking after the old people at the time of death and consequently migrants are usually ineligible.

Social control, then, with regard to remittance obligations is vested largely in the nature of the migrant's social network rather than in property considerations or legal sanctions. As long as his social ties are mainly with other Montserratians, there is a continuing general reminder about what the migrant should be doing for the people back home. The Montserratian migrant network in its broadest sense (i.e. the totality of links between all Montserratian migrants) mobilises no specific action against a migrant who does not send money home. In a more diffuse way, the defaulting migrant may suffer a loss of esteem among those who hear that his family at home is having a difficult time.

Within this overall network, however, the individual migrant is generally linked in a more specific set of relations and continuing interactions with other Montserratians who in turn are linked with each other. In short they are involved in what Bott (1957:59) has termed close-knit networks. Such networks are usually composed of kin, friends, or fellow villagers who are in a position to put pressure on the subject. This pressure is most marked when the migrant, and one or more other members of his network, share obligations to the same person. For example, when two brothers are involved in a network in London and one fails to support their mother, confrontations arise which may either resolve the problem or rupture the relationship. Networks which include a large number of siblings serve as effective channels for information about the fulfilment of remittance obligations. The following case further illustrates the point:

Two migrants in a close-knit network were from neighbouring households in Montserrat. One migrant sent his mother five pounds. In her return letter she said she gave ten shillings to the other migrant's mother because she was having a hard time. The first migrant was annoyed and confronted the second, asking him why he was doing nothing for his mother. The man said he was making payments for a van. He was then told: 'Man, you na pass through you van. You pass through your mother.' This stricture on the man's moral obligation to his mother for the difficulty she underwent in bearing and rearing him had a strong effect.

The argument thus far suggests that sanctions bearing on remittance obligations stem mainly from the nature of social networks which migrants form and from their 'migrant ideology'. Probably less than 20 per cent of Montserratian migrants now in England will in fact ever return to the island to stay. Yet almost all talk and *act* as if they will return. Actions taken by migrants, such as sending or withholding remittances, are viewed as having future consequences for their life in Montserrat. Their behaviour is influenced accordingly.

The fact that most Montserratian migrants' personal networks involve other Montserratians tends to maintain the migrant ideology with its emphasis on remittance obligations and an eventual return to the island. To some extent, the ideology influences the choices a migrant makes in forming his or her personal network. Theoretically, it should be possible for migrant ideology and the composition of a migrant's social network to change independently; in practice, this does not seem to happen. For example, some migrants have decided to stay in Britain permanently, and have cut themselves off from other Montserratians, sometimes without even repaying passage money loaned by family members and friends. Such radical rejection of the dominant ideology, however, is rare.

Remittances, despite erratic annual variations, tend to decline over time. It is misleading to interpret this as a reorientation of values. Rather, the migrant is faced with a continuing series of choices over the allocation of his scarce resources among competing obligations and interests. Providing support for one's mother, wife, or children; buying a house or a car, or a television, or drinks for one's friends; these are all valued actions for Montserratians, whether in the island or in England.

However, the migrant is removed from the system of checks and balances operating within the island which enables a degree of compromise to be worked out between competing ends. In the migrant situation, as indicated, the checks and balances are vested primarily in the worker's personal network. Montserratians, however, place little moral value on contact with other Montserratians; their continuing interaction is largely a matter of it being the 'comfortable' or the 'wise' thing to do rather than the 'right' thing to do.

A tendency for Montserratians to include other West Indians in their personal networks is already well under way; however, current attitudes appear to preclude for now any major inclusion of Asians or Whites. In the future, it seems possible that as the migrants' social networks encompass more and more non-Montserratians their commitment to the home society will decline.

My argument does not imply that changing remittance patterns are entirely bound up with the composition of personal networks. New obligations are continually arising in Britain. These are regarded, both by the migrants and the people at home, as legitimately reducing the potential of what the migrant can do for those in Montserrat. New obligations, in turn, may reduce the possibility of the migrant ever returning to the island. Finally, unemployment, inflation, sickness, and many other factors over which the migrant has little control also effect remittances.

Conclusion

The development of Montserrat's dependency on migration and its migrants has produced a particularly vulnerable social system. Given the adverse natural and economic conditions in which it developed, the manner in which migration has been incorporated into the social and cultural fabric of the island must be regarded as a relatively successful adaptation thus far. Yet the stresses in such a social system are great indeed; the island is dependent on legislation and economic conditions abroad over which Montserrat's population have no control.

Although recent efforts to improve the local economy have been reasonably successful, the prospects are very limited. Migration and remittances remain important. The flow of money from abroad is dependent on a migrant ideology which is patently unrealistic, stressing as it does ultimate return to the island. If a substantial proportion of the migrants returned to the island in the foreseeable future, whether through their own decisions or those of foreign governments, the social and economic consequences might well be calamitous.

NOTE

Two years' field research upon which this article is based was carried out in Montserrat and in London from 1964 to 1966. Continuing contact with the island and its migrants has been maintained since that time. I would like to thank the Research Institute for the Study of Man and the Canada Council for financial support and Alison de Pelham for typing the manuscript.

REFERENCES CITED

Ardener, Shirley, 1964, 'The Comparative Study of Rotating Credit Associations'. *Journal of the Royal Anthropological Institute* 94:201–29.

Banton, Michael P., 1959, *White and Coloured: The Behaviour of British People Towards Coloured Immigrants*. London: Jonathan Cape.

Beachey, Raymond W., 1957, *The British West Indies Sugar Industry in the Late 19th Century*. Oxford: Basil Blackwell.

Bott, Elizabeth, 1957, *Family and Social Network*. London: Tavistock.

Braithwaite, Lloyd, 1952, 'Social Stratification in Trinidad'. *Social and Economic Studies* 2(2–3):5–175.

Calley, Malcolm J. C., 1965, *God's People: West Indian Pentecostal Sects in England*. London: Oxford University Press for the Institute of Race Relations.

Comitas, Lambros, 1963, 'Occupational Multiplicity in Rural Jamaica'. *Proceedings* of the 1963 Annual Spring Meeting of the American Ethnological Society. Seattle: University of Washington Press.

Davison, R. B., 1962, *West Indian Migrants: Social and Economic Facts of Migration from the West Indies*. London: Oxford University Press for the Institute of Race Relations.

Davison, R. B., 1966, *Black British: Immigrants to England*. London: Oxford University Press for the Institute of Race Relations.

Frucht, Richard, 1968, 'Emigration, Remittances, and Social Change: Aspects of the Social Field of Nevis, the West Indies'. *Anthropologica* (n.s.) 10:193–208.

Gipson, Henry L., 1960, *The British Isles and the American Colonies: The Southern Plantations, 1748–1754*. New York: Alfred Knopf.

Glass, Ruth, 1960, *Newcomers: The West Indians in London*. London: George Allen and Unwin.

Goveia, Elsa V., 1965, *Slave Society in the British Leeward Islands at the End of the Eighteenth Century*. New Haven: Yale University Press.

Griffith, J. A. G. and Associates, 1960, *Coloured Immigrants in Britain*. London: Oxford University Press for the Institute of Race Relations.

Hall, Douglas, 1971, *Five of the Leewards, 1834–1870*. St. Laurence, Barbados: Caribbean Universities Press.

Henriques, Fernando, 1953, *Family and Colour in Jamaica*. London: Eyre and Spottiswoode.

Hill, Clifford S., 1963, *West Indian Migrants and the London Churches*. London: Oxford University Press for the Institute of Race Relations.

Jayawardena, Chandra, 1963, *Conflict and Solidarity in a Guianese Plantation*. London: Athlone Press.

Patterson, Sheila, 1963, *Dark Strangers*. London: Tavistock.

Peach, Ceri, 1968, *West Indian Migration to Britain: A Social Geography*. London: Oxford University Press for the Institute of Race Relations.

Philpott, Stuart B., 1968, 'Remittance Obligations, Social Networks, and Choice among Montserratian Migrants in Britain'. *Man* (n.s.) 1:465–476.

Philpott, Stuart B., 1970, 'The Implications of Migration for Sending Societies: Some Theoretical Considerations'. In *Migration and Anthropology* (ed.) Robert F. Spencer. Seattle: University of Washington Press.

Philpott, Stuart B., 1973, *West Indian Migration: The Montserrat Case*. London: Athlone Press.

Rose, E. J. B. and Associates, 1969, *Colour and Citizenship: A Report on British Race Relations*. London: Oxford University Press for the Institute of Race Relations.

Rubenstein, Hymie, 1976, 'Black Adaptive Strategies: Coping with Poverty in an Eastern Caribbean Village'. Unpublished Ph.D. thesis, University of Toronto.

Smith, M. G., 1966, Introduction to the Second Edition of Edith Clarke, *My Mother Who Fathered Me*. London: George Allen and Unwin.

Smith, Raymond T., 1956, *The Negro Family in British Guiana*. London: Routledge and Kegan Paul.

Smith, Raymond T., 1963, 'Culture and Social Structure in the Caribbean: Some Recent Work on Family and Kinship Studies'. *Comparative Studies in Society and History* 6:24–46.

Wright, Peter L., 1968, *The Coloured Worker in British Industry*. London: Oxford University Press for the Institute of Race Relations.

CHAPTER 5

NANCY FONER

The Jamaicans: Cultural and Social Change among Migrants in Britain

Jamaican migrants in England are caught between two worlds: they are no longer just like Jamaicans back home but they are also not exactly like, or fully accepted by, most English people. New cultural patterns as well as new patterns of social relations—neither wholly English nor wholly Jamaican—have emerged. Yet when academic commentators write about Jamaican, or West Indian, migrants' experiences in British society, the word assimilation (and sometimes the concept of 'cultural survivals') nearly always comes up. In my view, the way Jamaican migrants come to terms with their new environment is more akin to a process which has, in the West Indies, been labelled 'creolisation'.

Creolisation took place in the very formation of Jamaica itself. Jamaica, like other West Indian islands, is in V. S. Naipaul's (1970) phrase, a manufactured society. The original inhabitants of the island, the Arawak Indians, were decimated by disease and overwork during the period of Spanish rule; when England captured the island in 1655, the Arawaks had been completely wiped out. Jamaica was a plantation colony, made up almost entirely of immigrants from Europe and Africa. Few would argue, however, that African cultures survived unchanged in Jamaica or, conversely, that after emancipation the African slaves and their descendants became fully Anglicised in the image of the British colonisers. The term creole is in fact used to refer to 'things, habits, and ideas' native to the West Indies (Lowenthal 1972:32). Raymond Smith describes the social system that emerged in the West Indian territories after emancipation as creole society, and he argues that 'the population became increasingly creolised, rather than Anglicised, a process which affected Englishmen as well as others' (1967:234). Though this creole system was rooted in the political and economic dominance of Britain and was integrated around the conception of the moral and cultural superiority of things English (Smith 1967), it is clear that West Indian islands were not replicas of England. A new culture and a new social system were created in response to specific West Indian (and British) economic, social, and political circumstances.

Just as the term creole and the process of creolisation describe the creation of a new culture and society in the Caribbean, so too, when Jamaicans emigrate and settle in Britain, new cultural and social patterns begin to develop. Obviously, there are striking differences between immigration to Jamaica and Britain. Africans were, for a start, imported as slaves for plantation labour, whereas Jamaicans voluntarily emigrated to England as free labourers. And while migrants and descendants of recent migrants made up the majority of the Jamaican population in the nineteenth century, Jamaicans and other newcomers are a very small minority in present-day England. Still, I believe it is useful to think of a broadly analogous process of creolisation occurring among Jamaican migrants in England and to try to isolate the conditions which lead to specific cultural and social changes among them here. Indeed, to analyse Jamaican migrants' lives in England in terms of the familiar concepts of assimilation, on the one hand, or cultural persistences, on the other, is misleading.

Of course, Jamaican migrants in England carry with them much of the old and a 'memory of things past' (Jackson 1968:2). Yet, as Constance Cronin observes in her study of Sicilians in Australia, '... although individuals may attempt to establish some of their pre-emigration institutions, circumstances force the alteration of these institutions and eventually the values which relate to them' (1970:9). Faced with many new circumstances in England, a good many Jamaican 'traditional' beliefs, values, and cultural symbols—as well as 'traditional' behaviour patterns—inevitably undergo change. While some of their former beliefs and social institutions may persist, they may change in form and function in the new environment.

The fact that most Jamaican migrants' former cultural patterns and social institutions do not survive intact in England does not mean that Jamaicans become assimilated, however. Assimilation usually implies that migrants become absorbed into English society with their former traditions and values replaced by English ideas and customs. Undoubtedly, many Jamaicans conform to some English cultural patterns and social institutions, but they have not wiped out the old nor are they fully ready to be assimilated and socialised into the new. The concept of assimilation, in any case, is 'too simplistic to be of value in the analysis of migration in industrial societies' (Richmond 1968:277). As applied to Jamaicans in England, assimilation seems, in the first place, to imply that it is necessary and even desirable for Jamaicans to disappear as a separate social entity (Richmond 1973:239). Britain, like other industrial societies, is, moreover, quite heterogeneous, stratified, and pluralistic so that there is not always one set of institutions into which Jamaicans may assimilate. And even if we find similar behaviour patterns, for example, among Jamaican migrants and certain English people, this is not necessarily an indication of assimilation, in the sense of absorbing the new ways and values. Rather, these behaviour patterns may be independent responses to similar social and/or economic conditions which Jamaicans and English people face.

Admittedly, Jamaican migrants in England do want to be accepted by English people and they do want to be judged as individuals rather than simply as 'Blacks'. Still, most do not want to become carbon copies of the English nor do they want to preserve their 'traditional' beliefs and practices without any change. Whatever their preferences, the old and new seem in fact to have blended in many ways in response to circumstances in England. The following pages explore some of these cultural and social changes. Here changes in culture refer to changes in Jamaican migrants' beliefs, values, and symbols; social changes are changes in the pattern of their social relations (cf. Geertz 1965). Given the limitations of space, this paper cannot cover all the changes that have taken place among Jamaicans here. Instead, it focuses in detail on a few social and cultural changes and tries to give some idea of what these changes mean to the migrants themselves. To set the stage, I first look briefly at the background of Jamaican emigration to Britain and I outline the methods used in my research in rural Jamaica and in London. I then examine how, and why, two cultural symbols (blackness and education) have acquired a new meaning in England, and I consider some of the ways that family relations have changed in England. Whether these new cultural and social patterns will persist among the second generation in England or among migrants who return to Jamaica is the subject of the concluding remarks.

The Move to England

A variety of factors have 'pushed' and 'pulled' Jamaicans to Britain. 'It was sort of half and half,' one man told me. 'Half what I was leaving, not making much money, and half that I knew there were good jobs going in England.' The relative weight of the factors pushing Jamaicans to leave the island in contrast to the pull factors drawing them to Britain has been the subject of considerable study. Ceri Peach (1968), for example, argues that the pull factors—most notably the availability of jobs in Britain—were key, while Daniel Lawrence (1974) stresses the primacy of push factors— mainly the lack of economic opportunities in Jamaica. Undoubtedly both push and pull factors are important in understanding Jamaican emigration generally as well as the more recent emigration to Britain in the 1950s and 1960s—one of the largest emigration movements in Jamaican history.

First consider the push factors: Since the end of the nineteenth century, lower-class Jamaicans have faced poor living conditions, underemployment, and very limited opportunities for advancement in Jamaica. Most lower-class Jamaicans want to live, as closely as possible, in the style of the island's elite: to have a well-paid and prestigious job and the other accoutrements of respectability such as a modern home, new furniture, a car, and stylish store-bought clothes. The nature of the island's economy and polity, however, have made these achievements an unrealised dream for the vast majority of the population.

This is not the place to discuss at length the economic,

political, and social history of Jamaica. Besides, many West Indian social scientists have, in recent years, written excellent analyses of the political economy of the island (e.g. Beckford 1972; Girvan 1972; Jefferson 1972). The conclusion all of them come to is that the underdeveloped state of Jamaica's economy (a major cause of emigration) stems from the distorting effects of colonial rule, the domination of the island's economy by plantation agriculture, and Jamaica's continued dependence on neo-colonial powers and multinational corporations. Whether these conditions will be altered under Michael Manley's new regime of democratic socialism is still unclear. The discussion here refers, in any case, to the period prior to 1972, when Manley came into power.

In concrete terms what these conditions mean is that land distribution patterns, for instance, are stacked against small farmers. Farms under five acres in Jamaica, which in 1954 represented 70 per cent of all Jamaican farms, occupied only 14 per cent of the total farm acreage. Plantations, which were less than one per cent of all farms in that year, occupied 40 per cent of the total farm acreage. Plantations also monopolise most of the best quality land in the island.

It is not only that Jamaicans do not have enough farmland. It is that when they look for other ways to make a living, they are very often frustrated. Although the percentage of the Jamaican population engaged in agriculture has steadily declined in the past one hundred years—from 70 per cent in the 1880s to 38 per cent in 1960—this decline has not been matched by an equivalent expansion in other sectors of the economy. Indeed, the few new industries established in the past 25 years have not created many new jobs (see Jefferson 1972). Due to mechanisation, the major old industry, the sugar industry, employs fewer workers than before.

Combined with the lack of jobs is the fact that Jamaica has a rather severe overpopulation problem. Competition for decent jobs is often fierce. The unemployment rate in the island has in fact hovered around 20 per cent in the last few decades. For those lucky enough to find work, employment is often not steady. And all too frequently, the pay is very low.

No wonder that Jamaicans, since the end of the nineteenth century, have looked to emigration as one way to improve their situation. And here pull factors enter the picture. For the destination of Jamaicans has shifted in the past 100 years in response to employment opportunities and immigration restrictions in three main areas: other Caribbean islands and Central American countries; the United States and Canada; and Britain.

A look at a few figures gives some idea of these previous population movements (see Eisner 1961). More than 100,000 Jamaicans, for example, went to Panama in 1905 to help build the canal, and when this work ran out Jamaicans emigrated to Costa Rica to work on the banana plantations. After World War One many went to Cuba during the sugar boom there, and thousands emigrated to the United States in the first few decades of this century. Immigration restrictions in 1924 curtailed emigration to the United States, but many were recruited to work there during World War Two. The McCarren-Walter Act of 1952, however, once again limited Jamaican emigration to the United States, this time to 100 a year. Then Britain became the favoured destination.

Post-war Britain was experiencing economic expansion and many British workers were able to move into better jobs. This created gaps at the low ends of the occupational ladder, and Jamaicans, as well as other West Indians, Indians, and Pakistanis, were drawn in as a replacement population. Immigration restrictions in 1962, of course, ended Commonwealth citizens' right of free entry to Britain, and the flow of Jamaicans to Britain was then severely limited. In 1951 there were 15,300 West Indians in Britain, but two decades later 446,200 people of West Indian origin lived here, of whom 226,800 were born in the United Kingdom (Lomas 1973:39). Jamaicans make up the largest group from one island, over half of the West Indian population in Britain. To give some idea of the numbers involved, consider the most recent available figures for the number of Jamaicans (rather than West Indians) in the United Kingdom: by 1966 an estimated 188,100 Jamaican migrants lived in Britain, and the total Jamaican population in Britain at that time (including those of Jamaican descent born in Britain) was 273,800 (Rose 1969:99).

Jamaican emigration to Britain followed certain general patterns. It was, in the first place, what is usually termed 'chain migration'. In the early 1950s, many Jamaicans came to England on their own—pioneers as Price (1969) has called them, with no friends or relatives here. Subsequently, however, many prospective migrants learned of opportunities, were provided with transportation, and had their initial accommodation arranged 'by means of primary social relationships with previous migrants' (MacDonald and Mac-Donald 1964:82). These previous migrants were usually kin, but sometimes friends, of those they helped.

Typically, the man in the family came to Britain first, later followed by his wife (or common-law wife or girlfriend) and children. In many cases children stayed behind with grandparents or other relatives, while the mother and father saved enough money to send for them. Jamaican emigration to Britain was characterised from the start by a high percentage of women, but the proportion of men in the migration was especially high in the early 1950s. In most cases there was simply not enough money for the whole family to emigrate together, and men, as the expected family providers, probably received preference in gathering funds to pay for their passage. Also, some women preferred to stay in Jamaica, perhaps because child-rearing responsibilities were eased there by the presence of relatives or because they did not have ready knowledge (as men might have had) of job opportunities in England. 'My husband, he sort of chase me,' one woman said. 'In the end I made up my mind.' Male-female migration patterns affected living arrangements in England on arrival: Jamaican women in my sample generally lived at first with their husbands (or husbands-to-be), parents, or aunts and uncles; men lived on their own or with age peers such as friends, cousins, or siblings (see Foner 1976).

In the very early stages of the migration, skilled and semi-skilled workers seem to have predominated. As the migration progressed, the number of unskilled and farm workers rose (Rose 1969:50–1). This of course makes sense in that skilled workers were more likely than the unskilled to have the resources to finance their trip. Later, they could send money home (as gifts or loans) to cover the transportation costs of their relatives and friends. On the whole, however, the majority of the Jamaicans who came to Britain—those who came in the early as well as in the later stages of the migration—were skilled or semi-skilled by Jamaican standards, and they were more skilled than the average Jamaican (Wright 1968). Only a very small minority, probably less than 10 per cent, were white-collar workers at home. In fact, only 13 per cent of the men in my sample had been in white-collar positions in Jamaica; and only 38 per cent of the men were unemployed or in unskilled jobs (including farmers with under five acres of land) in the three months prior to emigration.

It is worth noting that the recent emigration to the United States, made possible by the new 1965 immigration laws, is different in several respects from the Jamaican emigration to Britain in the 1950s and early 1960s. More women than men are migrating to the United States. And the migrants tend to be more highly skilled than those who went to Britain. In 1972, for example, 30 per cent of the migrants to the United States had been in white-collar jobs in Jamaica and 40 per cent had been skilled workers or craftsmen (Kuper 1976:13). The higher percentage of skilled and professional workers in the emigration to the United States reflects United States immigration policies which favour those with professional and technical skills. It also undoubtedly reflects the fact that skilled and professional Jamaicans can simply earn much higher wages in the United States than they can in Jamaica.

The Two Studies: Rural Jamaica and London

When I lived in Coco Hill, a small rural Jamaican farming community, during 1968–69, emigration to Britain had already ended and those who wanted to go abroad set their sights on the United States or Canada. In any case, my study in rural Jamaica focused not on migration, but on the effects of national independence on the community—specifically, the influence of recent changes in the national political and educational systems (Foner 1973). Yet I could not ignore the role migration played in the villagers' lives. Indeed, villagers seemed to consider migration—both to Kingston and abroad —as part of the normal life course. Most wanted to travel, and despite the very close bonds between many kin, villagers thought it natural (and, from a financial point of view, desirable) to spend much of one's life—and perhaps the rest of one's life—abroad.

I was reminded in a variety of ways of how important migration was in the villagers' lives. Collecting genealogies showed that villagers usually had many relatives abroad, most often in England and the United States. The Post Mistress estimated that the village received about £200 a week in postal orders from abroad; and several houses were being built with money sent by people in England. Most men in the village had been abroad at some time in their lives: many worked, and some continued to work, in the United States on seasonal farm contracts; a good number had been to the United States during World War Two; and some of the older men had been to Cuba in the 1920s. Several villagers, moreover, were returned migrants from England. During my stay in the village I was besieged by requests to get people jobs and visas in the United States, and it seemed that nearly every week another woman left to go to the United States.

In rural Jamaica, my primary research method was participant observation. Four years later, however, when I studied Jamaican migrants in London I depended more on formal interview techniques. The people interviewed did not live in one neighbourhood but were scattered throughout working-class areas of South and North London. Most of them were located simply by knocking on doors. Mainly, I relied on a structured interview administered to a quota sample of 110, chosen to control for age, length of time in England, sex, and occupational mobility. While the 110 respondents were asked set questions, most of the questions were open-ended. I also spent many hours talking informally with most respondents after the formal interview ended. These informal talks, as well as depth interviews, gave me a feel for what the immigrants' lives are like in England and what the move to England has meant to them.

The people interviewed were typical in many ways of Jamaican migrants in England generally. Most were born in rural Jamaica; most came to England before they were 30 and had lived in England for 10 to 20 years; and nearly all were between the ages of 30 and 50. In addition, most were from rural Jamaican families in the upper ranges of the lower class. And nearly all had working-class jobs before they left Jamaica and had working-class jobs in London at the time of the study.

One of my main interests in the London study was to investigate the importance of status changes and status distinctions among Jamaican migrants. The reader should keep in mind that to give an overview of Jamaican migrants' experiences I speak of them here very often 'as if' they are undifferentiated. And I discuss many aspects of their experiences in England which most of them share. But there are important status distinctions among Jamaican migrants—for example, age and sex differences—and some have different experiences of status change in England than others (Foner, n.d.). Nevertheless, in the eyes of most English people, Jamaicans, as black people, are all one. Indeed, being black has a very different meaning in England than it did in Jamaica.

Being Black in England and Jamaica

'The black immigrant', Gordon Lewis (1971:22) writes, 'comes to feel less like a West Indian in English society and more like a black man in a white society.' The fact that black skin is more of a stigma in England does not mean, of course, that it was not a stigma back home. Black skin has long been devalued in Jamaica. This stems from Jamaica's history as a plantation colony based on African slavery. Whites were, in the days of slavery, masters, and throughout the colonial period, rulers. Indeed, a white bias has permeated the entire society since the eighteenth century: in the eyes of most Jamaicans, white stands for wealth, privilege, and power. To most lower-class Jamaicans—who not only comprise the majority of the population but who are, by and large, black— being black is another symbol, along with their poverty, of their low social position. Indeed, I would argue that it is mainly because being black stands for being poor in Jamaica that so many black Jamaicans place a negative value on black skin.

The colour-class hierarchy in Jamaica is a three-tiered one, and it is marked by a high degree of shade consciousness. Since slavery times, when free people of colour (the results of unions between white men and slave women) had economic and other privileges denied to slaves, it came to be expected, although never exactly realised, that whites should belong to the upper class, people of colour to the middle, and blacks to the lowest class (Mason 1970:301). Even though emancipation of the slaves in 1838 eliminated the legal distinction between black and white, colour continued to be closely correlated with status in Jamaican society. Expatriate and local whites continued to monopolise the highest ranking positions in the island, coloureds, the intermediate positions, and blacks, the lowest positions. This system has only begun to change in very recent years.

Another feature of the Jamaican colour-class system is that culture, occupation, and wealth can override skin colour in importance so that one can, in a sense, 'change' colour in Jamaica. Until the past few decades, high-status black and coloured Jamaicans were excluded from 'white society', and from the highest administrative and political positions in the island. Yet black or coloured Jamaicans who became doctors or lawyers, for example, or high-level civil servants, who acquired the cultural characteristics associated with English whites, and who maintained a 'respectable' standard of living, were often thought of 'as if' they were white by those of lower status. And they were recognised for many of their achievements by the whites as well.

Few, if any, such successful black or coloured Jamaicans live in rural communities. In any case, most villagers, including those in respected positions—primary-school teachers, low-level civil servants, and successful farmers, for instance—are black. Colour, as a consequence, is not a key factor in the villagers' daily lives.

Among Coco Hill villagers skin colour was a basis of prestige only when combined with other status attributes such as income and occupation. A poor light-skinned farmer, for example, was thought of as black if he lived and dressed in a manner associated with poor black folk in Jamaica. Skin colour was largely irrelevant in most villagers' day-to-day interactions. The vast majority had hardly anything to do with white people, and their friends, neighbours, church brethren, relatives, and the people they respected in the village were generally, like themselves, black or very dark-skinned.

It is true, however, that most villagers had an unquestioning acceptance of the superiority of white skin. This white bias was reinforced by the fact that the few whites with whom they had contact—estate owners, ministers of religion, doctors, and lawyers—they met in a dependent and subordinate position. And most of these whites conformed to the villagers' stereotype: they were well-off, maintained a middle-class or upper-class life style, and either were English or had acquired English culture. Although many villagers resented whites' privilege and power, and harboured hostility towards them, most still continued to denigrate their own blackness and to believe in the superiority of white skin and white (European) culture.

Life in Britain

For most Jamaican migrants, coming to England was a shock. As a character in one of Samuel Selvon's novels puts it: 'To English people every black man look the same' (Selvon quoted in Cheetham 1970:121). Whatever their shade and whatever their achievements, Jamaicans in England tend to be viewed as lower class and inferior by most English people.

Used to being a majority back home, blacks are a very small minority in Britain—about two per cent of the population. More important, English people are often racially prejudiced, and blacks are systematically exploited at every level in British society—in employment, housing, education, and the social services. Numerous studies have documented the widespread discrimination blacks in Britain experience in housing and employment (see Burney 1967; Daniel 1968; Hepple 1968; Smith 1974). They occupy the worst-paid, the dirtiest, and the most boring jobs: jobs that English people usually do not want. Jamaican men tend, on the whole, to be concentrated in such occupations as transportation and communication, the engineering trades, woodworking, and labouring. The women are often service or clothing workers. But aside from nursing, only a very few Jamaicans in Britain occupy professional, clerical or managerial occupations (for figures on occupational distribution of Jamaicans see Rose 1969:150–71). The Political and Economic Planning (PEP) studies show in fact that blacks with the highest qualifications face the greatest difficulties in getting the better white collar jobs (Daniel 1968; Smith 1976).

Why so few Jamaicans (and other West Indians) have moved into entrepreneurial activities here, where they would be self-employed or even employers, is hard to explain. It is particularly intriguing as Jamaicans' entrepreneurial success in New York relative to American blacks has been frequently noted. Indeed, enough West Indians prospered in New York 'to engender an American Negro stereotype of them as "Black Jews"—aggressive, efficient, acquisitive, calculating, and clannish' (Lowenthal 1972:227). Ivan Light (1972:32–6) attributes West Indian success in New York to a traditional institution: rotating credit associations (known as 'partners' to Jamaicans) which, he argues, provide West Indians with an important source of capital for business ventures. American blacks, by contrast, lacking traditional credit associations, have been more dependent on banks and lending institutions for credit, which they are frequently denied (Light 1972:36). The fact that 'partners' are found among Jamaicans in England as well as in New York seems to undermine Light's argument, however. It is true that Jamaicans in England may well have amassed financial resources for real-estate investment through 'partners'. Indeed, many Jamaicans (and other West Indians) are home owners here. Yet, it is unclear why they do not invest more of their savings in small-scale businesses, like so many Jamaicans in New York.

A complete analysis of this problem is beyond the scope of the present paper. Here I merely suggest two factors which may be important. One is that Jamaicans who emigrated to the United States generally had higher-status occupations in Jamaica than those who went to Britain. They may not only have had relatively advanced education but also prior managerial skills. Many may have held positions of prestige and authority back home and therefore felt confident about setting up their own businesses. Probably more important, Jamaicans in New York had a ready-made—and a rather large—constituency for their enterprises: the American, as well as the West Indian, black community. There are far fewer West Indians in British cities than blacks in New York to furnish a market for West Indian businesses. And the fear that English whites might not patronise black businesses could inhibit Jamaicans from investing their savings in small enterprises.

Jamaicans in this country have been the victims of discrimination in housing. One reason why they have scrimped and saved to buy homes is precisely because of the difficulty they experience, as blacks, in renting accommodations. Some undoubtedly prefer to remain in areas with large Jamaican settlements, but discriminatory practices do limit where they can buy homes. Jamaicans, and other West Indians, do not live in strictly defined ghettoes, but they have been forced to settle in the decaying inner and middle rings of large English cities. The PEP studies show that West Indians find it harder than whites and non-black immigrants to rent accommodation and to buy houses. The properties they have acquired tend to be markedly inferior to those bought by whites (Smith 1976). West Indians also appear to receive unfair treatment in the allocation of council housing: when blacks qualify for council housing, they often get inferior accommodation (Race and Council Housing 1975).

It is not surprising that Jamaicans in England are constantly aware of being black. On the bus, in the shops, and on the job, they can never forget that to English people their black skin marks them off as 'something less than human'. Most Jamaicans I met related recent incidents where they felt victimised because they are black. And many recalled earlier episodes. 'Soon after I came here (in 1959) I went into a pub,' one man told me, 'and I was drinking and minding my own business and this bloke was telling a joke quite loudly and he was talking about Sambo and thick lips and that sort of thing. They were all laughing and then they were dead quiet. I looked around and they were all looking at me.' He thought (perhaps because of the open debates over immigration and race relations, and the rise of Enoch Powell and the National Front) that whites were now more hostile than when he first arrived: 'At that time, they were really embarrassed and we ended up having a drink and shaking hands. I think people are different now. It's respectable to make bad comments about coloured people. When it comes to immigrants, they go out of their way to be nasty.' One woman explained: 'I don't push myself because insult is not a good invitation. I have English neighbours and we say hello. But if we meet on the high road, they look the other way.'

Much of the mystique of whiteness to Jamaicans has in fact been undermined in England. Because Jamaicans face such widespread discrimination in England and because white skin is no longer necessarily linked with other attributes of status and power, Jamaican migrants are not so awed by whiteness in England. While the whites encountered in Jamaica were usually in positions of prestige and authority, in England they are nearly all members of the working class. Indeed, judging by the migrants' former criteria, English working-class whites do not merit deference: like poor light-skinned Jamaican villagers, they have, besides their skin colour, none of the characteristics (wealth, good jobs, education, or cultural traits) which deserve respect. Yet Jamaicans seem to be less deferential to whites generally in England—including high status whites—than they were in Jamaica. And because they receive unequal treatment on the basis of their skin colour, a good number are, for the first time, seriously questioning and challenging the inferiority of blackness.

The Meaning of Education

While the aura surrounding white skin has been dramatically reduced in England, education also seems to have less symbolic importance, and indeed a different meaning, to Jamaican migrants than it did to Jamaicans back home.

Education has long been a powerful symbol of prestige in Jamaican society. Throughout the island's history, education has been a major avenue to occupational advancement. Secondary schools have provided Jamaicans with the skills to qualify for prestigious and remunerative jobs, and education is also linked with certain cultural characteristics (speech patterns, for example) which command deference when accompanied by high-status occupations. Until the past few decades, however, admission to secondary school was informally limited to children whose parents had relatively high income and status (and often light skin). A small number of rural children did manage to advance occupationally by passing certain examinations given in the primary schools and they became teachers and low-level civil servants. Yet recent changes have made it possible for increasing numbers of lower-class children to attend secondary school. Prior to 1953, for instance, no child from Coco Hill had attended secondary school, but by 1968 approximately 70 were attending, or had attended, secondary school in the past five years.

To Coco Hill villagers, these changes represented a tremendous advance. Since opportunities for upward mobility in Jamaica through agricultural and entrepreneurial activities were so limited, their enthusiasm is hardly surprising. Most were aware that education is a main route to success in Jamaica and they felt that the expanded opportunities to attend secondary school had been the most important change for the better in recent years. The need to finance their children's education was a constant topic of conversation, especially among women in the village. Many hoped that their children 'might not have it hard like me' and even villagers who planned to emigrate usually said that a major reason was to secure funds to educate their children.

I had thought that education would also be of central concern to Jamaicans in Britain. It is true that none of the people interviewed in London lived in Jamaica in 1968, the time of my study there. Educational opportunities, however, had begun to expand in the 1950s, when most of the migrants in my sample did live in Jamaica. It is reasonable to assume that the respondents were enthusiastic about these educational changes when they were home, especially since most are from relatively prosperous rural families—that is, the people who were usually most excited by educational changes in Coco Hill (Foner 1973). In any case, I expected the similarities in emphasis on education to be due, not to a persistence in attitudes, but to conditions in England and rural Jamaica. For one, education is a major channel to upward mobility in both countries. And since Jamaicans in England tend toward working-class jobs, I assumed that they would, like parents in rural Jamaica, transfer their own, still unfulfilled mobility aspirations to their children. Moreover, I supposed that the comparison between the previous, limited chances for secondary education in Jamaica would stand in sharp contrast to the wider availability of education in England. The responses of the people interviewed were not what I had predicted. Of course, parents in England, as in Jamaica, did value education and were aware that educational opportunities are better in England than in Jamaica. But education was rarely a topic of conversation with Jamaicans in London, and respondents only rarely mentioned education in the formal or informal interviews (Foner 1975a).

One reason why the emphasis on education differs among the two groups I studied is that among Jamaicans in Britain, unlike their counterparts in Jamaica, education is not the *sine qua non* for marked material improvement. Jamaican migrants have in fact improved their standard of living in England: most earn more money in England than they did back home; most have, at least so far, been able to find steady work; and most can afford to buy amenities that they would not have been able to afford back home. In rural Jamaica usually only the educated white-collar workers could afford modern furniture, a refrigerator, or an indoor toilet. In England, nearly all of the people interviewed had these amenities.

Also, in England secondary education is not, as it was in Jamaica, a scarce resource. It is in fact widely available, and it is free. Until 1973, when secondary school fees were eliminated altogether in Jamaica, the cost of secondary education was, to poor Jamaican families, a very heavy burden. Those children lucky enough to pass the required exams to gain entry to secondary schools (when I was in Jamaica) rarely won full scholarships, that is, scholarships which paid for books and uniforms as well as school fees. Usually children received half scholarships so that parents had to finance a considerable part of the school cost. Many parents told me that they sold land and cows to finance their children's education. In England (prior to the elimination of secondary school fees in Jamaica), migrants told me that they planned to school their children here before returning home because of the availability of free secondary education.

Parents thus seem less likely to dwell on education in England where attending secondary school is part of nearly every child's experience. Many migrants' children have, moreover, qualified for what their parents consider to be prestigious jobs—nursing and clerical positions, in the case of daughters, and skilled manual or low-level white-collar positions, in the case of sons. But access to elite educational institutions in Britain is indeed a very scarce resource, so scarce that it is not a realistic goal for the overwhelming majority of the migrants' children. And this has to do with racial prejudice and discrimination, perhaps the most important factor in understanding the different meaning that education has to Jamaicans at home and in England.

It is true that few Jamaicans I met in England spoke of racial discrimination as a barrier to their children's educational advancement. Objectively, however, racial prejudice and discrimination do seem to affect the meaning of education in England. It is not only that Jamaican migrants and their children experience blockages to occupational and educational advancement and that hardly any Jamaican migrants' children attend grammar school or university. What seems more important is that status distinctions based on education and occupation in England, unlike in Jamaica, are superseded by the importance of colour.

In rural Jamaica, education was an important basis of prestige. Those with advanced educational qualifications (white-collar workers) were sharply differentiated from manual workers. Teachers or nurses, for instance, claimed deference on the basis of their education, life style, 'refinement', and culture. And they commanded respect on the basis of these achievements regardless of their skin colour. In England, however, few Jamaicans have professional and managerial occupations. But whatever their occupation or education, Jamaicans tend to be defined as 'black' by English people. And this lessens the symbolic importance that education has to Jamaican migrants.

A last factor in analysing attitudes to education is also linked to racial prejudice. This is that many Jamaican migrants' thoughts of the future are dominated by the desire to return home. About half of the people in the sample said that they planned to return to Jamaica, either in the indefinite future or in the next ten years, and 43 per cent said that if they won the pools, they would use the money to return home.

In rural Jamaica, villagers' thoughts of the future centred around aspirations for their children. Too old to acquire the skills to alter their own status in the national society, they hoped that their children could succeed where they had failed. This hope has been nourished in recent years by expanded educational opportunities which have made it possible for more lower-class children to acquire secondary education and prestigious jobs.

Because they are black, migrants and their children are often frustrated and disappointed by life in England. Some (especially men who have also experienced a decline in their occupational status) react to their plight by defining their stay as a temporary one. The homeward orientation seems to shield migrants from some of the stings of racial prejudice: if England is not their real home, then they can more easily endure discrimination. Also, I sense that the homeward orientation appears to minimise some of the migrants' disappointments with their own failures and anxieties over their children's success by focusing on the return home. Most will probably stay in England permanently: migrants do not want to return home unless their savings will significantly alter their status in Jamaica, and many are used to life abroad and have friends and relatives here. Yet many continue to hope that they will go back one day and this, rather than anticipation of their children's success, is a dominant theme in their conceptions of the future.

Family Relations and Marriage

Racial distinctions and education, then, have different symbolic meaning for Jamaicans living at home and in England. These meanings also, obviously, differ from those of white English people. Family relations too have changed from what they were in rural Jamaica. At the same time, these patterns differ from those of English people in many ways, though there are some indications that Jamaican migrants are conforming to certain English family patterns. New meanings and new social arrangements that are a response to life in England appear to have taken shape among Jamaican migrants here, and it is in this sense that the analogy with creolisation in Jamaica, discussed at the outset, seems relevant.

Many social scientists have observed that Jamaicans (and other West Indians) in England seem to establish legal marital unions with greater frequency and at an earlier age than was generally true in Jamaica (Davison 1966; Fitzherbert 1967; Patterson 1965; Philpott 1973). Of course, deciding on the baseline in Jamaica from which to compare migrants' marriage patterns in England is not easy. This is due, first, to the various and sometimes conflicting analyses of the West Indian family (see Smith 1963 for a summary of these different views) and, second, to the fact that migrants have varying socio-economic backgrounds in Jamaica. Still, the following description is probably an accurate view of what the marriage patterns of most migrants were in rural Jamaica.

Marriage tended to occur relatively late in rural Jamaica—often not until the couple were in their early or middle thirties. Most men and women had a number of affairs in their late teens or early twenties, but these did not usually involve common residence. Instead, young men and women remained attached to their parents' households; the women helped with household chores and the men helped in the fields, worked for cash, and contributed money to the maintenance of their parents' household. Children from these non-residential unions usually remained with the mother. As the men grew older, they found that to maintain their economic and social freedom, they had to break away and set up their own homes. To do this required a mate, since a man needed someone to care for the house, to wash and cook, and to take his crops to the local market. Generally he rented rooms in the community and took up residence with the mother of his most recent children. When he achieved a minimal level of economic security—that is, accumulated enough money to buy his own home and some land (or inherited a home and land)—he usually got married. But even if a man did not achieve this level of economic security, there were pressures to induce him to marry. If a man had little security, William Davenport (1961) argues and then, through a series of non-legal unions, assumed responsibility for several illegitimate children, in addition to his obligations to his parents and grandparents, the resulting conflict of loyalties made his position difficult. 'The more frequent alternative is for a man to move toward a consolidation of all his obligations and potential assets by setting up a household around a permanent marriage. With meagre resources, this is extremely difficult, but it is the only way in which he can lay the groundwork for security in his own declining years and return to dependency' (Davenport 1961:440).

In England, other pressures seem to account for the fact that men and women often marry at an earlier age than at home. For one, Jamaicans are doubtless influenced by the norms of English family life. In addition, it has been argued that the migrants' improved economic position in England provides the economic supports considered necessary by Jamaicans for the establishment of legal unions at an earlier age—men can effectively play the role of steady and reliable family providers here. Another factor is that the tax relief associated with marriage makes such unions desirable and that migrants' isolation from kin in England propels many into unions backed by the sanctions of legal ties (cf. Patterson 1965:266–68).

It is not only that marriage patterns seem to have shifted in England, but attitudes to common-law unions also appear to have changed. Common-law unions were part of the Jamaican lower-class tradition, one stage in the life-cycle of most lower-class Jamaicans (see Smith 1956). Marriage was associated with respectability and with the middle and upper classes in the island; it was sometimes regarded, as R. T. Smith (1956:181) notes for Guyanese villagers, 'as being wrong for the lower-class villagers themselves. Even married persons will often say "marriage is not for we black people".' In England, Jamaicans expect to marry and they certainly consider this appropriate and normal behaviour. Some Jamaicans here do live in common-law unions. But 'those who cohabit for longer than a trial period preceding marriage (though this may last two or three years) are now the exception [sic] who must explain why they don't conform,' Fitzherbert (1967:34) writes. My impression is that many Jamaican migrants here view common-law unions, rather than marriage, as wrong if only because English people disapprove of such non-legal unions.

In this regard it is interesting that the majority of the 20 men and women interviewed in depth about their family lives in Britain said that if given the choice, they would prefer to be married and have no children than to have children without being married. This was the reverse of what I found in rural Jamaica. 'In Jamaica it didn't matter,' one woman said, 'if you have a child and don't marry, no one looks on it as anything. But here they look on it as funny.' A single woman I met who had previously lived with the father of her five children but who now lived alone, wore a wedding band and the children pretended at school that their mother was married. 'I like to be free and do what I want to do, but here there is more pressure on you to get married,' she told me. When I asked her if there were other reasons why Jamaicans got married in England she said: 'Here you are more lonely, just shut up by yourself. In Jamaica, there are plenty people and relatives to talk to.'

Division of Labour and Joint Activities

Another change among Jamaicans in England has to do with the sexual division of labour. The division of household labour is often more equitable here than it was in rural Jamaica. This seems related both to the absence of close kin (especially mothers) as well as to women's wage-earning status.

In rural Jamaica men rarely did housework, even when their wives had cash-earning activities. Work in rural Jamaica, however, did not usually take women away from home or out of the house for long periods of time. And although it was often very exhausting, women generally managed to combine work with child-rearing and domestic chores. Relatives also frequently helped out. If women had to go to the field or to market, their mothers or sisters might take care of their children. The mother of one higgler (market woman) I knew in Coco Hill, for instance, stayed with her daughter's children when her daughter was at the Kingston market. Salaried women, such as nurses or teachers, could afford to employ other women to care for their children and to do domestic tasks.

The move to England has not eliminated this rather strict sexual division of labour altogether. Jamaican migrant women, even those who work, do most of the cooking, cleaning, shopping, and washing. Men are responsible for household repairs. But even though men resent doing 'women's work' in England, they often help out—usually when their wives are working and when their children are still young. Men recognise that they cannot manage financially if their wives do not work, and they cannot afford to hire household help. Working women simply cannot shoulder all of the domestic responsibilities expected of them in England nor do they usually have close relatives to help as they did back home. Furthermore, when the children are young, women cannot enlist the aid of older children (daughters in particular) to help in the house. Thus many men whose shifts are different from those of their wives help care for the children and do some cooking, cleaning, washing, and shopping.

Further, couples seem to spend more of their leisure time together in Britain than in rural Jamaica. Men and women in Jamaica rarely, if ever, went out together as couples: the locus of male activity was outside the home, at work, in the rum shops, or on the road, while women's domain was the home. True, Jamaican men and women in England also tend to pursue separate recreational activities. Men go to pubs or parties on their own or with their mates while women visit, play bingo, or attend church with female friends and relatives. But many of the people interviewed about their family lives said that they jointly entertained friends at home with their spouses and occasionally went with them to parties, pubs, and the cinema. A few took family outings together on a regular basis. My impression was that a genuine companionship existed between a number of husbands and wives I met.

It is not that Jamaican men in England place a high value on joint leisure activities. Indeed, men usually prefer to be with their male friends rather than to stay at home or to go out with their wives. Yet women seem to put more pressure on their husbands to engage in joint activities in England than they did back home, and men seem more willing to oblige. The absence of kin in England, combined with the normative stress on the desirability of joint husband-wife activities in England, means that wives tend to look to their spouses for some of the comfort and companionship they formerly found with relatives. The fact that most women in England provide an important part of the family income also gives them a stronger position from which to make demands; in Jamaica, women were more often dependent on their spouses for financial support (Foner 1975b).

Men, too, may give in to their wives' demands, however minimally, because (among other reasons) they lack extensive kin networks in England. If they continually flout their spouses' demands, their wives might leave them, probably a worse fate in England than it would be in rural Jamaica. In England men do not usually have a choice of female relatives willing to perform domestic chores for them. The absence of kin in England, in any case, may draw men closer to their wives, and they may depend on them for security and emotional support.

The fact that Jamaican men in England often help with household chores and that they spend some leisure time with their wives and families is not unique to Jamaican migrants. This pattern has also been reported in several studies of English working-class family life (Klein 1965; Rosser and Harris 1965; Young and Wilmott 1957). Finding similar patterns of social relations among two groups, however, does not necessarily mean that members of one group are adopting the norms of the other, or that Jamaicans are becoming assimilated. Jamaican migrants are obviously influenced by the norms of English society, including those governing family relations. But the similarities of family patterns between the two groups may also stem from parallel social and economic forces. Studies of the English working class show in fact that, as among Jamaican migrants, it is when women work and when geographical mobility disrupts close kin ties that men engage in more joint activities with their wives and are more helpful in the house (Bott 1971; Rosser and Harris 1965; Young and Wilmott 1957).

Indeed, when conditions change among Jamaicans in England, there may be a partial return to 'old' patterns of family relations. It is true that second-generation Jamaicans will probably be socialised to many of the new family patterns by their parents and they will also be influenced by their English teachers, school fellows, work-mates, and the media. But it is probable that they will be affected by other circumstances as well. Most Jamaican migrants will probably remain in England rather than return home, and thus many members of the second generation will, unlike their parents, have mothers and other female relatives (especially retired relatives) to help them with child-rearing and domestic tasks. Men may then be less likely to help in the house than they do now. Second-generation Jamaican women in England may also rely more on their female kin for company in their leisure time and make fewer demands on their husbands for joint leisure activities. Whether the pattern of early marriage will continue among the second generation is also open to question.

Some Implications: the Second Generation and Returned Migrants

As these remarks about the second generation suggest, attitudes and behaviour do not necessarily pass unchanged from one generation to the next: as social, economic, and political conditions change, so too behaviour patterns and attitudes are also transformed. Indeed, this paper has shown that the move to England has, for the first generation of Jamaican migrants, led to the emergence of new cultural and social patterns—a kind of creolisation process, as it were. The meaning of two cultural symbols, education and black skin, as well as patterns of family life, are not the same as they were back home nor are they the same as those found among English people. Although one cannot predict future economic and political conditions in Britain, it seems very unlikely that these new cultural and social patterns will be passed down intact to the migrants' children. Rather, they will be modified and changed in tune with the experiences of the second generation. Born in Britain, young blacks have had, and will probably continue to have, very different life experiences than their parents. But they will not, however, become identical to Englishmen and women either. Like their parents, they straddle two worlds: the world of their parents, or first-generation migrants, and the world of English people.

Having grown up in England and having been schooled here, second generation Jamaicans are like the English in a good many ways—in food habits, for example, and dress. Yet 'it hardly seems likely', as Gordon Lewis (1971:12) observes, 'that they [the local born] will undertake for multi-racial Britain what the ... second generation had done, classically, in most migratory situations, that is to say, facilitate the cultural absorption of their group into the host society as they become, through education, social mobility, and intermarriage, the culture carriers of a new and enthusiastic patriotism.'

Young blacks find it difficult to get the type of jobs they want and they are often victimised by the police. Because most have more education and higher aspirations than their parents, they tend to be more resentful of the low-status jobs they are usually forced to accept. Whatever their aspirations, in the tightening economic situation they are extremely vulnerable to unemployment, more vulnerable than young whites.

It is precisely because second-generation Jamaicans are rejected by English whites that they are so bitter and so frustrated by racial prejudice and discrimination in England —usually much more bitter than their parents. Unlike their parents, most have never been to Jamaica and they cannot compare their situation with what it was like back home. Thus, young blacks will probably be more disappointed with the English educational system than their parents have been. British-born Jamaicans, moreover, cannot look forward to a return home, because they *are* home. Neither Jamaican nor fully English, they often look to their blackness as a basis for identification.

Little has been written which gives an in-depth and systematic view of young blacks' attitudes, values, and behaviour. My own study did not include second-generation Jamaicans. What has been written, however, suggests that certain characteristics and behaviour symbolise their identity as British-born blacks. Gus John (1972:82) writes, for example, that 'Black power. ... the growth of a distinctively black youth culture, all form the framework within which the black youth works out his stance to this society.' *Reggae*, the latest Jamaican popular music, has become 'THE urban black sound in England, spreading beyond the limits of the black population' (Midgett 1975:78). Youth clubs have become important meeting places for blacks in their late teens, and a youth dialect has emerged, 'a kind of generalized West

Indian English, which is not attributable to any single island but which has numerous Jamaican and Cockney elements' (Midgett 1975:75).

If members of the second generation differ from their parents in many ways, as well as from English people, then what about migrants who return to Jamaica? Will cultural symbols and patterns of family relations retain the meaning and form that they have acquired in England when migrants go back? Or will the objective realities of life in Jamaica subtly exert pressure on returned migrants to again act and perceive themselves and their society in the old ways?

The evidence, though very fragmentary, appears to indicate that both processes may operate. Certainly returned migrants have been a source of rising aspirations in Jamaica, bringing back with them tales of success and glory on foreign shores. Some are also discontented in Jamaica: having experienced a higher standard of living abroad, they are frustrated by the relatively poor conditions in Jamaica. One frequently cited cause of the Jamaican riots and disturbances of 1938 is the frustrated aspirations of migrants who returned from the United States and Central America during the depression years. More recently, many Jamaicans who have returned from England have suffered from 'the shock of reality' (B. Davison 1968). The 28 returned migrants whom Betty Davison interviewed in Kingston in the mid-1960s had been successful in Britain, but the years of striving often seemed to have been in vain. Many found it hard to get decent jobs and housing in Jamaica, and the cost of living there had risen markedly while they were in Britain. Their friends and relatives, moreover, were often jealous of them, expecting the returned migrants to be well-off and generous, on the one hand, but also fearing that they would buy their way into the few available jobs (B. Davison 1968:509). Many of Davison's respondents intended to return to Britain, and several people I interviewed in London had gone home to settle but returned. 'I went home in 1964,' one woman told me, 'but I get accustomed to life here. There is nothing to do there and things so expensive. Besides, I have more freedom here to do what I want.'

Constance Sutton and Susan Makiesky (1969) also suggest that returned migrants may bring back new values and beliefs

when they go back home. Returned migrants from the
United States, they argue, contributed to the awakening of
racial and political consciousness in the Barbadian village
they studied. While only a few returned migrants were
directly involved in introducing Black Power ideology and
writings into the village, most were 'conveyers of political
messages, however inadvertently. . . . What they did impart
of their experiences, however, reinforced in unintended ways
the use of black people as a reference group' (1975:138).

It is true that many Jamaicans sense that 'you can't', in
Thomas Wolfe's phrase, 'go home again.' The experience of
living abroad undoubtedly affects returned migrants' views of
the world. Moreover, Jamaica has changed in many ways
since they left for England. Yet, returned migrants may
revert to some of the old ways and old views when they go
back home. In the Jamaican context, these old ideas and
behaviour patterns not only 'make sense', but they are sometimes backed up by social sanctions. Thus Coco Hill villagers
who had lived in Britain seemed to accept the legitimacy of
common-law unions. From what I could tell, they also spent
leisure time activities with their friends and their relatives
rather than with spouses.

What seems clear is that whether we look at Jamaican
migrants in England or at the returnees in Jamaica, we must
consider the impact of both the past and the present. For
while Schumpeter (1955:111) reminds us that 'every social
situation is the heritage of preceding situations and takes
over from them . . . their cultures, their dispositions and their
spirit', it is the old and the new, as they combine in the
present, which affect the way Jamaican migrants act and the
way they view the world.

NOTE

The study in rural Jamaica was financed by a grant from the
United States National Institute of Mental Health; the study
of Jamaicans in London was financed by grants from the
National Institute of Mental Health, The City University of

New York, and The State University of New York. The author wishes to thank Peter Braham, now at The Open University, for his help in conducting the interviews and Anne Foner, Rutgers University, for her critical reading of earlier drafts of this paper and for helpful advice at all stages of the research.

REFERENCES

Beckford, George, 1972, *Persistent Poverty: Underdevelopment in Plantation Economies of the Third World*. London: Oxford University Press.

Bott, Elizabeth, 1971, *Family and Social Network*. Second Edition. New York: The Free Press.

Burney, Elizabeth, 1967, *Housing on Trial*. London: Oxford University Press.

Cheetham, Julia, 1970, *Social Work with Immigrants*. London: Routledge and Kegan Paul.

Cronin, Constance, 1970, *The Sting of Change: Sicilians in Sicily and Australia*. Chicago: University of Chicago Press.

Daniel, W. W., 1968, *Racial Discrimination in England*. London: Penguin.

Davenport, William, 1961, 'The Family System of Jamaica'. *Social and Economic Studies* 10:420–54.

Davison, Betty, 1968, 'No Place Back Home: A Study of Jamaicans Returning to Kingston'. *Race* 9:499–509.

Davison, R. B., 1966, *Black British: Immigrants to England*. London: Oxford University Press.

Eisner, Gisela, 1961, *Jamaica, 1830–1930: A Study in Economic Growth*. Manchester: Manchester University Press.

Fitzherbert, Katrin, 1967, *West Indian Children in London*. London: G. Bell and Sons.

Foner, Nancy, 1973, *Status and Power in Rural Jamaica: A Study of Educational and Political Change*. New York: Teachers College Press, Columbia University.

Foner, Nancy, 1975a, 'The Meaning of Education to Jamaicans at Home and in London'. *New Community* 4:195–202.

Foner, Nancy, 1975b, 'Women, Work and Migration: Jamaicans in London'. *Urban Anthropology* 4:229–49.

Foner, Nancy, 1976, 'Male and Female: Jamaican Migrants in London'. *Anthropological Quarterly* 49:28–35.

Foner, Nancy, n.d., *Jamaica Farewell*. Berkeley: University of California Press, in press.

Geertz, Clifford, 1965, 'Religion and Social Change: A Javanese Example'. In *Reader in Comparative Religion* (eds.) William A. Lessa and Evon Z. Vogt. 2nd Edition. New York: Harper and Row.

Girvan, Norman, 1972, *Foreign Capital and Economic Underdevelopment in Jamaica.* Kingston: Institute of Social and Economic Research, University of the West Indies.

Hepple, Bob, 1968, *Race, Jobs and the Law in Britain.* London: Allen Lane.

Jackson, J. A., 1968, 'Migration: Editorial Introduction'. In *Migration* (ed.) J. A. Jackson. Cambridge: Cambridge University Press.

Jefferson, Owen, 1972, *The Post-War Economic Development of Jamaica.* Kingston: Institute of Social and Economic Research, University of the West Indies.

John, Gus, 1972, The Social Worker and the Young Blacks. In *Social Work with Coloured Immigrants and Their Families* (ed.) J. P. Triseliotis. London: Oxford University Press.

Klein, Josephine, 1965, *Samples from English Cultures, Vol. I.* London: Routledge and Kegan Paul.

Kuper, Adam, 1976, *Changing Jamaica.* London: Routledge and Kegan Paul.

Lawrence, Daniel, 1974, *Black Migrants: White Natives.* Cambridge: Cambridge University Press.

Lewis, Gordon, 1971, An Introductory Note to the Study of Race Relations in Great Britain. *Caribbean Studies* 11:5–29.

Light, Ivan, 1972, *Ethnic Enterprise in America.* Berkeley: University of California Press.

Lomas, Gillian, 1973, *The Coloured Population of Great Britain.* London: Runnymede Trust.

Lowenthal, David, 1972, *West Indian Societies.* London: Oxford University Press.

Mason, Philip, 1970, *Patterns of Dominance.* London: Oxford University Press.

MacDonald, J. S. and L. D. MacDonald, 1964, 'Chain Migration, Ethnic Neighborhood Formation and Social Networks'. *Millbank Memorial Fund Quarterly* 42:82–97.

Midgett, Douglas, 1975, 'West Indian Ethnicity in Britain'. In *Migration and Development* (eds.) Helen Safa and Brian duToit. The Hague: Mouton Publishers.

Naipaul, V. S., 1970, 'Power to the Caribbean People'. *New York Review of Books* 14:32–34.

Patterson, Sheila, 1965, *Dark Strangers: A Study of West Indians in London.* London: Penguin.

Peach, Ceri, 1968, *West Indian Migration to Britain*. London: Oxford University Press.

Philpott, Stuart, 1973, *West Indian Migration: The Montserrat Case*. London: Athlone Press.

Price, Charles, 1968, 'The Study of Assimilation'. In *Migration* (ed.) J. A. Jackson. Cambridge: Cambridge University Press.

Richmond, Anthony, 1968, 'Sociology of Migration in Industrial and Post-Industrial Societies'. In *Migration* (ed.) J. A. Jackson. Cambridge: Cambridge University Press.

Richmond, Anthony, 1973, *Migration and Race Relations in an English City*. London: Oxford University Press.

Rose, E. J. B. et al., 1969, *Colour and Citizenship: A Report on British Race Relations*. London: Oxford University Press.

Rosser, Colin and Christopher Harris, 1965, *The Family and Social Change*. London: Routledge and Kegan Paul.

Runnymede Trust Staff, 1975, *Race and Council Housing in London*. London: Runnymede Trust.

Schumpeter, Joseph, 1955, *Imperialism and Social Classes*. New York and Cleveland: World Publishing Company, Meridien Books.

Smith, David J., 1974, 'Job Discrimination and the Function of Law'. *New Community* 4:55–61.

Smith, David J., 1976, *The Facts of Racial Disadvantage*. London: Political and Economic Planning (PEP).

Smith, Raymond T., 1956, *The Negro Family in British Guiana*. London: Routledge and Kegan Paul.

Smith, Raymond T., 1963, 'Culture and Social Structure in the Caribbean: Some Recent Work on Family and Kinship Studies'. *Comparative Studies in Society and History* 6:24–45.

Smith, Raymond T., 1967, 'Social Stratification, Cultural Pluralism, and Integration in West Indian Societies'. In *Caribbean Integration: Papers on Social, Political and Economic Integration* (eds.) Sybil Lewis and Thomas G. Mathews. Rio Piedras: Institute of Caribbean Studies, University of Puerto Rico.

Sutton, Constance and Susan Makiesky, 1975, 'Migration and West Indian Racial and Ethnic Consciousness'. In *Migration and Development* (eds.) Helen Safa and Brian duToit. The Hague: Mouton Publishers.

Wright, Peter, 1968, *The Coloured Worker in British Industry*. London: Oxford University Press.

Young, Michael and Peter Wilmott, 1957, *Family and Kinship in East London*. London: Penguin.

CHAPTER 6

ESTHER N. GOODY and
CHRISTINE MUIR GROOTHUES

The West Africans:
The Quest for Education

Ann (not her real name) aged nine, a Ghanaian girl fostered nearly all her life by a white professional English couple in suburban Surrey, can stay in their care, Sir George Baker, President of the High Court Family Division, decided yesterday. He said that he could not bring himself to send her back to Africa, where her real parents wanted to take her.... 'My answer in the best interests, present and future, of this girl—despite the blood tie, the race, despite colour, is that I cannot bring myself to send this child to Ghana, and I, as well as the girl, would feel a rankling sense of injustice were I to do so,' he said. (*Times,* 5 December 1972)

Judge Baker had begun his summing up by saying:

The reason why I am giving this judgement in open court is that I think the public, and particularly potential foster parents, ought to know of the practice, indeed custom, of West Africans and other coloured people who come to this country, which is that the husband is a student, often a perennial student, the wife works and the children, particularly those born here, are fostered out privately, often for many years, and often as a result of newspaper advertisements or cards in shop windows or by the introduction of friends. The children are brought up in and learn our British ways of life. When a strong bond of attachment and love has been forged between the children and the foster parents, the natural parents take them away, even tear them away, to go with them to West Africa or elsewhere. There is overwhelming evidence before me of this practice, and there have been two other cases before Judges of the Family Division in the last few weeks. (*Times,* 5 December 1972)

Ann was placed with English foster parents when she was two months old. Three months later, when it became clear

that the foster parents assumed they would adopt her, Ann's
parents took her home. After reassurances they allowed her
to return to the foster parents, but when she was four the
foster parents again pressed for adoption, and Ann was again
removed by her parents. Her father then wrote to the foster
parents:

I must make it clear to you that [Ann] belongs to us and nothing
can separate us and the baby, not all the riches in the world. The
child is ours, and will be ours forever and take it from me that
you will never see her again.
(Transcript: Re 'O' [a minor] High Court, Family Division, before
the President, Sir George Baker. December 4, 1972. Transcribed
from the tape by the Mechanical Recording Department.)

Later an agreement was reached and the foster parents
understood that Ann was to stay with them until she was 18,
and finish her education. When Ann's parents decided to
return to Ghana and wanted to take her with them, the foster
parents took action to retain custody over the child. On hearing in court that Ann must remain in England, her parents
were very upset, her father saying that since they were Akans
(a matrilineal people) his wife's relatives would hold him
responsible for returning without their child; that he dared
not return without Ann (*Times*, 5 December 1972, full tran-
scripts: Re "O"... in the Family Division before Baker,
P 4–12–72; Appeal in the Court of Appeal (CA) before Davies
and Megaw (Lord Justices), and Sir Seymour Karminski
26–2–73).

Like the High Court judges, social workers have assumed
that West African parents in England 'for one reason or
another are either unwilling or unable to provide a home for
their children' (Hill 1970:87). Estimates of the number of
West African children in English foster homes vary from
2,700 (*West Africa* December 25, 1965) to 5,000 (Ellis 1971:
21). Since these children are usually placed in English families
by private arrangement, there is no way of knowing what
proportion of the families are registered with the local social
services, and hence no basis for accurate figures. However,
one indication of the significance of fostering among West
Africans in England is the finding of Holman (1973) that
60 percent of the children in a sample of 143 private foster
homes in the Birmingham area were West African. Since,

according to the 1971 census, there were then only 880 people in Birmingham who had been born in West Africa in a total population of over one million, the proportion of West Africans being fostered is clearly very high. (Indeed, we found in our London study that many families had been forced to look as far as Manchester and Birmingham for suitable foster parents.) Significantly, Holman found no other immigrant groups which regularly fostered children. In the group of 296 West African families we interviewed in London, exactly half had placed one or more children with English foster parents at some time, although only one-quarter currently had a child being fostered. It would seem that fostering is 'normal' for West Africans in England.

These cases of contested custody over West African children, and the frequency with which they are placed with English foster parents raise a number of questions about West Africans in Great Britain: who are they, and why have they come here? Why are they willing to let other people rear their children if they care so much about them? Is the West African conception of parenthood different from our own? And perhaps most fundamental of all, what is the meaning of the judge's assumption that not only he, but the Ghanaian child Ann, would feel 'a rankling sense of injustice' if she were sent back to West Africa?

There are relatively few West Africans in England, compared with several of the other minority groups discussed in this book. In the 1971 census the total number of those born in the three largest Commonwealth countries of West Africa (Nigeria, Ghana, and Sierra Leone) was 46,065. This figure of course represents adults born in their home countries. The census also gives figures for children born in this country of parents born abroad, and 19,440 were born here of parents born in all parts of Africa. Some unknown proportion of these are children of West African parents. A further source of probable underrepresentation arises from the fact that census figures inevitably represent only those recorded on census forms. Those who originally entered this country on visitors' or students' permits, and who have since taken a job or ceased to study are not likely to wish to be officially recorded, and may avoid the census taker. It is impossible to estimate how many West Africans have remained here after their permits expired. However, the figure of 46,065 from the 1971 census is almost certainly too low, even for adults.

The popular stereotype of West Africans in this country is that they are students, here for university degrees or technical qualifications unavailable in their own countries. This is a view that is held by West Africans themselves, though they often add that many are not very *serious* students. In 1970, as part of a larger study, we carried out a survey of all the West African families living in selected enumeration districts in four inner London boroughs. The results surprised us, for we found that in our sample of 296 families, 96 per cent of the men said that they had come to England in order to obtain professional or technical qualifications. As our sample was based on married couples with children, we included no student hostels; yet nearly every man we spoke to considered himself to be a student, and gave this as his reason for coming to England. It is true that in answer to further questions many explained that they had been unable to continue as fulltime students due to the responsibilities of supporting a family. The most common pattern was one of alternating study and work, with some periods of halftime or evening study combined with a job. Despite this, many had succeeded in obtaining necessary preliminary qualifications ('O' and 'A' levels), and in entering degree courses or specialist professional and technical courses (in law, accountancy, engineering, and the like). Some had completed these and were waiting to return home until their wives finished their training, or until, with both of them working, they could save enough to buy a car or other major item of equipment that was difficult to obtain at home. A number had even gone on to get a second qualification, adding economics to law, or a business course to a qualification in accounting. West Africans in England do indeed seem to be students, and if they are forced to pause in their studies from time to time in order to support themselves and their families, they are doggedly persistent in returning to their education. This persistence is the more surprising when one realises that three-quarters had been here for six years or more, and over 40 per cent for at least eight years. The men are thus substantially older than most English students, with 80 per cent over 35 years of age.

Education and Occupational Stratification in West Africa

Even when working fulltime, and not enrolled in any course, West Africans often prefer to describe themselves as students. The significance of the role of student can only be understood in the context of contemporary West Africa.

Centuries of Western trade, followed by Christianity and Colonial rule have set in motion processes which in turn have led to the flow of West Africans seeking qualifications in England. The major and most far reaching change has been in the economic structure of society, and particularly in the occupational system. Where previously nearly everyone farmed, and chief and citizen (and slave) shared much the same style of life, by the mid-twentieth century an occupationally differentiated and clearly stratified social system was emerging. Salaries of clerks were many times the yearly income of an ordinary farmer, while business men, civil servants or members of the professions lived in large western-style houses, had many servants, drove large expensive cars, and sent their children to private schools. Unlike Europe and Asia, privilege here was not the result of landed property, but rather followed mainly from the income attached to occupations in the modern sector of the economy. And the key to occupational mobility was education.

It is impossible to overstress the suddenness of these changes. Following explorations of the coast in the fifteenth century, European forts became a focus of trade at many points along the West African coast. Enclaves of African middlemen grew up around the forts, and as early as the eighteenth century some of the wealthier families sent sons to be educated in Europe to enable them to keep accounts and deal as equals with the foreign merchants. But there was virtually no contact with the peoples beyond the coastal strip until the mid-nineteenth century. The following century of Colonial rule still saw relatively little change. There was never a European settler population in British West Africa (malaria and the apparently impenetrable high forest made the costs too high). But enough administrators and soldiers were sent from England to carry out the work of governing.

So there were, even in the early twentieth century, relatively few occupations within the westernised sector of the economy.

This situation was reflected in the provision of schools. Most jobs then allocated to Africans could be carried out with only a primary education, and in 1920 there were in Ghana only three secondary schools with a total enrolment of 207. Despite a Colonial policy of improving facilities for education, expansion did not begin to keep pace with demand. A report on admission to government secondary schools in Eastern Nigeria in 1960 notes that whereas in 1944 there were 513 candidates for 28 places, in 1950 2,800 candidates were seeking the 112 available places, and in 1958 there were 9,000 applicants for 140 places. At the time of this report there had been requests for 28,000 application forms for the 1960 entry (Wareham 1962:62). Foster wrote of Ghana in the 1960s that 'the academic secondary school has become increasingly vital for social mobility, since it commands entry to nearly all significant roles within the public service' (which accounted for 60 percent of all wage and salary employment). Secondary education was 'also a prerequisite for employment by the larger commercial companies' (1965:197).

If the difficulty of entry into secondary school was a serious obstacle to occupational mobility, a second hurdle appeared at entry into sixth form. Foster's (1965) study of education in Ghana showed that only a few secondary schools had a sixth form. Furthermore, these were all government, or government assisted schools, and it was virtually impossible for students from private secondary schools to get a place. Since their number was so small, those who successfully completed the sixth form course were practically assured of a place at university. But for pupils in the private secondary schools (which made up 86 of the total of 101) both sixth form accreditation and higher education were effectively ruled out. While we neglected to ask those we interviewed in London whether they had been able to secure a sixth form place in West Africa, the proportion who began their studies here by taking 'O' and 'A' level courses supports the strong inference that this bottleneck in the educational system was often responsible for their coming to England to study.

When the West Africans we talked to in our study arrived

in England, during the early or middle 1960s, higher educational qualifications were the key to occupations carrying the greatest rewards in both wealth and prestige. With a civil service or professional position virtually assured, a period of study abroad seemed a good investment. This was doubly so because the new West African elites—who ran the Colonies under the British, and took over their governments on independence—were the educated occupants of professional and bureaucratic positions (Lloyd 1966). One trained not only for an occupational career, but also for entry into the governing stratum of these newly independent countries.

The policy of West African governments towards training in the professions has radically changed in the early 1970s. The opening of a number of new universities and professional schools has made it possible to become a fully qualified doctor or lawyer without leaving Nigeria or Ghana, and resources have been concentrated on improving the training available at home, rather than on scholarships to send students abroad. Indeed, doctors and lawyers who do train abroad are now required to take additional courses to acquaint them with the medical and legal problems particular to their own countries. However it seems likely that it will be many years before there are sufficient places in the West African universities for all those seeking to qualify in these and other professions. Perhaps a more effective restraint on the numbers seeking to train abroad will be the growing scarcity of openings in government employment for those with higher qualifications. What seemed like an insatiable demand for qualified personnel in 1960 (Hollander 1962), has become in the mid-1970s a glut of secondary school leavers in relation to the jobs available, and fewer and fewer openings for university graduates in the government offices which formerly supplied the majority of all white collar and professional employment. It has also become more difficult to enter Britain as a student. Since 1968 immigration officials have been required to seek evidence that a would-be student has a place at a recognised school or university, to satisfy themselves that he is capable of following such a course and that he has sufficient financial support to see him through his studies. Such requirements would have turned away many of the students we talked to in our study, since they often arranged their courses after arriving in Britain, and few had sufficient funds for more than the first few months.

This then, is the background to the steady stream of West Africans who have come as students to Britain from Nigeria, Ghana, the Gambia, and Sierra Leone since the Second World War. The Colonial administration presided over the transformation of their countries' political and economic structures, and by the coming of independence some qualification through higher education was the *sine qua non* for participation in the emergent elite which replaced ex-patriots in government and commercial firms as the dominant class. There is a further thread to untangle. For it is not accidental that the people of these countries come for preference to England.

Language is of course a tremendously important factor, since at least the later years of primary education, and all further education is in English. But more than this there was the conviction that life and training in England held some kind of extra virtue. The most probable origin of this view is to be found in the years of Colonial domination, when judges, administrators, soldiers and technicians who were English held both power and the knowledge on which it seemed to be based. Thus until very recently many West Africans felt that a lawyer or doctor trained in England must be more skilled than one who had studied at home. Such a person, a 'been-to' (been-to England), was likely to be given preference in competition for a job, and in promotion, and in any case received added respect from colleagues, friends, and kin. Now for many reasons, the trip to England is losing its mystique; perhaps at the same time that it is becoming both more difficult and less necessary for occupational advancement.

This search for educational qualifications has brought thousands of West Africans to study in England, but while living here they have made a practice of placing their children in English foster homes. Judges and social workers assume that this must mean that the parents either do not care about their children, that they reject them; or that they are unable to care for them through poverty or incompetence. Such a judgment follows logically from our own views concerning the 'natural' expression of parenthood as succinctly expressed by Judge Baker:

The practice of fostering for the convenience of the natural parents is contrary to our ideas and social beliefs, and particularly the belief that a young child should if possible spend its early formative years with its own natural parents or at least with its mother. (Re 'O' *Times*, 5 December 1972)

But does West African culture necessarily hold the same premises concerning the ways in which parents can best carry out their obligations to their children?

Traditional Education in West Africa

At the time of consolidation of Colonial rule over the peoples of the interior around 1900, West Africa contained a bewildering variety of societies. Pastoral groups in the savannahs of the north moved with their cattle to find grass and water; settled agricultural communities in the savannah grew grains while those in the forests were dependent on root and tree crops. And in the sophisticated inland cities Muslim philosophers debated law and wrote poetry, traders grew rich or fell into debt, and the courts of kings were centres for dependents seeking office and generals urging that the next campaign was sure to be successful. In the technologically simple rural societies, sons learned farming or herding skills from their fathers, and daughters the difficult techniques of soap and oil making, the spinning of cotton and other domestic arts from their mothers and grandmothers. Every child grew up watching adults doing the tasks which he in turn would be responsible for. More than this, every child was expected to contribute in his own small way to these tasks. Little girls swept and washed pots, and took responsibility for younger siblings. Small boys chased chickens and carried dinner to the men in the farm; when they were older they took charge of the cows grazing near the village and spent long days in fields of ripening grain, driving away hungry birds. This was 'on the job education'; apprenticeship with a stake in the firm. It continues in the same way on the farms and in the villages today.

However in many West African societies, of whom the Gonja of northern Ghana are probably reasonably typical, parents try to arrange for some of their children to grow up

with other relatives (E. Goody 1970). Such children joined
their foster parents when still quite young. There is a feeling
that until the age of five or six a child lacks the sense to benefit from precept or correction, but after that he is ready and
able to learn. So children were usually sent around the 'age
of sense'. This is done for several reasons, the most fundamental of which is that parents feel that a child gets a better
education away from home, and that if he remains with them
he is likely to be indulged and become lazy. But the rearing
of children by kin also serves to keep distant members of the
family in touch, because of their common interest in the child,
and through the exchange of visits. Indeed, in Gonja it is
felt that relatives have rights in one anothers' children, and
it is difficult for a parent to refuse a request for a child to
rear. Elderly grandparents seek children for companionship
and to run errands for them; women are always eager to have
extra girls in the household to help with the endless chores of
carrying water from the stream, collecting firewood from the
forest, bringing food from the farm or market, cooking,
washing clothes and looking after children; and men hope to
have as many lads as possible to help on the farm. Parents
are often sad to see so little of a growing child, though
travellers from his village will carry messages and keep them
informed of his welfare, and visits back and forth occur every
year or so. But parents do not fear the loss of such a fostered
child, because all accept that the links to parents and natal
home are stronger than any other, and that as an adult his
place is in his father's community, where he may succeed to
office or have a traditional role in the religious system. It is
simply inconceivable to the Gonja that it would be possible
to sever the links which bind a child to the father who begot
him and the mother who bore him, and his identity in adulthood is seen as arising from these primary links.

Gonja is still essentially a rural society, but there were, and
are, many urban centres in which life in general, and economic roles in particular are more complex. In centres like
Kano, Bornu, or Timbucktoo there are many alternative
occupations to which a parent might aspire for his son. A
father might hope that a child would enter trade; he might
want him to learn the Koran, and to understand the com-
mentaries so that he could become a Muslim legal authority

or a priest; he might wish him to become skilled in a craft such as carving, or metal or leather work, or the making of fine embroidered gowns. Of course many sons followed their fathers' occupations, but others were sent to live with and work for men who could teach them different skills.

In this new home education followed much the same model as in rural societies. A child was given increasingly more difficult tasks and was from the beginning expected to contribute to the productive effort of the household. Where a child was placed with a Mallam for a religious and legal training, he usually worked on the teacher's farm during the day, and attended lessons in the early morning and in the evening. Older students took beginners' classes and spent less time on the farm. Since parents living in rural areas might aspire to placing their children in more lucrative and prestigious urban occupations, a child was often sent to live and work with a relative, or friend of the parents, in the town.

These apprentice-fostered children lived as members of the master's family. They ate the same food, slept with the sons of the family and were given the same clothing to wear. As they grew up, they not only mastered the skills of their chosen occupation, but they became familiar with others doing the same work, and were often gradually allotted customers and clients of their own. As adults they might remain as dependents of their former master, benefiting from his established clientele, or they might set up business on their own, sometimes in another town where they acted also as agents of the old master. In short, their training not only gave them the necessary skills with which to practise an occupation, but helped them to establish vital contacts with clients and colleagues. Usually parents did not pay for a son's education, since he contributed his labour which grew increasingly more valuable, and he would always remain a loyal follower of the man who trained him. The master was a 'kind of parent' and could expect the sort of obedience and respect due to a parent.

In traditional West African societies parents used apprentice-fostering arrangements to place their children in desirable occupations and secure for them contacts with people in a position to be able to help them in the future. These same strategies were adapted to the new circumstances of the emerging educated elite of coastal societies. This is perhaps clearest in the Creole communities of Freetown and Monrovia (Banton 1957; Fraenkel 1964) where the institution of wardship appeared during the nineteenth century. Established Creole families were the elite of Liberia and Sierra Leone, and educated their children as a matter of course. But they also took in children from the rural hinterland, and sent them to local schools (rather than to the boarding schools which their own children often attended). When these wards reached adulthood the foster parents were expected to help them find a suitable job, preferably in a white collar occupation. These wards came to form a network of loyal followers of the elite families and, if they were successful, in their turn took in wards to educate and as help in the household. Teachers and clergymen were also likely to be offered children to educate as they were viewed as morally admirable, and thus able to provide a good model for children, and at the same time they represented successful mastery of Western religious and cultural norms. Here again, as with traditional education, the child was expected to learn from simply being in the household of the foster parents, without special instruction in morality or western culture.

West Africans in London

In an attempt to understand both the determination of West Africans to study abroad, and the pressures and traditions which led to the placing of their children with English foster parents, we carried out a dual-focus study of West Africans in London between 1970 and 1972. Our first problem was to find some way of getting a sample which was, even in a crude sense, representative of West Africans who come to England. This required quite a large sample, but the information was necessarily relatively superficial. To balance this we decided to carry out a second phase in which Christine Groothues worked intensively with 20 couples, half of whom were from Ghana and half Nigerian.

For the first phase of the study we had originally hoped to be able to locate lists of West Africans living in London from which we could draw a representative sample for interview.

However this proved impossible as all available lists were either incomplete or seriously biased. In the end we decided on an essentially pragmatic approach. Four central London boroughs known to contain concentrations of West Africans were selected for study. Using the results of the 1966 ten per cent sample census we were able to rank order the enumeration districts within each borough in terms of the proportion of residents born in Africa. All enumeration districts with 5 per cent or more African-born population were taken as the universe for the survey. The interviewers then went to each address in these enumeration districts and listed the country of origin of the heads of all the households (being especially alert for multiple occupancies). The sample consists of all households in this census which met our criteria of two West African parents who had at least one child with them in this country. (On the basis of this census we estimate that between 80 and 85 per cent of the West African couples living in these boroughs had at least one child with them.) We were finally able to interview about 70 per cent of the sample or 296 couples. There are obvious limitations to the selection of a sample in this way and generalisations beyond the residents of the four boroughs studied can only be tentative. Information from these interviews will be referred to as based on the survey.

The couples for the second phase of the study were located through informal contacts and some of them with the assistance of the Commonwealth Students' Children's Society. The couples were selected so that half were from a major Nigerian ethnic group and half from a Ghanaian one; with each of these two sub-samples, half of the couples had fostered a child and half had never done so. Extensive notes were kept on visits to these couples over a period of several months, and background information systematically collected from each. Pseudonyms are used in referring to the couples who contributed to the intensive phase of the study, and details have been altered where these seemed likely to permit identification. By now the majority have probably returned to West Africa. The purpose of the second phase was to gain an insight into the mechanisms which underlie patterns of work, study and the care of children. Here we were not concerned with generalising to a wider population so much as with understanding how different factors interact to create the pattern of West African life in London.

Among the most striking findings of the survey were the universality of the intention to study in England, and the length of time which the men had already spent here (over 40 per cent had been here at least eight years). Despite this, only two per cent planned to remain here permanently. We have seen why the ambition to gain qualifications abroad is so important in contemporary West Africa, but the length of time involved seems to be far longer than originally planned for. This in turn has a number of consequences for life in London. But why should it take so long to complete studies?

First of all, there is the obvious problem of finances. Only 11 per cent of the families depended mainly on grants, loans or help from relatives. As we were interested in families with children, we did not include student hostels in our survey; had we done so the proportion of government-sponsored students would have been higher. A further six per cent received supplementary help from some outside source. The remaining four-fifths have no outside support at all. Relatives at home, although a potential source of help, are rarely able to support a student once he is over here, even if they have been largely responsible for financing the trip itself and expenses during the first few months. Only five per cent of our survey sample listed relatives as a major source of financial support, though many mentioned that they had sent money at first and still occasionally sent small amounts. Because the civil war in Nigeria impoverished many families there, the flow of money was often in the other direction. Relatives at home tend to think that money is easily found in England, and they expect to see something of it, even before the migrant returns.

With such a high proportion having to be self-supporting it is not surprising to find that two-thirds of the men in the survey were currently working, nearly all of these full time. Only one-quarter were devoting all their time to studies. But the picture is yet more complicated. The typical pattern is alternating periods of full time study with periods of work-plus-study when a shortage of funds makes full or parttime employment necessary. While 43 per cent were both working and studying at the time we talked to them, an additional

34 per cent had done both at some time during their life in England. Less than one-quarter had never tried to combine work and study.

The men we spoke with varied greatly in how clearly defined their goals were. Several of those in our intensive sample came intending to do a particular course, set about getting the necessary 'O' and 'A' level qualifications, enrolled for the course, and completed it with no apparent indecision as to the best plan of action, even when there were difficulties and delays for other reasons. Others, however, came intending to do 'business studies' or medicine or engineering and found for one reason or another that this was impossible. It is significant that they did not then give up and go home, but found some other, more realistic vocation for which they could train. Again this often meant a period of preparation before actually beginning, but men seem to be willing to think and plan a long way ahead in order to be able finally to return home with a qualification that will ensure good career prospects. Mr. Achebi, for instance, originally intended to study medicine in Yugoslavia. He found the language a serious problem, and when with the outbreak of the war in Nigeria his grant came to an end, he came to England where his wife was already studying. Although he did two 'A' levels here, he still could not get a place in a medical school, and when finally convinced of this decided to do law. He has passed the first year examinations but failed the Part I, so is now preparing to sit this again. He feels that although he managed to complete his 'A' levels by correspondence course while working, that his law studies have suffered from the lack of concentration this involves. He is very anxious to find a foster mother for his two small boys so that he can work nights and do full time studies during the day. At present he has to be at home during the day because his wife is working in an accounts department in conjunction with her training in accountancy.

Many men find that they must first obtain 'O' and 'A' levels to satisfy matriculation requirements before they can begin the course they have chosen. When Mr. Bankwah first came to England he had to begin by doing 'O' level English and then the three 'A' levels he was advised were necessary for university entrance. After this he began to study law, but gave this up as a 'useless subject'. In 1971 he began a degree course in economics. He had worked in the family business for some time before coming to study in the United Kingdom and keeps in touch with this by trips home in the vacations. From his business interests he receives enough, together with what his wife earns (working fulltime and overtime in a toy factory) to study full-time and work only during the vacations.

Because of the pattern of part-time and interrupted education, a man often finds his stay in England lasting far longer than he originally planned. Loneliness, together with the prospect of a long delay before he is ready to return, may lead him to send for the wife he left behind in West Africa. Among the survey families there was a mean difference of two years between the length of time the husband and wife had been in this country. From the husband's point of view there are probably two main reasons for asking his wife to join him. One, obviously, is to relieve the loneliness and provide a few home comforts in a land where food, climate, and language are all foreign. Another reason is that by getting a job in this country, she may enable him to give up working, or to work only parttime, and thus to give more time to his studies.

Of the 296 wives in the survey, 45 (15 per cent) had come on their own to study or train and married while in this country. The proportion of our intensive sample which came independently of their husbands is even higher; six, or nearly one-third, had come on their own to train in England, and then married here. But many of those who were already engaged or married also came to study. About one-quarter of the survey wives accompanied or followed their husbands with the intention of studying in this country, and a further 30 per cent joined their husbands expecting to both work and train. In all, 70 per cent of the survey wives came to the United Kingdom hoping to obtain a professional or technical qualification of some kind. The proportion in our intensive sample is very similar: three-quarters of the wives came intending to train or study, though in this group too, many knew they would have to work as well.

Women in West Africa are famous for their enterprise as traders and their industry as farmers. Although women's economic roles vary appreciably from one society to another, in the societies of the coast and forest belt which send migrants to England, a woman assumes that she will work in addition to looking after the household and the children. The question is not *whether* she will work, but at what? Thus when a man brings a wife to this country he is securing not only companionship and a homemaker, but both he and his wife assume that she will work as well. Often her earnings are an important, or even essential, contribution to the family finances.

Among the twenty intensive study couples, only one of the five women who did not make a major contribution to the family budget was not working at all. She had been nursing fulltime until a difficult pregnancy, and in fact, resumed fulltime work just at the end of the study. The others worked full or nearly fulltime, but because their husbands were earning more, their own contribution was proportionately lower. None of the wives in the intensive sample was a housewife only. Even those with no skill or training work in factories, and one woman taught herself how to sew, and then worked her way up to a well-paid machinist's job.

But although they know they must work, West African women come to this country with their own ambitions. What do they hope to learn? About 20 per cent of the survey wives intended to enter a profession, nearly always nursing; another 20 per cent were thinking in terms of secretarial work, while a further 20 per cent planned to prepare for setting up a business. This last group is largely made up of women doing dressmaking, hairdressing, and catering and domestic science courses. The choices are the same for the intensive sample. Nursing is the most commonly chosen career among those who came to study on their own and married in this country. Although some of the wives in the intensive sample who followed their husbands hoped to become nurses, the need to earn money to help their husband's studies, and the arrival of children had led them to switch to a less demanding course of study.

Perhaps equally revealing of the commitment of this group to educational goals is the fact that of those wives in the intensive sample who initially came to join their husbands without having specific plans for study, all but two have, in fact, taken courses—in hairdressing, wig-making, English and typing. One of the remaining two had plans for intensive study when her husband finished his course. Clearly, although they are wives and mothers, and also working, these women have their own goals and see a period in this country as giving them a chance to further their own education, whether they came intially as students or as wives with responsibilities for helping to support the family. This determination to achieve some form of educational qualification while in England was readily expressed. One woman compared the motives for coming to this country with the competition between villages at home, each seeking to do better than the other. In education 'the best' is thought to be English, and by coming to this country to train, she said 'you can topple your rival on your return with ease'. Another wife remarked that 'People who come to England are proud when they return, and you feel you're missing something.' These sentiments also effect the men who come to study in this country, and indeed are very important in their decisions to do so. But whereas *all* the men were here to better their prospects by training, there would seem to be no *a priori* reason why their wives should share this ambition. Nor were these merely optimistic hopes. Fourteen out of the twenty wives in the intensive study had already completed qualifications in this country.

The Delay-Companionship-Responsibility Cycle

Broadly speaking these West African families are of two kinds. One kind is the recently married, where the couple either met in this country or where the wife came over as a new bride. The second kind of family was already established when the husband decided to study in the United Kingdom. The wife remained behind at first, but later joined him. A common arrangement is for children who are already in school to stay behind with relatives in West Africa. If there are younger children, they may accompany their mother when she comes to join her husband, or they may remain with a grandmother or other relative at home. One-third of the families in the survey had left at least one child behind, while another 13 per cent had sent one or more children home from England. In contrast, only 6 per cent had brought a child to join them after both parents were settled here.

Such a pattern is confirmed by the age distribution of the children of West Africans in this country. The largest group is in the infant and pre-school category, while the primary and secondary school age groups are relatively small. This is the sort of distribution one would expect from a young married population. Yet 80 per cent of the husbands are over 35 years old, and only 14 per cent of the wives are under 25 years of age, usually the most fertile period for women. As this distribution of child ages suggests, there are strong pressures on both kinds of family to have children while in England. In the newly-established families, the relatives back home are naturally anxious to be assured that the marriage will be a fertile one, and the partners themselves share this concern. While many couples are fully aware of the difficulties involved in raising small children while trying to work and study, they are also anxious to begin a family before they are any older. Ironically, the tradition that a West African woman should be able to rear a large family while pulling her full weight either on the farm or in trading leads these women to feel that they ought to be able to manage even under the changed circumstances of life in London. It is expected of them and they expect it of themselves. The pressures on an established family to continue having children may be only slightly less severe. As the years go on and the date of a return home is still not certain, so the couple grows older, and the remaining years of childbearing dwindle. If they are to have even a moderate size family, they cannot just miss out six or eight years during which they could be having children.

This situation in which West African couples so often find themselves may be described as the 'delay-companionship-responsibility cycle'. It is a pattern of interrelated role conflicts involving husband and wife which ultimately affects the children. When the husband finds his training will take several years, he sends for his wife, or arranges to marry. The wife comes to join her husband in England to help, both as companion and wage-earner, but she brings along her own set of needs and ambitions. Now there are two people trying to combine work and study. At the same time, the creation, or reunion, of the conjugal couple leads to the birth of children which makes still more difficult the balance between work and study, and greatly increases the difficulty of finding suitable accommodations. The added difficulties mean further delays in completing courses and training programmes. This is likely to mean another child, more responsibilities and yet more delays.

Strategies of Childrearing

An English couple confronted with a similar set of role conflicts will almost certainly resolve them by the wife giving up her studies to care for the children, while a combination of parental support and government grants finances the husband's continued studies. If they are particularly fortunate, there may be a grandmother or aunt near enough to look after the children so that the wife can continue to study, at least on a parttime basis. But the wife is expected to be ready to give up her career for her children's sake if there is any conflict between the requirements of the two.

Given this contrast between English and West African responses to the same kind of problem, it would seem that mothers' aspirations for their own training were likely to be a central factor in the resort to fostering of young children. However the picture is not so simple. Our data from the intensive sample suggest that there is no very strong link between the decision to foster and the determination of a mother to complete her training. Of those whose studies were completed before the birth of children, about half nevertheless subsequently fostered a child; the same number used neither foster parents nor daily minders. Of those whose training was not completed, nearly all made use of either fostering or daily minding, but the same pattern holds for those who had no clear career plans on coming to this country. There is however a link between fostering and the wish to complete training in particular cases: Mrs. Boateng says that their daughter was fostered at the age of nine months because she could not manage to work fulltime and keep up with her evening classes as well as caring for the baby. And when Mrs. Kotoko found that she was pregnant, although still not finished with her midwifery training, she immediately set about looking for a foster mother, as she never even considered the possibility of giving up her training when she had so nearly reached the end.

The frequent use of foster parents and daily minders by women who are not strongly career oriented reflects several other factors which also influence choices about child care. Among the constraints which operate in this way, poor accommodation and the father's efforts to complete his qualifications are without doubt important. But we have also seen that nearly all mothers work. Some, indeed most, do so for financial reasons, and if young children threaten to interfere they must be entrusted to someone else's care. Thus Mrs. Ikoye is very anxious to have the two youngest boys at home, despite the fact that they are very satisfied with the foster parents with whom they have lived since infancy. But they cannot manage without the wages she brings home, and as the boys are not yet in school she would have to give up her job to look after them during the day. Similarly, when Mrs. Idusi came to England specifically in order to support her husband through the remainder of his studies, their son was sent immediately to foster parents so that she could take a fulltime job. He remained there until old enough to start school, and is now at home since he can stay with a neighbour until Mrs. Idusi gets back from work.

But if some children are fostered because the mother must work in order to support the family, in other cases women work because they want to. Often, as with Mrs. Bentum, this seems to be associated with having achieved a high level of skill and holding a responsible job. She finds her work in Whitehall as a stenographic secretary extremely interesting. When her first child was born she nursed her for three months and then sent her home to her mother in Ghana. The second child, a son, stayed longer, and was sent first to a daily minder, and then to a foster parent before they decided that he too would be better off with his grandmother. Mrs. Bentum says she cannot imagine giving up her work to look after the babies, and as her mother is very pleased to have them this is not necessary. She would certainly find it difficult to combine their care with her present job, as she not infrequently works until ten at night. Mrs. Molomo was fully qualified as a nurse before she married, and when her daughter was born she stayed home for only a month before beginning to seek nursing jobs through an agency. The child was placed with a daily minder who was most carefully examined before the arrangement was completed. Mary Molomo was soon back to working virtually fulltime, and though she says this is because they are trying to arrange a mortgage on their new house, she also adds that she could not imagine staying at home with the baby all day.

Even women who have few skills to exercise seem to need the outlet of a job. They also value the major household goods which this enables them to buy: washing machines, refrigerators and almost always a sewing machine. But women also need to feel some degree of independence from their husbands. As one wife put it, 'I cannot always be asking him for money to buy my toilet articles, I must have something of my own.' In addition, it is important to remember that women in West Africa are expected to contribute actively to the domestic economy. Thus Mrs. Obemi struggled to keep up with her factory sewing throughout a difficult fourth pregnancy in five years until she became ill. In referring to this she said simply that it was her duty to do what she could to help with the family finances.

Conjugal Roles and Child Care

Since all mothers work, this factor alone cannot be used to explain why some couples foster children and others do not. And it seems that women's aspirations for gaining qualifications while in England are not directly related to the use of fostering. Nor is it simply a matter of the age of the child, with parents of infants sending them to be fostered, while those with school-age children can manage with them at home (although this pattern does appear). There are two main ways in which couples cope with pre-school children at home. They may send them to a woman who looks after children during the day, a daily minder. Or they may so synchronise their schedules that one or the other of the parents is always at home. Examples from the intensive sample of how spouses coordinate their schedules are a husband who works on the night shift in a factory while his wife is a secretary during the day, and several cases of women who do night nursing and thus are able to be at home during the day while their husbands are working or attending classes. It should be noted that husbands who share the responsibility for seeing that someone is always with a young child do not necessarily do anything about the maintenance of the household. The man on night shift tries to sleep during the day, and does only the minimum necessary to keep the toddler clean and fed. Husbands whose wives are working at night will, of course, get up with the children if they cry, but often do not expect to do anything more. However one man feeds and dresses the children before his wife gets back.

All women 'must' work, as they see this as part of a wife's responsibility. Those with infants and pre-school children can only work if they can find some way of caring for the children while they are away. If the husband is willing, and if his regime of study and work allow, he can often fill this function. But if the husband's commitments are such as to make such a careful meshing of schedules unworkable, then some other course must be found. Many of the survey couples said they had tried to get places in local authority nurseries for their children, but had been unsuccessful. Our impression is that local authorities do not treat such requests very seriously, perhaps because they feel the wife should be at home looking after the children herself. Seven per cent (20) of the 296 survey couples had been able to place a child in day nurseries of all kinds, and of these four per cent had also made use of foster parents.

In a classic study of London families Bott (1957) suggested that there was a significant difference in the pattern of conjugal relations with different styles of extra-family networks. Her categories were based on the extent to which a couple carried out the various activities of marriage and family life jointly, either taking turns or working together; or where their roles were segregated each having a separate sphere of competence and responsibility. Bott found that those couples whose pattern of task performance was segregated tended to spend their leisure time separately, each with kin or friends of the same sex who knew one another. The network of each spouse was 'connected'. Each spouse would depend on his or her own friends for assistance and companionship in the activities for which they were responsible, rather than turning to the other partner. Those couples with a joint activity pattern had common friends, but these tended to be unknown to each other; their network was 'unconnected'. Friendship activities—dinners, outings—involved husband and wife together and jointness was carried over into leisure pursuits. Husband and wife turned to one another for assistance in domestic activities rather than to kin or friends of the same sex outside the conjugal family.

In traditional West African societies the division of virtually all spheres of activity into 'male' and 'female' is pronounced, and this is nowhere clearer than in domestic matters. Women cook, and wash clothes and care for children as a matter of course, in addition to their work as traders or farmers. In the homes of the modern elite servants do most of the domestic work, and thus jointness in roles is unnecessary. While some leisure activities are shared, many are not. The husband has his career, and the wife either a career or some kind of job which occupies her during the day. Their home is a common ground on which they share interests, above all in their children (see Oppong 1974 and Harrell-Bond 1975). Thus in traditional West African societies, and often still to a notable extent, conjugal roles are highly segregated, both in terms of interests and task performance. When West Africans who have spent some time in Europe return home, they often comment on the difference between this pattern and life abroad where 'we did everything together'. One of the things we looked at in our work with the couples of the intensive sample was the organisation of domestic and leisure activities and the kinds of social networks within which these couples moved.

There were quite clear differences between couples from Ghana and those from Nigeria in the organisation of conjugal roles; these are related to the different types of descent system followed by each group, and the consequent differences in traditional marriage roles. However the case material suggests that at least some of those couples who share responsibility for decisions, child care, family expenses and leisure activities here in England are doing so because their customary alternative sources of assistance and support are absent.

Their roles are joint-under-duress, rather than as a result of fundamental changes in ideas about how responsibilities ought to be shared. In one case, for instance, while the wife was ill her husband took care of the baby, did all the shopping, housework and cooking, but once she recovered they reverted to the pattern of the wife having responsibility for domestic chores and children, with the husband helping with the shopping at weekends.

Patterns of leisure time activities are particularly revealing. Over half of the couples (11/20) had highly segregated leisure roles, with only four being fully joint. Generally, friends tend to overlap to a considerable extent, since both know many people from home who are also in London. But each spouse tends to have some friends not shared by the other—either school or work friends from home, or people from current or past study or work situations in England. Husbands rarely take wives along to sporting events and pub sessions with friends from work, and one husband who had a band treated this part of his life as entirely separate from his family. On the other hand some of the Nigerian couples attended meetings of their home town union together, and couples from both countries often had friends and relatives from home who celebrated a birth or wedding or the achievement of a degree, or who had to be welcomed or sent off home with a party. Even here, however, the husband would often attend while the wife stayed at home with the children. This was likely to be her own choice, for with job and studies and the house to look after, women tended to be very tired most of the time, and to prefer a quiet evening at home to a large gathering where they would feel called upon to participate fully. Husbands' social networks also extend beyond those of their wives because men are freer to attend parties and gatherings uninvited; if they know someone who has been invited they may go along with him, but a wife is not included in such an arrangement.

We were surprised by the number of couples who had relatives in Britain. Only one of the twenty couples in the intensive study did not have at least 'distant cousins' from home who were also in London at the time of the study. While there were quite frequent visits, unless these relatives were living close by there was very little exchange of services.

Although this is contrary to the West African ethic of kinship solidarity, it is perhaps hardly surprising in view of the full and complex lives which both men and women lead here. Anyone, man or woman, who is in London is likely to be trying to work, study and raise a family in some combination, and thus to have little time to help out kin with similar problems. The fact that relatives tend to be dispersed, and not to live in the same neighbourhood (unless, as sometimes happens, they are sharing a house) adds to the difficulties of helping out. Transport is a perpetual problem, both because of the extra time involved and because of the cost. Couples with cars tended to share significantly more leisure activities than those without. This isolation is, for many couples, compensated for by extensive use of the telephone for keeping in touch, and information circulates rapidly among relatives and those from the same home community.

We tried to select the couples of the intensive sample in order to have equal numbers who had fostered a child, and who had reared their children entirely at home. This turned out to be more difficult than we anticipated, because many couples try a series of arrangements due both to changing circumstances and to the difficulty of finding one with which they are satisfied. In the end we found that of our twenty couples, eleven had used foster parents at some time, while of the remaining nine, four had placed their children with a daily minder. Only five of the twenty couples had never used either form of child care. In Table 1 the degree of conjugal

Conjugal Role Structure	**Arrangements for Child Care**		
	Fostering	Daily Minding	Parents only
Joint	1	1	3
Intermediate	5	1	2
Segregated	5	2	0
	11	4	5 N = 20

TABLE 1   Relationship between Child Care Arrangements and Conjugal Role Structure: Intensive Sample.

role segregation is related to the kind of arrangements made for child care. Although with such small numbers we can do no more than indicate trends, it is striking that none of the couples with highly segregated roles had reared their children entirely at home, while only one of the five couples scored as having fully joint conjugal roles sent a child to foster parents. This could be interpreted in either of two ways: it may be that couples with highly segregated roles cannot manage to synchronise their schedules and share responsibility sufficiently to allow them to keep a child at home while both parents are working or studying. When there is no sharing of responsibility and tasks, and the mother is working and possibly also studying, she may simply not be able to cope with a child as well. Since West African conjugal roles are, traditionally, highly segregated, this may be a common source of pressure on West African parents to place a child with foster parents. The other interpretation of this pattern would be that parents who have defined their conjugal roles in terms of sharing tasks and responsibilities are those who have also adopted the view that it is harmful for a child to be reared by anyone other than his own parents. Both these attitudes characterise the stereotype of the modern Western family where companionate marriage and close bonds between parents and children are idealised. It seems likely that both these interpretations may be correct, and that both kinds of pressure are influencing decisions about child rearing.

Conclusions: Educational Fostering as a Cultural Paradigm

We have tried to show why education in England is so important to ambitious West Africans, and to indicate the kinds of problems they encounter in trying to secure it. But there remains the question of why West African couples so often attempt to meet the conflicting demands of earning a living, studying, and rearing a family by placing young children with foster parents. English families do not see this as a possible solution to similar problems, nor do other migrant groups. Pakistani, Indian, Irish, and Cypriot families all appear to closely resemble English families in this respect.

West Indian families do make considerable use of daily minders, but rarely send children to foster parents (see E. Goody 1975). It is here that West African traditions are crucial. Explanations of fostering by West Africans in England must be seen in terms of fostering as a cultural paradigm for the education of children.

As noted earlier, in many traditional West African societies children are sent to be reared away from home in order to learn adult skills and sound moral values. In the more complex West African societies, both traditional and modern, specialised skills are learned in apprentice-fostering. Today, families from rural areas place children with city people as housemaids or wards. And there is a well-established practice of sending a schoolchild to live with a teacher or clergyman in order that he may receive help with his studies. All these forms of fostering are based on the underlying premise that parents are not necessarily the best people to rear their own children, and may very well not be able to provide them with the opportunities and advantages available in a foster home. Thus, the West African parent sees private fostering arrangements in England in a very different light than the English child care officer well-versed in child psychology from Freud to Bowlby. Faced with crowded living conditions, and the demands of work and studies on both parents' time and energies, English foster parents appear able to provide their children with just those positive advantages that they themselves came here to seek: familiarity with English culture and language and a basis for later social mobility. Judge Baker's supposition that the Ghanaian child Ann would feel a 'rankling sense of injustice' if she were sent back to West Africa suggests that many English people also feel that an English upbringing conveys special advantages. It is hardly surprising that couples who have come to this country in order to receive an English education are eager to provide their children with the same opportunity.

NOTE

The research on West African families in London was supported by the Social Science Research Council, and owes much to the advice and assistance of the Commonwealth Students' Children's Society, and especially to Mrs. Pat Stapleton. The analysis of traditional education is based on several periods of work in Ghana by Esther Goody. The London study was jointly planned by the two authors; Christine Groothues organised and supervised the survey, and carried out the observations on the twenty families in the intensive sample. Esther Goody is responsible for the analysis of the data and the writing of the paper.

REFERENCES CITED

Abernethy, David, 1969, *The Political Dilemma of Popular Education: An African Case.* Stanford: Stanford University Press.

Banton, Michael, 1957, *West African City: A Study of Tribal Life in Freetown.* London: Oxford University Press.

Bott, Elizabeth, 1957, *Family and Social Network.* London: Tavistock Publications.

Ellis, June, 1971, 'The Fostering of West African Children in England'. *Social Work Today* 2(5):21–24.

Foster, Philip, 1965, *Education and Social Change in Ghana.* London: Routledge and Kegan Paul.

Fraenkel, Merran, 1964, *Tribe and Class in Monrovia.* London: International African Institute.

Goody, Esther N., 1966, 'Fostering of Children in Ghana: A Preliminary Report. *Ghana Journal of Sociology* 2:26–33.

Goody, Esther N., 1970, 'Kinship Fostering in Gonja: Deprivation or Advantage?' In *Socialization: The Approach from Social Anthropology* (ed.) Philip Meyer. London: Tavistock Publications.

Goody, Esther N., 1971, 'Varieties of Fostering'. *New Society* 5: 237–9 (August).

Goody, Esther N., 1973, *Contexts of Kinship.* Cambridge: Cambridge University Press.

Goody, Esther N., 1975, 'Delegation of Parental Roles in West Africa and the West Indies'. In *Socialization and Communication in Primary Groups* (ed.) Thomas R. Williams. The Hague: Mouton.

Harrell-Bond, Barbara, 1975, *Modern Marriage in Sierra Leone.* The Hague: Mouton.

Hill, Clifford, 1970, *Immigration and Integration.* Oxford: Pergamon Press.

Holman, Robert, 1973, *Trading in Children: A Study of Private Fostering*. London: Routledge and Kegan Paul.

Hollander, E. D., 1962, 'Observations on the Labour Market in Ghana'. In *Educational and Occupational Selection in West Africa* (ed.) A. Taylor. London: Oxford University Press.

Lloyd, Peter, 1966, *The New Elites of Tropical Africa*. London: Oxford University Press.

Muir, Christine and Esther Goody, 1972, 'Student Parents: West African Families in London'. *Race* 13:329–36.

Oppong, Christine, 1974, *Marriage among a Matrilineal Elite*. Cambridge: Cambridge University Press.

Wallerstein, Immanuel, 1964, *The Road to Independence in Ghana and the Ivory Coast*. Paris: Mouton.

Wareham, A. K., 1962, 'Methods of Selection for the Government Secondary Grammar Schools in Eastern Nigeria'. In *Educational and Occupational Selection in West Africa* (ed.) A. Taylor, London: Oxford University Press.

CHAPTER 7

JAMES L. WATSON

The Chinese: Hong Kong Villagers in the British Catering Trade

The Chinese are undoubtedly the least understood of all Britain's immigrant minorities. Only a handful of scholars have studied this group and, as a consequence, the published results are rather sparse. Government-sponsored bodies and volunteer agencies, such as the Community Relations Commission and the Runnymede Trust, admit openly that they know little about the Chinese minority. The mass media have simply exacerbated the problem: after completely ignoring the Chinese for over a decade, British newspapers have begun a series of sensationalised reports focusing on gangland activities in Soho—thus giving the general public a totally unrepresentative view of the Chinese community. As I hope to demonstrate here, the general lack of understanding that surrounds this hard-working minority is a direct result of a unique pattern of settlement that sets the Chinese apart from most other immigrant groups in Britain.

The vast majority of Chinese immigrants are associated with the family restaurant trade and are thereby dispersed in urban neighbourhoods, suburbs, and small towns throughout the country. It is now almost impossible to find a town in England (and, increasingly, in Scotland) with a population of 5000 or more that does not have at least one Chinese restaurant or take-away shop. Except for a small ward in Liverpool and the Soho district of London, the Chinese have not stayed together and, hence, do not represent a very significant 'problem' for local authorities. Even the two settlements in Liverpool and London cannot be described as ghettoes in the usual sense of the term. Most of the Chinese in this country live and work in areas where they have easy access to a large middle-class clientele. For their own part, the restaurant workers prefer to keep a low public profile and do not seek close personal ties with members of the host society. The adults seldom venture beyond the security of the catering trade and, on average, their children rarely constitute more than about five per cent of the local school population. Even though many Chinese have decided to settle permanently in Britain, few are interested in assimilation. The majority cling tenaciously to their cultural heritage and continue to identify with kinsmen in rural Hong Kong.

In this essay, I will attempt to explain how the Chinese have managed to remain so aloof from British society and how this pattern of immigration first emerged. My own research began in 1969 with a seventeen month study of a traditional village in Hong Kong's rural hinterland (Watson 1975). The village is an 'emigrant community' with an economy completely dependent on remittances from abroad; eighty-five to ninety per cent of the community's able-bodied males work in Britain or in other parts of Western Europe. Immediately following this study I conducted a brief survey of emigrants from the same village who were working in the London metropolitan area (Watson 1974). After moving to Britain myself in 1973, the research has been continued on a part-time basis.

Like many other contributors to this volume, I am convinced that it is difficult, if not impossible, to gain a true picture of immigration as a *process* without investigating its impact at *both* ends of the migration chain. In keeping with this view, the present essay is divided more or less equally between the effects of emigration on the sending society and the immigrants' experience in Britain.

Background: The British Side

Immigration and census statistics dealing with the Chinese are notoriously difficult to use but, according to best estimates, at least 60,000 now live in Britain (based on data from Chan 1976 and Campbell-Platt 1976). This figure covers the main group of immigrants who work in the catering trade; it excludes approximately 6000 full-time students and 2000 nurses who are better classified as educational transients. London has the largest concentration of Chinese with over 14,000 distributed throughout its 28 metropolitan boroughs. Liverpool is the next largest centre with 1500, while Manchester and Birmingham each have approximately one thousand. In the last decade, Scotland's Chinese population has grown from a mere handful to well over three thousand. Glasgow and Edinburgh now claim 1400 and 900 respectively. As discussed in more detail later, the majority of these immigrants are British subjects who were born in the Crown Colony of Hong Kong, one of the last surviving outposts of Empire.

The Chinese expansion into Britain is a direct result of an economic boom that occurred here during the late 1950s and early 1960s. At that time, the British people began to change their eating habits and developed a taste for foreign cuisine, most notably Indian and Chinese. The Chinese restaurant trade grew rapidly in the decade between 1956 and 1965, and the rate of immigration from Hong Kong rose accordingly. This restaurant boom continued unabated until the market reached a saturation point around 1970. By then economic recession had curtailed further expansion and many restaurants were forced to close or retrench. The number of Chinese catering businesses, including restaurants and take-away shops, has levelled out at approximately 4000.

Economic stagnation is also the principle reason why many Chinese restaurateurs and their families chose to leave Britain in the last decade and reemigrate to Continental Europe. The movement across the Channel began as early as 1960 among certain emigrants who had learned to adapt rapidly to opportunities from abroad. In the village I studied, for example, the earliest emigrants settled in Britain but their sons and nephews soon branched out into Holland, Belgium, and West Germany. There are now at least 10,000 Hong Kong Chinese living in Holland where they compete with Indonesian immigrants in the restaurant trade. West Germany and Belgium have been much stricter on non-EEC immigration and have kept the local Chinese populations at 4000 and 2000 respectively (London Report 1972–3:28–9). This may change in the near future, however, because under EEC rules holders of British passports endorsed with the 'right of abode' in the United Kingdom may eventually be admitted without restrictions to member countries (London Report 1972–3:23). It takes only five years of residence in Britain to obtain the necessary endorsement.

Increasingly, therefore, the Chinese community in Britain cannot be understood in isolation from its extensions on the continent. Holland, Belgium, West Germany, and Scandinavia were once treated as pioneer outposts into which the Hong Kong Chinese ventured only after they had established a base in England. Given the present state of the European economy it is not surprising that these outposts have already surpassed Britain as the Promised Land for most immigrants. The small towns of West Germany, along with the cities of Scandinavia, are the new frontiers for Chinese restaurant development.

Background: The Hong Kong Side

As noted above, the vast majority of Chinese in Britain come from Hong Kong, either as British subjects born in the colony or as 'stateless aliens' who left China to settle in Hong Kong after the Chinese Communist revolution. The earlier emigrants originate from a handful of villages in Hong Kong's rural hinterland, known as the New Territories. This 365 square-mile section of Chinese mainland was leased from the Manchu government in 1898 for a period of 99 years, ostensively as a military buffer zone for the island of Hong Kong. It has since become an integral part of the colony. Although Hong Kong is renowned for its cosmopolitan urban centres (the cities of Victoria and Kowloon are among the most densely-populated in the world), significant elements of the traditional peasant culture still survive in the rural areas.

Until the post-World War Two era when Hong Kong was flooded with refugees from all over China, three distinct ethnic groups inhabited the New Territories: Cantonese, Hakka, and boatpeople. The Cantonese-speaking *Punti* ('native settlers') are generally thought to be descendants of northern Chinese pioneers who gained control of South China by the tenth century. The *Hakka* ('guest people') speak a separate language and arrived several centuries after the dominant Punti group. Since they were latecomers, the Hakka settled in the hilly areas of what was later to become the New Territories. The boatpeople managed to survive in this highly competitive social environment by occupying a niche on the fringe of the other groups' territory. As the name implies, the boatpeople are fishermen who spend most of their lives aboard the junks and boats in Hong Kong's many harbours (see Ward 1965). These three ethnic groups make up the indigenous population of the New Territories; all would be roughly categorised as Southern Chinese to distinguish them from Northerners who speak Mandarin. Approximately 70 per cent of the Chinese in Britain are Cantonese-speaking Punti; 25 per cent are Hakka and the remainder are Northerners (mostly from Taiwan) and Singaporians (who speak Hokkien, yet another Southern dialect). Due largely to their traditional status as a despised minority and their consequent lack of financial backing, Hong Kong's boatpeople rarely find their way to Europe.

Although the people of the New Territories have lived under British colonial rule for nearly 80 years, they have not become 'Anglicised' and they have not forsaken their cultural traditions. Most of the villagers share a common peasant culture with the other residents of Kwangtung, China's southern-most province. This densely-populated region is best known to anthropologists as the site of the largest and most complex lineage organisations in the world (see Baker 1968; Freedman 1958, 1966; Potter 1968). In the Chinese context, lineages are property-owning corporations based on land which was set aside by wealthy predecessors. The members of a lineage (all of whom are males, women do not inherit) share a common surname and trace direct lines of descent to a founding ancestor, usually a Punti pioneer who arrived in Kwangtung during the frontier era. Chinese lineages often reach an historical depth of 30 or more generations in one locality and incorporate members who represent nearly every class in the society. Until the Communist revolution in 1949, competing lineages dominated the political and economic life of rural Kwangtung. Soon after the revolution, however, these elaborate kinship organisations were singled out by the Communists as 'feudal' institutions and were eradicated within a few years. For reasons that are still

not entirely clear, the Chinese did not reclaim the colony
of Hong Kong after the civil war. It is only by chance, therefore, that a handful of powerful lineages have survived in
British territory where they continue to function.

Over the centuries these elite kinship organisations have
formed exclusive communities known as 'single-lineage
villages'. Many of the Cantonese-speaking Chinese in Britain
come from villages of this type. A good example is San Tin,
located in a remote corner of the New Territories. In 1970,
San Tin had a population of approximately 4000—including
over 1000 emigrants who were working in Europe at the
time. Except for a handful of shopkeepers, all males in the
village share the surname *Man* and trace descent from a
founding ancestor who settled in the San Tin area over six
centuries ago. Surname exogamy (i.e. marriage outside the
surname group) is strictly observed in this part of China
which means, of course, that all wives must be brought in
from other lineages. San Tin is a remarkably closed and
resilient community. 'Outsiders' (defined as anyone beyond
the boundaries of the lineage) are not suffered easily and the
local residents prefer to keep the outside world at arms length
as much as possible. Just being born into a lineage like this
sets one apart from the mass of ordinary peasants and confers
high status in the regional political arena. Traditionally, the
lineage served as an intermediary institution for all contacts
outside the community. As outlined in more detail later, this
intermediary role is still important in some lineages and it
helps explain how the people of San Tin were able to capital-
ise so readily on the European restaurant boom in the early
1960s.

Although it is difficult to be certain, I estimate that no
more than one-third of the Cantonese-speaking Punti in
Britain can claim elite lineage membership (there are five
dominate lineages in the New Territories, see Baker 1966).
The other Punti come from smaller, more heterogeneous
communities known as 'multi-lineage villages' and from the
traditional market towns that are fast becoming cities in their
own right. The Hakka immigrants ordinarily live in small
hamlets scattered throughout the hills and islands of Hong
Kong (Aijmer 1967). Some of these settlements are inhabited
by males of a single lineage, but they are too small and too

weak to compete in regional power circles. Few, if any, of the Hakka in Britain can claim to be members of the traditional elite.

The recent migration of New Territories peoples to Europe is not an isolated historical phenomenon. Kwangtung and the neighbouring province of Fukien have been the staging grounds for successive waves of Chinese emigrants since the mid-nineteenth century (see e.g. Chen 1939; Purcell 1965; Skinner 1957). These migrants settled in Southeast Asia and the Pacific, known collectively as the *Nanyang* ('Southern Seas'), as well as in the New World—from California to the Caribbean. Ninety per cent of today's Overseas Chinese originated from a handful of districts in Kwangtung and Fukien that, for various historical and ecological reasons, specialised in sending males abroad. For example, most of the Chinese in Hawaii came from Chungshan District which adjoins the Portuguese colony of Macao. The search for origins can be narrowed even further until one discovers that most Hawaiian Chinese trace descent to early cane workers who emigrated from twenty emigrant communities in one small county in Chungshan, called Lung Tou. A similar pattern of migration existed in the Sze Yap Districts of Kwangtung and in the region surrounding the city of Amoy in Fukien Province. The majority of California's Chinese population came from the Sze Yap ('Four Counties') region, while the Philippine Chinese emigrated predominantly from six rural districts near Amoy. It is not surprising, therefore, that most of the Chinese in Europe originate from a small parcel of land—the New Territories—which is roughly equivalent in size to the traditional emigrant districts mentioned above.

It is difficult to determine how many emigrant communities actually exist in the New Territories. There are over 600 villages in this region and a comprehensive survey of migrant labour has yet to be carried out. For the purpose of this study, an 'emigrant community' is any village, hamlet, or town that depends upon regular remittances for 50 per cent or more of its income; most communities of this type are characterised by an absence of men, at least half of whom are abroad at any one time. In order to avoid confusion, it is best to reserve the term 'emigrant community' for settlements

that have a high rate of *international* emigration as opposed
to internal or rural-to-urban migration. By these defining
criteria there may be more than 30 emigrant communities in
the New Territories. However, most of these are very small
Hakka hamlets consisting of 50 or fewer households.

A recent development affecting the population ratio of the
Chinese in Britain is the immigration of 'stateless aliens' who
do not hold British passports. With the introduction of the
Commonwealth Immigrants Act in 1962, it became increasingly more difficult for Hong Kong-born Chinese to enter the
United Kingdom. The need for Chinese labour continued
unabated, however, and many restaurateurs were forced to
import aliens not covered by Commonwealth restrictions.
Coincidentally, the Chinese Communist government relaxed
its vigilance along the Anglo-Chinese border for a short
period in 1962, resulting in the influx of several thousand
newcomers—most of whom were young people in their early
twenties. These aliens constituted a pool of cheap labour
upon which the established restaurateurs would draw when
necessary. As might be expected, some of the larger restaurant chains exploited this new class of immigrants during
the 1960s. However, by 1973 the loophole allowing Chinese
aliens to enter as a separate category was closed and all
labourers from Hong Kong are now admitted under the same
work permit scheme. Approximately 10,000 'stateless'
Chinese found employment in Britain between 1963 and
1973 (Watson 1975:113; Immigration Reports 1970–74).
These immigrants are firmly entrenched abroad and constitute, by conservative estimate, at least one-sixth of the
Chinese community in Britain. Most of the 'aliens' are
Cantonese-speaking Punti who came originally from rural
Kwangtung; culturally they have much in common with the
Hong Kong-born Punti who dominate the European res-
taurant trade.

Organisation of Emigration

If everyone in the New Territories who wanted to emigrate
during the last two decades had managed to do so, Britain's
Chinese population would now be double or even triple its

present size. The lure of highly-paid restaurant jobs was such that nearly every village in rural Hong Kong went through a period of 'emigration fever'. The prospects of striking it rich abroad created a bandwagon effect that helped allay the fears of the older generation and convinced even the most conservative of them to allow their sons to emigrate. However, only a small minority of people in the New Territories were ever in a position to take advantage of the new opportunities in Europe. It took more than money. In order to succeed, a prospective emigrant needed *contacts* with people already established abroad.

The earliest Chinese immigrants in Britain were sailors who lived in the dock areas of Liverpool and London. These hardy adventurers were recruited from New Territories villages to serve aboard European freighters, but most jumped ship at the first opportunity. The majority failed to make their fortunes and returned to Hong Kong almost as poor as the day they left. By the 1950s only a handful had managed to survive as the proprietors of small laundries and chop suey shops in working-class neighbourhoods. The laundries soon disappeared with the advent of electric washing machines but the eating establishments, however modest they may have been, served as the foundation for Britain's Chinese restaurant boom. The market potential was not fully realised until the original sailors were joined by kinsmen who had more capital and entrepreneurial ability. Jobs in the expanding restaurants were not dealt out indiscriminately; instead, the owners gave preferential treatment to their immediate kinsmen and the new openings became the exclusive property of specific families or lineages. Even though this pattern of recruitment has broken down somewhat in recent years (due to a labour shortage), Chinese restaurateurs still prefer to hire kinsmen whenever possible.

The exclusiveness of the Chinese in Britain is also reflected in the way they organise themselves for emigration. With few exceptions they follow a system of chain migration, best defined as a 'movement in which prospective migrants learn of opportunities, are provided with transportation, and have initial accommodation and employment arranged by ... the previous migrants' (MacDonald and MacDonald 1964:82). In the Chinese case, kinship ties—either those of the immediate family or of the patrilineage—often constitute the links in the chain, but it is also possible to find elaborate networks based on shared dialect or common district of origin. The latter criteria were utilised in the organisation of the Overseas Chinese settlements in Southeast Asia (see e.g. Crissman 1967; Willmott 1970). In Europe the emerging Chinese settlements have been small enough to rely on kinship as the primary means of labour recruitment and community organisation.

Prospective emigrants from San Tin make use of lineage ties at every stage in their movement abroad. The first step is finding suitable employment and, in 80 per cent of the cases examined, jobs were arranged in advance by kinsmen. Most villagers, in fact, work in restaurants owned by fellow lineage members. Before leaving Hong Kong, the emigrants need passports and entry certificates; these too are obtained with the help of lineage leaders who act as intermediaries for all transactions with government bureaucracies. Passage money is ordinarily provided by employers as an advance on wages. Even the flights are handled by a prominent member of the *Man* lineage who owns a successful charter service that operates between Hong Kong and Europe. On the London side, lineage members take care of all formalities required by the British government, including work permits and job guarantees. The ever-tightening immigration laws have worked to the advantage of the established kinship groups because it is nearly impossible for new emigrants who lack proper contacts to break into the catering trade. As I have argued elsewhere (Watson 1975), emigration has strengthened the *Man* lineage as a social institution and made individual members even more dependent on their kinsmen than they may have been in the past. The lineage is so well suited to the requirements of chain migration that it has been converted into a kind of 'emigration agency'. It should be noted, however, that the *Man* lineage is an exceptional case; most of the Chinese in Britain are organised along different lines. Among the majority, the critical links in the chain are formed by members of an extended family—usually sets of brothers and their sons. Ordinarily there is little cooperation with neighbours or other non-kinsmen, including affines (relatives acquired by marriage) in San Tin's case. As might be expected, the closed nature of the migration chains has important implications for the character of the Chinese community in Britain.

Economics of the Restaurant Trade

The Chinese are involved in all types of catering in Britain, from first-class restaurants to neighbourhood fish and chips shops. Until recently, it was very difficult to find authentic Chinese cuisine in this country because the earlier immigrants believed that the British public could not tell the difference. Most restaurants are still categorised by the workers themselves as 'chop suey houses' in which the food is prepared for quick sale to an undemanding clientele. However, in the last three years there seems to have been a marked improvement in the quality of Chinese food served in larger cities; and, as a consequence, the British public has begun to appreciate, and demand, a more sophisticated cuisine. The Chinese catering trade finally 'arrived' for most Britons when the 1975 *Michelin Guide* awarded a single star to one of London's Cantonese-style restaurants.

The growing market for authentic Cantonese and Peking-style food is paralleled by a phenomenal expansion of Chinese immigrants into the take-away trade. In the Midlands and the Northwest, Chinese have nearly taken over the old English institution of the fish and chips shop. The reason, of course, is that the migrants are willing to work longer hours and offer a wider range of food than any of their competitors. In Manchester, for example, the established friers with their traditional opening hours cannot compete. (A typical, English-owned fish and chips shop in that city maintains the following hours: closed all day Monday and most of Sunday, open for lunch Tuesday through Saturday 11.45–1.30, closed for tea every day except Friday 4.45–6.30, open evenings 8.45–11.15 except Monday and Thursday; closed during all public holidays. A Chinese take-away shop in the same neighbourhood is open 14 hours a day, every day of the year except Christmas.)

Another advantage that the Chinese bring to the take-away trade is their exclusive reliance on family labour, thus avoiding high wages and overtime problems. In 1976, a fish and chips shop in the Manchester area cost, on average, around £35,000. After the initial outlay of capital, the Chinese family can expect to turn a profit within a few years of hard work and self sacrifice. The goal of every immigrant is to reach this level of independent proprietorship, but most begin as cooks or waiters in the larger restaurants.

The Chinese restaurant trade reached its highest level of expansion in the mid-1960s and, since that time, there have been many changes in management and ownership. The majority of restaurants were established as partnerships during the boom phase. The usual arrangement was for the ownership to be divided among the workers and the resident manager. For example, a cook might own two shares, a young waiter one, and the manager four—there may be a dozen shares in even the smallest restaurants. Increasingly, however, there is a movement toward individual ownership and a number of restaurant chains have emerged. This concentration of ownership is due largely to the sale of shares by junior partners who need to finance their move into the take-away trade. They are replaced by younger migrants, usually kinsmen, who are recruited in the New Territories. In 1976, the average wage in London's larger restaurants was £40–45 per week. These rates will continue to rise as it becomes more difficult to import new workers. The restrictions on Commonwealth immigration have created a serious labour shortage in the Chinese restaurant trade—a shortage that cannot be filled by indigenous workers. In smaller towns it has become so difficult for Chinese restaurateurs to find help that a number have had to hire Spanish waiters.

The Chinese have built up their catering establishments with remarkably little help from institutions or individuals outside their own ethnic community. The capital for most restaurants derives from the personal savings and family resources of ordinary immigrants. Partnerships are especially useful when a new venture is started in an unfamiliar neighbourhood or town, thus cushioning the owners if it should prove to be a total failure. British bank loans are sought in a minority of cases, but these are only available after the applicant has established himself and has access to other collateral.

A handful of restaurateurs in Britain have become spectacularly successful, largely on the strength of their own entrepreneurial abilities. The owner of one of England's largest Chinese restaurant chains arrived in 1961 and started as an ordinary cook in London. Fifteen years later he was sole owner of four restaurants and the dominant partner of seven others scattered throughout the country. Another success story involves a member of the *Man* lineage who began his career as a sailor stranded in England during the Second World War. He left San Tin in his early twenties with little more than the clothes on his back but, by the late 1960s, he had risen to become the proprietor of five lucrative restaurants in London and the Midlands. He now lives as a British 'tax exile' on a Mediterranean island and makes only periodic inspection tours of his holdings in England. This entrepreneur is well known to the residents of his home village as a leading contributor to civic projects undertaken by the *Man* lineage.

The Restaurant Niche

The economic niche that the Chinese control allows the migrants to live, work, and prosper without changing their way of life to suit British social expectations. My research corroborates the earlier findings of Ng (1968:88) and Broady (1955:74; 1958:34) who maintain that the Chinese are by far the least assimilated of all Britain's immigrant minorities. The catering establishments are virtual islands of Chinese culture in the larger British society, isolated pockets where the migrants can interact with the outside world on their own terms. Many cooks and kitchen workers do not learn more than a few words of English, even after years of residence abroad. The waiters have a better command of the host language but few are fluent enough to carry on extensive conversations with their customers. In order to overcome the language barrier, each restaurant hires at least one employee who is competent in English and, thus, is able to act as a mediator for the others. In most cases, the migrants I have met are not particularly interested in making English friends or in changing their way of life. Chinese culture, in their view, is infinitely superior to the European cultures they encounter abroad. They have few illusions about their role as workers in an alien society, however, and prefer to maintain a low profile.

The catering trade is ideally suited to the needs of an immigrant group of this nature because it forms an unobtrusive niche on the fringe of the British economy. Unlike so many other Commonwealth immigrants in Britain, the Chinese do not compete directly with English workers for jobs in commerce or industry. This may be one reason why the Chinese as a group are not perceived as a 'problem' by government authorities. Broady observed nearly 20 years ago that the Chinese in Liverpool were well treated 'precisely because they had not attempted to become assimilated' and had not threatened the livelihood of English workers (1958: 34). This is still generally true in Britain today. Catering is dominated by immigrants; few English work in this sector, except at management levels or in neighbourhood tea shops. The franchised food outlets and hamburger chains employ Spanish, Turkish, and Italian workers, while most of the independent restaurants are managed by migrants (Greek Cypriot, Italian, Bengali, etc.) who recruit labour in their own homelands.

So far, few Chinese of village origin have taken up occupations outside the catering trade. New openings and opportunities have appeared in the wake of the restaurant boom: travel agencies, hire cars, gambling halls, specialised grocery shops, food processing and distribution, and cinemas. Most of these services are directed at the larger community of catering workers; only a small proportion of their income derives from non-Chinese customers. The Chinese have restricted themselves to these protective economic niches largely in response to intense competition from other ethnic minorities in Britain. Corner grocery stores have long since become a monopoly of the South Asians (from East Africa and Pakistan) and the Cypriots. Similarly, neighbourhood sub-post offices and dry goods shops in the larger cities are increasingly dominated by South Asians. The Chinese compete vigorously with the Cypriots and the Bengalis in the catering trade but they do not carry the same spirit of entrepreneurial adventure with them into the wider society.

This is not to say, of course, that all Chinese in Britain are employed in catering or in related service industries. There are many professionals working in this country who were reared and educated in Hong Kong, including doctors, solicitors, architects, teachers, university lecturers, bankers, and business executives. However, few of these people trace their origins to New Territories villages: they are highly-educated urbanites who learned English in their youth and attended Western-style universities. The Chinese professionals form a separate and distinct class in the British overseas community. Migrants from rural Hong Kong occasionally call on members of this professional class for assistance, but the two groups have very little in common and rarely identify with each other. The professionals interact more readily with their English counterparts and a number have effectively 'dropped out' of Chinese culture altogether. Little is known about this section of the Chinese population because, to date, all research has focused on the majority who work in the catering trade.

Development of a Chinese 'Community' in Britain

In what sense, if any, do the Chinese in Britain constitute a cohesive and self-conscious social group? Social scientists often use the term 'community' when discussing immigrant minorities but few bother to explain or justify their usage. In my view, the Chinese in this country do indeed conceive of themselves as members of a loosely-organised 'community' which incorporates all migrants (and second generation residents) associated with the restaurant niche. The Chinese caterers do not have a centralised authority structure and they do not live in an identifiable settlement. However, in an abstract sense, members of this minority have so much in common and maintain such close ties—irrespective of where they reside—that they constitute a community of mutual interests. Also, as noted earlier, the restaurant niche allows the Chinese to remain 'encapsulated' within the larger society. In other words, they may be enveloped by British society and scattered throughout the country but they maintain a separate culture.

There are, of course, real divisions within the Chinese community, based on kinship, dialect, and village of origin.

But, these divisions are not as strong as the perceived difference between Chinese and non-Chinese. In Europe, this fundamental dichotomy is paramount. The effective social universe for the caterers is restricted almost exclusively to the overseas Chinese community. Outside this community is the realm of the 'foreigners' (*wai ren*, literally 'out people'), and most Chinese make few meaningful distinctions between various categories of outsiders—beyond 'European', 'Indian', and 'Black'.

The focus of Britain's Chinese Community and its main centre of activity is Gerrard Street in London's West End, known to the immigrants as *Tong Yahn Gai* (Cantonese for 'Chinese People's Street'). This small street, along with the surrounding mews and passageways, is the core of an incipient Chinatown complex and is thus an interesting urban development in its own right. Prior to World War Two, an earlier Chinatown emerged to serve the Chinese in the Limehouse area of London, but this centre was obliterated during the blitz (see Ng 1968:18–20). Later, in the mid-1960s, several Chinese restaurants opened in rapid succession on Gerrard Street. Not the usual 'chop suey' establishments, these restaurants served authentic dishes previously unavailable in Britain and catered almost exclusively to the growing Chinese population. During my early field research in London, non-Chinese customers were discouraged from visiting some of these restaurants, but the proprietors soon learned to accommodate outsiders. Nevertheless, Gerrard Street's restaurants continue to be the major gathering places for Chinese all over Britain and, to a surprising extent, Europe as a whole. On their days off, cooks and waiters from as far away as Manchester may drive down to 'Chinese People's Street', often in convoys of two or three cars. Here they spend their time with friends and relatives who have made similar pilgrimages from other cities. In one sense, therefore, Gerrard Street's larger restaurants have taken on the function of the traditional 'teahouses' which are found in all important market towns and cities in South China. In rural Hong Kong, teahouses are multi-storied restaurants that serve drinks, meals, and snacks; as in London, these establishments are the arenas for social exchange between widely scattered people and groups.

Entrepreneurs who hope to stay on top of the British catering trade must 'hold court' every Sunday morning at a
specific time in a particular Gerrard Street restaurant. Aspiring entrepreneurs and ordinary workers can be seen making
the circuit of these restaurants where they receive and pass
on news (regarding recent arrivals from Hong Kong, restaurant failures, new partnerships, prospects for expansion on
the continent, etc.). A very similar pattern of entrepreneurial
activity is found in Hong Kong's teahouses (Young 1974).

Besides authentic restaurants, London's incipient Chinatown offers a variety of recreational and service facilities that
cater primarily to the Chinese community. These include
gambling halls, cinemas, printing shops, travel agencies,
barber shops, grocery stores, book shops, solicitors' offices,
and private taxi companies—all with Chinese clerks and
proprietors. The gambling halls are of special significance
because they are (with rare exceptions) strictly off limits to
non-Chinese. Due to lack of alternatives, gambling is the
main form of recreation for many Chinese workers. However,
it should not be assumed that gambling is as much of a social
problem as the popular press sometimes implies; the Gerrard
Street halls are used by most workers as convenient places to
meet their friends, and as informal labour exchanges.

The restaurants, recreational facilities, and specialised
services give this part of Soho the elemental characteristics
of a Chinese urban settlement, although on a much smaller
scale than the Chinatowns of San Francisco, New York, and
Bangkok. The growth of London's new Chinatown complex
has been limited by excessively high rents on private and
commercial properties in the West End. A more important
reason, however, is the dispersed nature of the Chinese
catering trade which precludes congregation in one or more
urban districts.

Chinese Associations in Britain

In one respect the Chinese community in Britain is different
from almost every other settlement of first-generation Chinese
migrants: it is not organised on the basis of voluntary
associations. With few exceptions, the Chinese who migrated

to Southeast Asia, the Pacific, and the New World used associations as a means to insulate themselves from unfamiliar surroundings and to mediate with the wider society—often dominated by a colonial regime. New migrants were recruited into these organisations on the basis of common dialect, surname, or district of origin. The leaders of all major associations (representing the primary divisions within the overseas community) sat on the governing board of an overriding body, usually referred to as a Chinese Chamber of Commerce, that spoke for the immigrant minority as a whole (see e.g., Crissman 1967; Freedman 1960; Willmott 1970). The Chinese in Britain have founded a number of clubs and welfare societies, but these associations do not play a central role in the lives of their members. Furthermore, in spite of persistent efforts on the part of some leaders, the 'British Chamber of Chinese Traders' has never managed to establish itself as an important intermediary institution, and it cannot claim to speak for the Chinese community in this country.

The few associations that have succeeded reflect the narrow concerns of a specific segment of the migrant population. For instance, the oldest surviving Chinese welfare club in Europe is a clan association, restricted to people who share the surname Cheung. It has a membership of about 200 and holds a reunion banquet once a year, during which new officers are appointed. Besides the banquet, this association sponsors welfare work in the Chinese community and holds Chinese language classes for caterers' children in its Soho headquarters. Language classes and English tutorials provide the organisational focus for most of the other active Chinese associations in Britain. One of the best known is the 'Overseas Chinese Professional Association', composed primarily of doctors, solicitors, and university lecturers who devote some of their spare time to help Chinese school children in central London prepare for their 'O' level examinations. Significantly, the caterers themselves do not play an active role in this association; it is directed by Western-educated, middle-class professionals who originated from Hong Kong's urban centres.

It is generally true that, in order to succeed, a Chinese association in Britain must either appeal to the narrow interests of a specific group of migrants who are already linked by some pre-existing tie (such as common surname) or it must be directed and organised by an 'outside' interest group (middle-class professionals, church members, or political activists). Most of the 'clubs' and 'societies' that survive long enough to be listed in successive issues of a commercial directory entitled *Overseas Chinese in Britain Yearbook* (published in London) are gambling halls and recreational centres. Leaders who do try to form associations for mutual benefit and general welfare invariably fail. One such association, which was started specifically to draw immigrants away from the Gerrard Street gambling clubs, opened with much fanfare and official goodwill in 1970. Less than a year later the organisation was bankrupt and its most enthusiastic members had lost interest. The unhappy fate of the 'Edinburgh Chinese Association' is equally instructive. Leaders of the Chinese catering trade in Scotland banded together in 1971 to form a central association, equivalent to a chamber of commerce, thus signalling to the wider Chinese community in Europe that they were no longer dependent on London. A grand opening ceremony with representatives from Hong Kong and most of the major European centres was held in the new headquarters and a formal membership drive began soon after. Restaurateurs, ordinary workers, and government agencies contributed money to help cover the initial operating expenses. Nevertheless, within six months the association was in financial trouble and members were unwilling to donate more money, even to save it from total collapse.

The reason for the failure of these and other Chinese associations in Britain is that they have little to offer the migrants in return for participation and support. Unlike some earlier Overseas Chinese settlements, notably in Southeast Asia, the economic niche that the migrants have filled in Britain is not controlled by specific associations. Membership in a voluntary association is not a prerequisite for employment in catering or related service industries. As noted earlier, for most migrants it is the tie of kinship—either family or lineage—that opens the door to a job in the Chinese restaurant trade. Even the clan association mentioned above does not act as a monopoly agency; the bond of common surname is not enough to insure advantage in Britain. (In the Chinese kinship system a 'clan' is distinguished from a 'lineage' in that the former is based on shared surname and

the lines of descent are often fictional. A 'lineage', on the
other hand, is based on known descent from a specific ancestor
and is usually localised in a given village. Lineages are landowning, multiplex corporations while clans are amorphous,
single-purpose organisations with a voluntary membership.)

Another reason for the inherent weakness of Chinese associations in Britain is the undeveloped status hierarchy at this
end of the migration chain. In Hong Kong, leaders compete
vigorously for positions as chairman, vice-president, secretary,
board member, etc., of the many associations found throughout the colony (G. Johnson 1971). These positions, most of
which are honorary, are expensive to acquire but carry great
prestige in the local community. Some associations create up
to 16 vice-presidencies in order to accommodate all those
who are willing to bid for the title. Significantly, a number
of important restaurateurs who are normally resident in
Europe compete actively for these positions; yet, they are
not concerned with the incipient associations in London,
Edinburgh, or Amsterdam. For many first-generation
migrants, therefore, Britain is still a backwater. They feel
that any effort expended to build up a formal leadership
position for themselves on this side will be wasted because
it cannot be readily translated into status at home. It is more
logical, in their own view, to channel all of their energy and
organisational ability into the catering trade itself—and *buy*
a position when they return to the New Territories. It is
irrelevant whether or not the entrepreneurs in question
actually do retire to their home villages when the time comes;
all that matters is that they believe they will and act accordingly. There are signs that this pattern of leadership is beginning to change, but it may take at least another generation
before the Chinese community develops its own self-
appointed and highly visible leaders on the model one has
come to expect of South Asian minorities in Britain (see chapters two and three).

Social Problems

Until recently, the Chinese catering trade consisted largely
of males who had left their wives and children at home in

the New Territories. However, with the rise of family emigration during the late 1960s and 1970s (see Watson 1975:119–122, 131), the Chinese community became less self-sufficient and individual workers were faced with the difficult task of raising their children in an alien environment. The language barrier was (and still is) the most critical problem. Few of the migrants learned English before leaving Hong Kong and, as noted earlier, many had managed to get by for years without understanding a single word of any European language. The younger workers were better able to pick up some English once they had settled in Britain but these men usually did not have wives and children waiting to join them. It was precisely those members of the Chinese population least able to handle themselves in the host society—males aged 35 and over—who brought their families to Britain. Once here, the migrants found themselves having to cope with problems they had never confronted before: housing, shopping, public transportation, medical treatment, and schooling for their children.

During the early phase of my research (1969–70), two-thirds of the *Man* children born in Europe (including some by European mothers) were handed over to their paternal grandmothers to be raised, and educated, in San Tin. This pattern of childrearing, which I chose to call 'grandparent socialisation', had profound implications for behaviour because the children were treated in a very lenient manner and were seldom, if ever, disciplined (Watson 1975:184–95). Although I cannot be certain until a restudy is completed, it appears that the *Mans*, like most other Chinese migrants in Britain, have abandoned this form of socialisation in favour of keeping their children with them abroad. As a consequence, they now have to deal directly with the state-supported school system in Britain. This is, without doubt, a problem that has caused considerable anxiety for migrant parents.

Again, it is the highly-dispersed nature of the Chinese community that is at the heart of the problem. Except for a few schools in London, Liverpool, and Manchester, Chinese children rarely constitute more than a tiny minority in the overall student population; in most cases, there are only a handful in each school. British teachers often complain that they cannot 'communicate' with their Chinese pupils and, in response, several conferences and meetings have been held on this issue in recent years (sponsored by the Community Relations Commission). The children may in fact be withdrawn and quiet in class but this is expected behaviour in the Chinese context; village children are socialised to be circumspect in public. The Hong Kong Chinese place a high premium on education and often make great sacrifices to ensure that their children, of both sexes, receive proper schooling. The same values are stressed by the Chinese here. However, this is not to say that the parents are completely enthusiastic about the British school system. In common with other minorities, such as the South Asians and West Indians, what the Chinese fear most is that their children will be seduced by English life-styles and become *fei jai* (Cantonese for 'Teddy Boys' or soccer hooligans). These fears are especially pronounced in the larger cities.

Superficially, it may appear that Chinese children are languishing in British schools and that they are making little progress (see e.g., Jackson and Garvey 1974), but this is a narrow view taken by observers who have had little, if any, experience in Chinese schools. In my own research into this problem I have been struck by the remarkable adaptability of Chinese children in Britain—given that most have come directly from New Territories villages and that they have been in this country for only a short time. The majority, in London at least, are reasonably proficient in the language of their English age mates and are capable of switching codes (English to Cantonese and back) with ease. Children often play an indispensable role in the family as interpreters, especially for their village-orientated mothers who find it extremely difficult to adjust. In the long run, the mothers may constitute more of a social problem than their children because they rarely make an effort to learn English and are, with few exceptions, unhappy with life in Britain (for more on migrant women see Watson 1975).

The emigration of wives and children also means that the Chinese community is now confronted with problems of housing, medical treatment, and general social welfare. During the early years of migration, all-male households, like the ones described elsewhere in this volume for Sikh workers in Leeds (see chapter two), were the rule; housing was provided by the employers, usually above or near the restaurant. Chinese workers with families must compete for scarce housing along with everyone else in Britain. Most caterers rely on private accommodation in order to be near their work premises. Also, the late hours kept by Chinese restaurants and take-away shops make it impossible to depend on public transportation and, hence, reinforce the need to live close by.

Medical treatment is another problem that worries all Chinese families in this country. The constant stress of life in an alien environment contributes to a high level of psychosomatic illness among Chinese adults, especially women. Hong Kong's mild climate does not prepare them for the cold, dreary English winters that last—in their eyes—for most of the year. This, coupled with the widespread inability to communicate in English, makes the prospects of illness even more frightening. To ease the burden, catering families try to use Chinese doctors who practise with the Public Health Service. Many rely on a Cantonese-speaking Indian physician who has lived in Hong Kong and now practises in London. Even after moving his office from Soho to a South London suburb, members of the Chinese community continue to call on him. The increasing immigration of Hong Kong-trained nurses has made it easier for Chinese patients who find themselves in British hospitals. At one time, hospital trips were terrifying for migrants whose only experience with such institutions had been negative in the extreme (villagers traditionally associate hospitals with death houses).

Although the Chinese are generally aware that they have certain welfare rights under British law, in comparison to other minorities they have made few demands on local authorities. The rare cases in which Chinese workers do ask for public assistance almost always involve housing subsidies (cf. Lai 1975). Some migrants, such as the *Mans* from San Tin, have their own informal system of welfare to help people in distress. In 1970, for instance, members of this kin group took up a collection in London to send one of their lineage mates back home to San Tin (he had lost all his money when a restaurant failed and was too old to start again). Although the *Mans* are exceptional in this regard, most migrants can rely on personal networks of one kind or another for emergency aid. Furthermore, the general shortage of

Chinese labour in the British catering trade ensures that un-employment is not a major problem. The Chinese have little patience with the official welfare system and even less toler-ance for the red tape involved. Stories circulate in London's recreational centres about the perils of approaching British authorities for help. One popular myth relates how a migrant was deported on the same day that he visited a welfare office. Chinese attitudes toward government officials in this country closely parallel those held by their relatives back home in the New Territories: villagers learn at an early age to avoid contact with authority of any kind.

Interethnic Relations

As noted in the introductory chapter, ethnicity is an analy-tical concept that only has meaning when two or more identifiable groups interact or compete, usually for control over economic resources or political power. In this sense, modern Hong Kong may be one of the most heterogeneous societies in the world. Since the 1949 Chinese Communist revolution, Hong Kong has been inundated with immigrants who represent a variety of distinct ethnic groups, separated by dialect as well as culture. The original Cantonese (Punti) farmers who pioneered the New Territories region had little trouble controlling their traditional rivals—the Hakka—but their hegemony is now threatened by aggressive immigrants from China. Many of these newcomers are highly-skilled vegetable farmers who rent fields from Punti landlords; and, much to the chagrin of indigenous villagers, the immigrants have managed to dominate agriculture in Hong Kong (Aijmer 1973; Topley 1964). It did not take long for the new arrivals to begin pressuring the colonial administration for representa-tion on consultative councils ('Rural Committees'). The immi-grants also began to compete openly in the market place and, for the first time in nearly six centuries, the indigenous Punti lineages lost their monopoly over the regional economy.

Ethnic hostilities between Chinese dialect groups (e.g., Cantonese, Hakka, Ch'ao Chou, Shanghainese, etc.) are now very pronounced in many parts of the New Territories, yet they are not of primary significance in the European overseas community. The traditional dichotomy of Cantonese versus Hakka is maintained in Britain but there is little open hostility between the two groups. The reason, perhaps, is that Hakka and Cantonese caterers do not perceive each other as direct competitors; their primary rivals are the Bengalis and the Cypriots. Furthermore, the two Chinese groups have much in common in Britain and find it to their mutual advantage to underplay ethnic differences (a similar 'dampening' of ethnic hostilities is evident in the Cypriot community in London—see chapter eleven). The 'new' minorities in Hong Kong, such as the Ch'ao Chou and the Shanghainese, have not been able to break into the Chinese restaurant trade in Europe, due largely to immigration restrictions.

In comparison to other minorities discussed in this volume, the Chinese sense of ethnic identity has changed very little as a consequence of life in Britain. The Jamaicans, by contrast, have adapted to the British social environment and are currently undergoing a process of redefinition, or 'creolisation'. Foner shows how these West Indians are forging a new ethnic identity for themselves which is neither English nor exclusively Caribbean; it is a unique combination of both (see chapter five). A similar transformation among young Sikhs is described in chapter two. The Ballards demonstrate that second-generation Sikhs in Leeds no longer perceive themselves as traditional South Asians but, because of British racism, they are not fully accepted into the majority society. In response, they have 'rediscovered' parts of their cultural heritage, including the turban, and have begun to construct a new identity that only has meaning in the British context. Although I have made a concerted effort to find evidence of a similar transformation in the Chinese community, none has yet appeared. The Chinese caterers, including even the younger migrants, have not begun to redefine themselves as a consequence of exposure to British society and culture. The evidence that does exist is misleading: young waiters dress in the latest West End fashions, some drive flashy cars and attend Rod Stewart concerts while others dream of becoming film stars. At first sight this seems to indicate a rejection of Chinese culture or, at the very least, a fundamental change in attitude. However, the same elements of 'Western' culture are prevalent among contemporary youth in Hong Kong. In fact, young workers in Britain may actually lag behind many of their Hong Kong counterparts in terms of 'westernisation'.

The changes in clothing and life style that one sees in Soho, therefore, are not necessarily the result of 'assimilation' or 'acculturation' in Britain. In most cases these modifications are rather superficial and it must not be assumed that they herald a simultaneous change in personal identity. During my earlier research among the *Mans* I found that the insecurities of work in an alien society could actually reinforce traditional attitudes, causing migrants to identify even more strongly with their lineage than those who had stayed at home. Given the history of Chinese settlement in other Western societies, notably the United States and Canada (see e.g., Hsu 1971; Sung 1967), I doubt that the relative imperviousness of the Chinese in Britain will last beyond the first generation. As yet, however, an Anglo-Chinese or a Sino-British culture has not materialised. It is significant that the Chinese are not included in the wider British category of 'Asian'. Twenty years ago, when English landlords posted 'No Coloureds' signs in their windows, Chinese students were generally exempt from that category as well. The Chinese in this country have always been a separate and relatively unique minority. The English have had little reason to feel threatened by them until recently. Unfortunately, this is beginning to change as the British press discovers that the Chinese have 'news' value.

It can hardly have escaped the attention of any newspaper reader in Britain that the Chinese are now identified with drug smuggling and extortion rackets. In the last two years dozens of newspaper articles and at least two prime-time television programmes have focused on these problems. Several murders involving Chinese victims have occurred in London and in Amsterdam (widely reported in the British press). Most of these underground activities are related to the traffic in illegal drugs between Asia and Europe; a less visible offshoot is an extortion racket run by a handful of young and disaffected migrants in Soho. It is undeniable that members of the Chinese community have been involved with the British heroin traffic (a disproportionate number seem to be from Singapore and Malaysia, and not from rural Hong

Kong). However, the offenders represent a very small group indeed; police authorities are always careful to stress that the Chinese as a whole are perhaps the most law-abiding minority in the country.

Nevertheless, newspaper reports usually stress the ethnic aspects of drug cases: the word 'Chinese' often appears in the headline, the drug is identified as 'Chinese heroin' whether or not members of this ethnic group are even mentioned, and almost invariably the traffic is said to be controlled by 'secret Chinese Triad societies'. A content analysis of the same reports (1975–77) reveals that there are nearly as many non-Chinese as Chinese involved. The term 'Triad' is now widely used in Britain and, with it, a new stereotype of the Chinese restaurant worker as an infiltrator and a dangerous purveyor of drugs is emerging. In 1970, when I began my research in Britain, if the English had any views about the Chinese at all their attitudes were generally positive: caterers were variously described to me as 'hardworking', 'quiet', 'industrious', and 'a credit to the community'. By 1976, many of the same English informants believed that Chinese restaurants were fronts for heroin pushers and that the migrants were 'threatening' and 'secretive'. This drastic change in public attitudes, I would argue, is directly due to sensationalised and often prejudicial coverage in the mass media. There is, in fact, little concrete evidence that drug smuggling is controlled by international 'Triad' organisations; the word is now used in the press to characterise any criminal activity—which by definition is clandestine—that involves Chinese. British reporters are easily misled by secretive behaviour that has the appearance of true Triad societies that once operated in China (see Chesneaux 1971). The result is that 'Triad' and 'Chinese' have become synonymous in the minds of many English people.

Ties to the Home Villages

I have emphasised repeatedly that the Chinese maintain close ties to their villages of origin; it is now time to document this claim (see also Watson 1977). Many Hong Kong villages, such as San Tin, subsist almost entirely on emigrant remittances.

Although the subject was difficult to probe, informants on both sides of the migration chain agreed that the average remittance for a married man with a family of three living in San Tin was between £20 and £30 per month in 1970–1971. Of course, not all dependent families in the New Territories received this much, but those who did were assured of a comfortable life. Caterers in London insist that the monthly remittances have kept pace with inflation in the 1970s (I have not been able to verify these claims yet).

Perhaps the clearest evidence of the migrants' continuing ties to their native villages is the housing boom in Hong Kong's emigrant communities. Many migrants buy land with their savings but an equally attractive investment is to build 'sterling houses' (named after the remittances that pay for their construction). These are modern-style, two-storey homes which are larger and more comfortable than the traditional, single-storey village houses. In San Tin, sterling houses constitute over a quarter of the livable homes. It is impossible to ignore these new houses because they loom high above the neighbouring structures and dominate many New Territories villages, thereby announcing the presence of successful emigrants.

Unlike land, investments in sterling houses are non-productive because they depreciate in value over time. Yet, by building in the New Territories the owner believes he will always be able to return to a comfortable home in a secure social environment after retirement. Furthermore, the expensive houses are used by the emigrants as the ultimate proof of their stake in the community of their birth. It should be noted that the private housing boom is not restricted to the older restaurateurs who are approaching retirement. During my stay in San Tin, I witnessed the construction of over 20 new houses, half of which were financed by workers in their mid-twenties and early thirties.

Besides investing in their own homes, almost every year the absentee workers are asked to contribute to the construction of new public buildings or other civic projects in the New Territories. In San Tin, the response has been so overwhelming that the village now has a new temple, a renovated ancestral hall, three new community halls, and a relatively new school. Although these contribution drives are voluntary, the emigrants and their families are under strong social pressure to donate as much as possible. In return the worker has his name, along with the exact amount donated, posted for public display during the grand opening ceremony. He is also given the satisfaction of knowing that he and his fellow emigrants are indispensable members of the community even though they work abroad.

Prior to 1960, Chinese in Britain travelled by ship and seldom returned to Hong Kong until they were ready for retirement. Under the circumstances it was difficult for the absentee workers to keep abreast of events in the New Territories or to have more than a passive influence on village affairs. These patterns have changed in the last 15 years, however, and migrants are now able to exercise a direct, active, and important influence on their home communities. Inexpensive charter flights that cater to New Territories workers are the primary cause of this change. Rather than gradually cutting themselves off, therefore, the contemporary migrants have closer ties to the home society than their predecessors—the pioneers of the Chinese catering trade.

New Territories migrants return on the average once every three to five years. During these trips, which are usually scheduled to coincide with the lunar new year festival, the workers play an active role in the life of their communities. Important family decisions, such as the education of children and the division of property, are postponed until the men involved are home on holiday. Younger migrants normally return to the New Territories to marry. 'Mail order brides' were once common in the European overseas community (Watson 1975:175ff), but it is now considered bad form for a worker to bypass the village ceremonies. The regular flow of people between Europe and Hong Kong also constitutes an effective communication network, thus enabling the absentee workers to keep up on local news. Many restaurateurs make this trip several times each year.

Conclusion: The Paradox of Change

When I first began my research in Hong Kong it seemed only logical to assume that emigration would have a 'modernising'

effect on the home communities. However, the longer I
stayed the more apparent it became that this view was too
simplistic. In San Tin, as in many other emigrant communities, the new sources of money and regular remittances
have allowed the villagers to maintain a traditional style of
life that no longer exists in other parts of the New Territories.
The returned emigrants themselves rarely behave like change
agents; and, when they retire, they often become enthusiastic
proponents of traditional values.

It is undeniable, of course, that emigrant communities in
rural Hong Kong have been affected by the outside world.
Japanese consumer items are found in every home, American
television programmes (dubbed in Cantonese) are followed
with great interest, and modern schools are widely available.
Although these influences are important, it does not follow
that the villagers have been stripped of their traditional
culture. The most salient feature of Chinese emigrant communities is their conservatism (Hsu 1945, E. Johnson 1977,
Watson 1975). San Tin, for instance, has remained relatively
aloof from the economic and social changes that have swept
the New Territories in recent decades; it stands out in striking contrast to nearby villages that have high rates of rural-
to-urban migration. These neighbouring communities are
immersed in Hong Kong's cut-throat economy and the local
residents do not find their traditional institutions, such as the
lineage, to be particularly useful (cf. Baker 1968:207-8;
Potter 1968:169-72).

The emigrant communities in rural Hong Kong are now
caught in a dilemma: by converting so rapidly and whole-
heartedly to labour migration during the boom years, the
people in these villages are no longer able to compete in the
local society. The dependence on remittances leaves them in
a precarious position indeed. The catering trade may be well
suited to the needs of migrant workers, but it is highly
susceptible to economic recessions in Europe. Furthermore,
the villagers are painfully aware that it is becoming harder
every year for new migrants to settle in Europe.

The future is equally uncertain for Hong Kong migrants
already established in Britain. Immigration restrictions
threaten to disrupt the kinship networks that are the basis for
continuing ties to the home villages. A British-educated

second generation is growing up without learning to read and write Chinese, thus causing great anxiety for parents who consider this skill an essential part of being 'Chinese'. And, finally, a problem that the majority of Chinese in this country must face is the future of Hong Kong itself. The 99-year lease on the New Territories expires in 1997 but it is well known that the Chinese People's Republic can reclaim the entire colony at any time. British Hong Kong has only survived this long because Peking finds it useful to have a window on the West. If the political climate should change and the colony does revert to China, the Chinese in Britain will have to make some difficult decisions about their own future.

NOTE

The author wishes to thank the Foreign Area Fellowship Program (American SSRC), the Center for Chinese Studies at the University of California (Berkeley), and the School of Oriental and African Studies (London) for supporting the research upon which this chapter is based. I would also like to express my gratitude to Victor Chan and Stuart Webb-Johnson of the Hong Kong Government Office in London.

REFERENCES CITED

Aijmer, L. Göran, 1967, 'Expansion and Extension in Hakka Society. *Journal of the Hong Kong Branch of the Royal Asiatic Society* 7:42–79.

Aijmer, L. Göran, 1973, 'Migrants into Hong Kong's New Territories: On the Background of Vegetable Farmers'. *Ethnos* 38: 57–70.

Baker, Hugh D. R., 1966, 'The Five Great Clans of the New Territories'. *Journal of the Hong Kong Branch of the Royal Asiatic Society* 6:25–47.

Baker, Hugh D. R., 1968, *A Chinese Lineage Village: Sheung Shui*. London: Frank Cass.

Broady, Maurice, 1955, 'The Social Adjustment of Chinese Immigrants in Liverpool'. *Sociological Review* 3:65–75.

Broady, Maurice, 1958, 'The Chinese in Great Britain'. In *Colloquium on Overseas Chinese* (ed.) Morton H. Fried. New York: Institute of Pacific Relations.

Campbell-Platt, Kiran, 1976, 'Linguistic Minorities in Britain'. Briefing Paper. London: Runnymede Trust.

Chan, Victor, 1976, 'Immigration Statistics, 1971 to 1976'. Information Report. London: Hong Kong Government Office.

Chen Ta, 1939, *Emigrant Communities in South China*. Shanghai: Kelly and Walsh.

Chesneaux, Jean, 1971, *Secret Societies in China*. London: Heinemann.

Crissman, Lawrence W., 1967, 'The Segmentary Structure of Urban Overseas Chinese Communities'. *Man* 2:185–204.

Freedman, Maurice, 1958, *Lineage Organization in Southeastern China*. London: Athlone Press.

Freedman, Maurice, 1960, 'Immigrants and Associations: Chinese in Nineteenth-Century Singapore'. *Comparative Studies in Society and History* 3:25–48.

Freedman, Maurice, 1966, *Chinese Lineage and Society: Fukien and Kwangtung*. London: Athlone Press.

Hsu, Francis L. K., 1945, 'The Influence of South-Seas Emigration on Certain Chinese Provinces'. *Far Eastern Quarterly* 5:47–59.

Hsu, Francis L. K., 1971, *The Challenge of the American Dream: The Chinese in the United States*. Belmont, California: Wadsworth Publishing Company.

Immigration Reports, 1970–74, *Annual Departmental Reports*. Director of Immigration. Hong Kong Government Press.

Jackson, Brian and Anne Garvey, 1974, 'Chinese Children in Britain'. *New Society* 30 (no. 626): 9–12.

Johnson, Elizabeth L., 1977, 'Emigration and Social Change: A Case Study from Hong Kong'. *Reviews in Anthropology*, in press.

Johnson, Graham E., 1971, 'From Rural Committee to Spirit Medium Cult: Voluntary Associations in the Development of a Chinese Town'. *Contributions to Asian Studies* 1:123–43.

Lai, Linda Yeuk-lin, 1975, 'Chinese Families in London: A Study Into Their Social Needs'. Unpublished M.A. thesis, Brunel University.

London Report, 1972–73, *Annual Departmental Report*. Hong Kong Government Office in London. Hong Kong Government Press.

MacDonald, John S. and Beatrice K. MacDonald, 1964, 'Migration, Ethnic Neighborhood Formation and Social Networks'. *Milbank Memorial Fund Quarterly* 42(1):82–97.

Ng Kwee-choo, 1968, *The Chinese in London*. London: Oxford University Press for the Institute of Race Relations.

Potter, Jack M., 1968, *Capitalism and the Chinese Peasant: Social and Economic Chance in a Hong Kong Village*. Berkeley: University of California Press.

Purcell, Victor, 1965, *The Chinese in Southeast Asia*. Second Edition. London: Oxford University Press.

Skinner, G. William, 1957, *Chinese Society in Thailand*. Ithaca: Cornell University Press.

Sung, Betty Lee, 1967, *Mountain of Gold: The Chinese in America*. New York: Macmillan.

Topley, Marjorie, 1964, 'Capital, Saving and Credit among Indigenous Rice Farmers and Immigrant Vegetable Farmers in Hong Kong's New Territories'. In *Capital, Saving and Credit in Peasant Societies* (eds.) Raymond Firth and B. S. Yamey. Chicago: Aldine Press.

Ward, Barbara E., 1965, 'Varieties of the Conscious Model: The Fishermen of South China'. In *The Relevance of Models for Social Anthropology* (ed.) Michael Banton. London: Tavistock.

Watson, James L., 1974, 'Restaurants and Remittances: Chinese Emigrant Workers in London'. In *Anthropologists in Cities* (eds.) George M. Foster and Robert V. Kemper. Boston: Little, Brown and Company.

Watson, James L., 1975, *Emigration and the Chinese Lineage: The Mans in Hong Kong and London*. Berkeley: University of California Press.

Watson, James L., 1977, 'Chinese Emigrant Ties to the Home Community'. *New Community*, in press.

Young, John A., 1974, *Business and Sentiment in a Chinese Market Town*. Taipei: Orient Cultural Service.

CHAPTER 8

SHEILA PATTERSON

The Poles: An Exile Community in Britain

In 1903 an early Polish exile in Britain, Joseph Conrad Korzeniowski, who had been nearly thirty years away from Poland, wrote to a friend:

And you may take my word for it... that in the course of my navigations on the earthly globe, I have never departed in mind or heart from my native country.

Conrad's sentiment is probably still shared by the great majority of Polish exiles in Britain today. This minority community dates back to the Second World War and its aftermath, as do over three-quarters of its members (Sterminski 1976:23). Its basic orientations are still those of a 'wartime' or a 'fighting' *emigracja* (exile community), 'political' in a patriotic and martial sense.

In the 1930s there were only a few thousand Polish-born residents of the Christian denomination in Britain (Zubrzycki 1956:47). The majority were labourers and artisans, settled in East London, Manchester, and Lanarkshire. Unlike the Polish ethnic groups in the United States, Canada, and France, the 'Old Poles' in Britain were insufficiently numerous or organised to dilute or influence the huge stream of political exiles which poured into Britain after 1939. In its original orientation, this exile group seemed closer to the elite and messianic 'Great Emigration' from Poland in the earlier decades of the nineteenth century than to the mass 'economic migrations' of Polish peasants and workers to Western Europe and the Americas in subsequent decades. Later, a partial resemblance between the Polish *emigracja* in Britain and the second, economic type of migrant community was to emerge with increasing clarity as the rank-and-file members accommodated themselves to permanent civilian life in Britain.

The post-1939 Polish settlement in Britain began as a government and armed forces in exile. Its earliest components were the civilian officials of the Polish government-in-exile in France and some wives and families of servicemen (about 3,000 in all); and about 27,500 members of the Polish armed forces, most of whom arrived after the fall of France in June 1940.

The next major addition to the Polish strength in Britain came in late 1941, following the entry of Russia into the war, and the amnesty proclaimed for the 1,500,000 Poles deported to the Soviet Union after the Soviet invasion of Eastern Poland in October 1939. General Wladyslaw Anders raised a Polish army in Russia of 100,000 men. The Polish Second Corps, or the 'Anders' Army' as it came to be known, was to become the inflexible backbone of the organised Polish post-war community in Britain. Most of its original members had spent nearly two years in Soviet Russia as prisoners-of-war, political prisoners, or civilian deportees. This shared experience and suffering was increased by the front-line community of the next few years and by Anders' Army's relative isolation from G.H.Q. in London. The army became a little exile world of its own, first in Palestine and later in Italy, with its own ethos and organisation. When it arrived in Britain in mid-1946 most of its members were unfamiliar with the English language or the British people, politically embittered and facing indefinite exile because their home provinces had been incorporated into the Soviet Union.

Other elements subsequently joined the Polish exiles in Britain. One large group was composed of over 21,000 prisoners-of-war, liberated from German camps and brought to England by Polish units. Of these the most active element were the Home Army units, captured after the Warsaw uprising of August–September 1944. Another small but important group consisted of over 2,000 political prisoners who had survived German concentration camps.

The small civilian minority of 1940 received its first large reinforcement of 33,000 when Polish military families and dependants were brought to Britain between 1945 and 1950. The uneven sex-ratio in the Polish exile group was somewhat reduced after the arrival of at least 14,000 European Volunteer Workers of Polish nationality from the displaced persons' camps, of whom nearly half were women. The highly-organised ex-combatants, proud of their war record and superficially more or less at home in Britain, at first felt ashamed of this ragged, uprooted, often turbulent addition to their group. Soon, however, the gap closed and the majority of E.V.W.s were drawn into Polish community life, usually in the provinces.

These then were the main elements of which the future exile community was to be formed, although they did not remain in Britain *en bloc*. In the first five years or so after the war 10,000 Poles emigrated under official schemes alone, mainly to the United States, Canada, and other American countries and Australia. Individual emigration continued at a reduced rate thereafter. Repatriation to Poland was minimal after the first post-war returns. The majority remaining in Britain included the personnel of the government-in-exile, most military leaders, and thousands of ordinary people. Many of those who stayed in Britain instead of emigrating also tended to be those who, in their own words, 'kept a suitcase packed' for return to Poland.

Since that period the Polish community in Britain has received no major group accessions by immigration: individual newcomers have included 'distressed relatives' and other close kin, fiancées, and disabled refugees from Germany and Austria. To reinforce the general 'political' tendency, there have also been small but significant contingents of active political exiles from Communist Poland, ranging from more traditional anti-Communists to—in the last decade—younger, left radical dissidents. The 1971 Census indicated the presence in Britain of 13,470 persons (75 per cent of them women) born in Poland who had arrived in this country between 1950 and 1971. Since then the steady annual trickle of several hundreds per annum has continued, with about 2,600 persons (most of them women) settling in Britain over the period from 1972 to 1975.

Vital and Other Statistics

It must be emphasised that census and other statistics concerned with birthplace and nationality can give only a blurred and approximate picture of the size and characteristics of the real or potential Polish exile community in Britain. It is necessary, but extremely difficult, to distinguish between ethnic affiliation and legal/territorial nationality or citizenship. In the Polish case, one must take into account not only the lack of congruence between birthplace, ethnic loyalty, and past or present nationality, but also the absence of published data about the increasing number of British-born children of parents born in Poland.

Pre-1939 Poland was an ethnically plural society which included unassimilated Jewish and Ukrainian communities (recorded as 'national groups' in census and other statistics) as well as smaller numbers of assimilated Jewish and Ukrainian Poles. As in earlier migrations to other countries, a large number of Polish-born Jews and Ukrainians dissociated themselves from Polish state loyalties and joined local Jewish or Ukrainian communities after their arrival in Britain.

In 1960, with only the 1951 Census and the Home Office alien and naturalisation figures to go on from the statistical side, and information derived from Polish community sources on the other, 130–135,000 seemed an acceptable estimate for the Polish exile community in Britain. This included ethnic Poles born inside and outside Poland, naturalised adults and children of Polish or half-Polish parentage (then estimated at 16–18,000). The figure excluded most Jews and Ukrainians born in Poland and also an unknown minority of ethnic Poles who had cut themselves off from Polish exile ties and become more or less integrated or assimilated into British life (although some of these were, as it later emerged, to return to *polskość*—'Polishness'—eventually).

By late 1976 there was general agreement among exile sources that the Polish community in Britain (born in Poland, Britain, and elsewhere) had decreased between 1960 and 1976 from 130–135,000 to a total of approximately 100–105,000. This was mainly because of its atypical age-structure, producing more deaths than births, and its uneven sex-ratio, resulting in a smaller second generation with both parents Polish, and also in considerable out marriage, frequently followed by depolonisation (assimilation) of the offspring. Data from three successive decennial censuses— 1951, 1961, 1971—provide some confirmation of this (Sterminski 1976:19–28).

The data which have so far been published for the Poland-born population from 1961 and 1971 Censuses (by which period the Polish exile community was more or less settled) are by no means so detailed or wide-ranging as those for the different 'New Commonwealth' or 'coloured' populations. The somewhat impressionistic account of educational background and occupational change given below cannot therefore be verified or checked against more objective census data. There is, however, one set of special 10 per cent sample tabulations available for the years 1961 and 1971: they relate to economic activity by country of birth for males and females aged over 15 years and born in Poland. This not only gives a picture of comparative economic distribution, status, and trends over the ten-year period which supports more subjective accounts, but also illustrates the changing age structure within the Poland-born population, including post-war accessions.

The ageing of this particular ethnic population is clearly indicated by the increasing number of retired persons: from just over six per cent of males in 1961 to nearly eleven per cent in 1971, and from 3.5 per cent of women to 19.4 per cent over the same ten-year period (the steep rise for women is presumably attributable in part at least to the lower retiring age in Britain).

There is no room here for detailed comment on the type and trends of economic activity indicated in the Census. For men, the data seem to support the subjective picture of a relatively large self-employed sector (probably including a considerable proportion of self-employed professional men), and a somewhat 'declassed' but upwardly mobile working population. The percentage of professional employees rose modestly over the ten-year period, as did the percentage for managers, foremen, and supervisors. Among women born in Poland, there was an increase in the total of economically active persons over the period and a decrease in the number

of economically inactive women, accounted for by the growing number of retired. This suggests that a fair number of
women were returning to full- or part-time work once they
had ceased to be full-time mothers. The overall distribution
of economically active and inactive women, with only about
two out of five working, does however indicate a relatively
settled and modestly prosperous community as early as 1961
(cf. Patterson 1968:29 for the situation in Croydon in 1958–
1960).

Religion and Occupation

The 1948 statistics of the Polish Resettlement Corps are the
only source of information about the religious affiliation and
the educational and occupational background of the Poles
who opted for exile in Britain. Nearly 86 per cent of the
102,200 were Roman Catholic, under 4 per cent Greek
Catholic, just over 4 per cent respectively Orthodox and
Protestant (mainly Augsburg Evangelical), and nearly 2 per
cent Jewish. This contrasts with the situation in pre-war
Poland where, out of a total population of nearly 32 million
in 1931, 65 per cent were Roman Catholics, 10.5 per cent
Greek Catholic, 12 per cent Greek Orthodox, 2.5 per cent
Protestant and 10 per cent Jewish. The P.R.C. figures indeed
suggest that the army-in-exile was already on the way to
being a cohesive 'Polish' exile community rather than a cross-
section of the former plural state.

Detailed data are available on the pre-war occupations of
adults in the Polish Resettlement Corps. This group included
approximately 6,000 professional officers and non-commis-
sioned officers, 2,600 civil servants, over a thousand teachers
and lecturers, and many lawyers, writers, artists, and doctors.
There were also nearly 10,000 skilled technicians, craftsmen,
and qualified engineers. The number which had been engaged
in Poland's agriculture was surprisingly low, a fact that was
to prove disconcerting to the British Ministry of Labour,
which had hoped that many Poles would settle as farm-
workers. There were just over 6,300 former farmers and landowners, but only 2,500 agricultural workers of all kinds.

These figures sketch the picture of a group that was top

heavy in the professions, fairly typical of political exile or refugee groups, but quite unlike the average economic migrant group. The exile Poles were clearly equipped to accommodate themselves more easily to the new environment than a comparable population of unskilled rural or even urban migrants would be. On the other hand, many professional and military exiles were too old to requalify in their former professions and were compelled to enter the British economy at a far lower level. This tended to leave them dissatisfied and eager to compensate for their lost status by active participation in exile community life and organisation.

Of those with pre-war professional qualifications, the doctors, dentists, and engineers had the best chance of continuing their professional careers. The 1951 Census showed 504 Polish-born registered medical practitioners, along with 35 dental practitioners, and by 1958 six hundred Polish doctors and eighty dental surgeons were practising in Britain, with up to 2,000 engineers and technicians. Requalification was harder in the legal profession, but in 1958 six barristers, ten solicitors, and twenty legal consultants were practising, most of them in London (Jezewski 1958:178). A number of younger architects also managed to requalify in Britain and others were trained after 1942 in the Polish Architectural School in Liverpool. Moreover, as a result of the generous terms of the resettlement, over 10,000 younger Poles received grants for higher or technical education between 1947 and 1960 and passed into the British or Commonwealth economic structure at the appropriate professional levels. In addition, by 1960 approximately fifty Poles were on the academic staffs of British universities and other institutions of higher education, and the number has risen considerably since then.

Apart from three main groups—(a) the professional minority whose qualifications were transferable to the new environment; (b) a small group of civil servants, entrepreneurs, journalists, and artists who found employment within the exile community; and (c) a rather larger group of disabled and elderly—the bulk of the Polish exiles (80–90,000) entered the post-war British economy as unskilled workers, irrespective of their education and occupational background. They were for the most part directed to the heaviest, least attractive, least secure or lowest paid sectors of industry, where local labour shortages were most acute. These included industries such as agriculture, mining (only pre-war miners were acceptable to the mineworkers' union), brick-making, domestic work, the hotel and catering trades, textiles, building and the iron and steel industry.

Here they stayed for several years but, as restrictions eased and the opposition of local workers and unions moderated, and, as they themselves acquired a greater aptitude and knowledge of the language, an increasing number began to move up the industrial hierarchy into semi-skilled white collar and more responsible jobs. And as the suspicion, exclusiveness and, in some cases, the political objections of the skilled unions decreased, the qualified artisans also began to find appropriate skilled work. The majority of older members of the pre-war intelligentsia, however, remained occupationally declassed (Zweig 1954:93–105), although in many cases their children have managed to revert to their parents' pre-war status.

While social and political work within the exile community helped to compensate many for their occupational declassment, others with lesser qualifications or ambitions in that direction found compensation by setting up small businesses. Some became home-owners and small-scale landlords. The Polish Year Book for 1958–9 estimated that there were at least 6,000 Polish home-owners in Britain, and this number has increased at least three-fold since then. Residential mobility has also been widespread among those who could not achieve upward occupational mobility, with moves to 'better' areas and 'nicer' housing (Patterson 1968:27–9).

Like home ownership, small or one-man enterprises are fairly characteristic of the Polish exile community, reflecting a widespread desire for security and self-sufficiency after the losses of the war years. As early as 1954 Ferdynand Zweig gave the number of Polish-owned business establishments at about one thousand. In 1960 the annual directory published by the Union of Polish Merchants and Industrialists in Britain listed about 2,500, three-quarters in London. By 1976, however, the number of commercial and craft establishments had decreased, as their proprietors died, retired, or were squeezed out of business. Most of those that survived had become larger and more prosperous.

Patterns of Settlement

With the exception of Scotland, the early post-war settlement patterns of the Poles in Britain were associated with the areas in which various units of the Polish forces had been stationed during the war or were located for resettlement. Thus airmen often settled in such towns as Nottingham, Leicester and Blackpool while naval personnel and merchant seamen returned to Portsmouth, Plymouth, Cardiff and other ports. In Scotland, however, which had been the war-time home of the bulk of the Polish Army in the West, there were only 9,250 Polish-born residents (not all exiles) as early as 1951, and deaths or emigration overseas or southwards to better economic opportunities in England had reduced their number to an estimated four thousand by 1976.

The Polish Resettlement Corps camps, and later the E.V.W. hostels, catered mainly for those who arrived in Britain after the war ended. They were scattered widely over England where labour was short and accommodation could be found. The establishment of these forty-odd camps and hostels served to minimise and postpone any competition and conflict with local people over scarce housing. For the exiles themselves, these Polish towns in miniature eased the initial years of accommodation to a strange civilian life, promoted community reintegration and retarded assimilation (depolonisation). Many who found work continued to live communally for some years, but the 1950s saw a steady movement out of these camps and hostels, off the land and into the nearest towns offering private accommodation as well as work, and by 1959 only three hostels were left. In 1976 there remained only Penrhos in Wales, now owned and run by the Poles themselves for some 220 older exiles (together with some other, more recently established homes for the old and ill).

For those leaving the camps, towns with an existing nucleus of Polish residents, or 'good towns' such as Bradford, where a local businessman who had been a prisoner-of-war in Poland during the 1914–18 War started a hospitality scheme for Polish servicemen in 1942, exerted a particular magnetism. So above all did London, the wartime seat of the Polish Government and General Staff and the cultural focus and organisational centre for most Polish exiles in Britain and elsewhere. By 1961 the regional settlement patterns had more or less crystallised. Internal community estimates gave London as by far the largest Polish settlement, numbering perhaps some 30–35,000. Next came Birmingham and Manchester (originally an 'Old Polish' settlement) with some 4–5,000 each; Bradford (c.3,000); and Wolverhampton, Leeds, Nottingham, Sheffield, Coventry, Leicester, and Slough, with 1,500–3,000 each. By 1976 the main residential changes had occurred inside and not between settlements.

Within each town or city Polish settlement patterns have largely been dictated by the availability of accommodation and later of capital for house-purchase. Like most immigrant groups, the Poles have tended to cluster together, although there are no Polish 'ghettoes' as such. Apart from a minority of well-to-do individuals, they bought cheap houses in central areas such as Brixton (South London) or Moss Side (Manchester) and then, after accumulating sufficient capital, followed the retreating British lower-middle class to more 'desirable' areas. In London the principal districts of Polish settlement in 1960 were indicated by the siting of the ethnic 'parishes'—Islington, Brompton, Clapham, Lewisham, Brockley, Willesden, Highgate (from 1960), Ealing, Croydon (for a detailed account of this area of exile secondary settlement cf. Patterson, 1968:27–30), and Wimbledon (from early summer 1959). The three latter indicated the westward and southward drift of socially-mobile home-owners. The Islington parish, with its own church building, is a traditional survival of an 'Old Polish' settlement in East London, but its Polish community has greatly declined.

Family and Kinship Ties

There are few first-generation Poles in Britain who do not retain some social and cultural links with other exiles and also the homeland, through informal social contacts, associational life, both lay and religious, through the Polish exile press, and over the last twenty years, increasing through first-hand contacts with Poland. Probably the greatest of these links are those of family and kinship. The losses and separations of several decades have only strengthened the links between those relatives who are left. A very common form of obituary notice in the exile press illustrates both the world-wide dispersal of the Polish exiles and the maintenance of close family ties between different communities:

A. G...., member of Pilsudski's Legions, soldier of the Second Corps... mourned by his wife, daughter and son-in-law in England, his son, daughter-in-law and grandchildren in Poland, his son and grandsons in the United States.

I have not encountered any Poles in Britain who do not maintain regular contact with and send regular assistance to relatives in Poland. One of the larger Polish parcel firms in London alone sent 110,000 items to Poland in the peak year of 1957. Since then the pattern has changed in that fewer parcels and more money transfers (in hard currency at an advantageous exchange rate) are sent. The amounts sent are said to have decreased, because of improved standards of living in Poland and the increasing numbers of visitors from Poland.

The increase in direct and indirect contacts between Poland and the exiles since the 'Polish October' in 1956 has had varying repercussions on organisational and community orientations in Britain. Regarding family and kinship ties, however, increased contact has reinforced the exiles' 'Polishness' (*polskość*) and helped to reinforce or to inculcate this attachment in the second generation. It has also resulted in a number of marriages between male exiles and women from Poland, where there was an excess of women over men. For the past two decades the personal column of the *Polish Daily* (published in London) has carried matrimonial enquiries not only from lonely male exiles but from Polish women visiting Britain, and sometimes from women in Poland.

Even in the case of mixed marriages family links with Poland are usually retained. At the end of the war the Polish Military Families Office gave an approximate figure of 4,000 British-Polish marriages, but the total has greatly increased since then, particularly among the younger generation (one reliable informant estimated that about half of all recent marriages have been mixed marriages). Many of the wartime mixed marriages were between Polish men and Scottish women. Later, as most Poles moved south, the number of English-Polish or Irish-Polish marriages increased. Ultimately such marriages can lead to the near-assimilation of the Polish husband and total assimilation of the children, although some British wives have made a positive effort to share their husbands' cultural and social interests, to learn the Polish language and Polish cooking, and to bring up the children with some knowledge of their Polish heritage.

On the whole, however, whatever efforts the British wife may make to understand her husband's background and cultural needs, the marriage itself tends to facilitate the husband's social and cultural adaptation, and his acceptance by the receiving society. With his wife as a sponsor the husband accommodates himself rapidly to British life. He usually speaks English adequately and often neglects to teach his wife and children Polish. He can satisfy his Polish cultural needs by joining an ex-servicemen's group, attending a Polish mass, reading a Polish language newspaper. He and his children, however, have an entrée into the 'heart' of British life through his wife and her family.

Organised Social Life

It is almost unique for an exile group to begin its life in a new country with a ready-made set or nucleus of institutions and associations, as the Poles in Britain did just after the Second World War. There was a London-based exile state with a complete military, civilian and religious organisation, in contact with virtually every Pole in the country. There was a party-political network along with a number of welfare associations like the Polish Red Cross, the Polish Y.M.C.A., several servicemen's clubs, and a prolific Polish-language press. Of the latter, indeed, a war-time Minister of Information, Brendan Bracken, made the comment: 'If you were to plant two Poles in the middle of the Sahara Desert, they would certainly start a newspaper.'

The existence of such an organisational nucleus was an important factor in maintaining group unity and social control after the withdrawal of British recognition of the Polish government-in-exile and the gradual demobilisation of the

Polish forces in Britain. Its strength probably inclined the British authorities to handle the economic resettlement of Poles in Britain by means of the novel policy of gradual integration through Polish or Anglo-Polish organisations. The British Government could not work directly through the de-recognised bureaucratic machinery but in practice it took over many of its functions. Between 1946 and 1949 Poles were gradually passed into civilian economic life through the Polish Resettlement Corps, a non-combatant demobilisation unit officered by Poles under War Office command. The existing network of Polish educational institutions was also taken over and adapted for resettlement purposes by the Committee for the Education of Poles in Great Britain.

Even after they had found civilian work the majority of Poles were, as noted earlier, housed for several years in all-Polish camps or hostels. This aspect of resettlement policy was, incidentally, one which could not have been applied in the case of unskilled coloured immigrants from the New Commonwealth entering Britain more or less freely after the late 1950s. It was utilised for the 29,000-odd Asian refugees who arrived in Britain from Uganda in 1972–73, but its application was partial and short-lived, the camps and the resettlement operation being wound up after only one year. For the Poles, the use of camps and hostels lessened the tension over housing in the immediate post-war period, but it also meant that for several years these Poles remained socially, culturally, and linguistically segregated from the receiving society and dependent upon Polish voluntary associations for the satisfaction of most non-economic needs.

Many of these associations were in existence by the end of the war and a number had from the beginning adequate funds to purchase or rent houses and carry on their activities. The major association, the Association of Polish ex-Combatants (*Stowarzyszenie Polskich Kombatantow*), developed, like the smaller Polish Air Force Association and Polish Naval Association, out of the armed forces organisation. Initially the S.P.K. was even organised along the lines of the wartime military hierarchy, but it was subsequently reorganised on a localised and more democratic basis. Between 1948 and 1953 its membership grew from 9,300 to 14,600, organised in 197 local branches. By early 1961, however, membership had dropped to 6,411 (including about 450 women). The number of local branches had also dropped to 107. To a considerable extent this drop was due to the closing of various Polish residential hostels in country districts and large-scale emigration overseas. Other factors which influenced the membership and dynamism of this and most other exile organisations during the 1950s were losses by death, the increasing preoccupation of individual exiles with their own economic and family life and a resurgence of apathy towards organised exile affairs as a result of internal political disputes and the relative liberalisation in Poland itself after October 1956.

By the mid-1960s, however, a process of reconsolidation of community ties occurred and some younger exiles began to return to organisational life in place of those who were ageing or had died. The number of S.P.K. branches went down to 97 in 1965, with a membership of 6,500. Thereafter, the branches rose to 100, while the membership remained at 6,500 until 1973, after which it began a slow but steady rise (despite the loss of 600 members, including 240 deaths) to 7,000 in 1974 and 7,200 in 1975. A breakdown of the 1974 membership by age-group showed that younger generations were joining the organisation. Some of these younger members derive from the Polish army schools set up in the Middle East for boys and girls who had been evacuated from Russia after 1941, or else from the Polish Scout and Guide movement.

The S.P.K. in Great Britain is the largest of nearly twenty such associations in countries of Polish exile settlement. These are linked in a world federation with its headquarters in London. In Britain and elsewhere the S.P.K. has for thirty years fulfilled a wide and expanding variety of functions. As well as preserving the feeling of war-time comradeship and purpose, it provides financial and legal assistance, cultural facilities, and social activities for its members. Since about 1970 the S.P.K. has increasingly assumed the stance of a permanent Polish exile institution in relation not only to the exile community but to Poland itself. The report presented at the Tenth S.P.K. World Congress in London in November 1976 referred to the resurgent opposition in Poland by workers, intellectuals, and the Church to the Communist regime. It also stressed the need for the S.P.K. and the whole political *emigracja* to serve their countrymen at home with material assistance and continuing ideological support for national independence and Polish culture.

The preservation of 'Polishness' (*polskość*) into the next generation has become an increasingly important objective for the S.P.K., as for other exile organisations. It is promoted by a network of special Saturday schools, by organised sports, and by Polish Scout and Guide companies. In 1960 the S.P.K. was directly responsible for running 54 Saturday schools to teach the second generation the Polish language, history, and culture. The schools were staffed by 188 teachers and were attended by 3,300 children. Sixty other schools with an over-all attendance of approximately 3,000 children were run or assisted by the Polish Education Society Abroad, and by eight Polish ethnic parishes. Standards of teaching were uneven and the results varied correspondingly. In the 1960s this teaching activity languished and the number of pupils declined, but in recent years enrolment has picked up again.

In 1975 there were 88 special schools in all (42 of them run by the S.P.K.), with over 5,000 pupils. It is estimated that the total rose to 7,000 in 1976. Polish was being taught up to 'O' and even 'A' levels for some pupils, and regional festivals of song and dance were becoming increasingly popular. A note of caution was, however, sounded in a 1974–5 report, which referred to the 'accelerating process of deterioration' in the standard of Polish language within the exile community. It was deplored that 'young parents are ceasing to use Polish in conversation with their children—new ranks of children are growing up who could be the first non-Polish speakers.'

There is an umbrella association—the Federation of Poles in Great Britain—to which are affiliated some 60 smaller Polish associations, mostly of an *emigracja* type (Jezewski 1976). A new, more specifically *Polonia* (ethnic community) type of institution was formally set up in 1964—the Polish Social and Cultural Association (P.O.S.K.). Initiated by members of the Polish University College Association Ltd., in conjunction with the engineers' association, P.O.S.K.'s objective was to provide for present and future generations a centre in London to accommodate all major exile voluntary associations and education-cultural enterprises (including the large and efficient Polish Library). This ambitious project gained the support of many, though not all, existing organisations, including the financially-strong S.P.K., and has also attracted an increasing stream of individual donations. The large, modern P.O.S.K. building on King Street, Hammersmith, was opened in December 1974, but the enterprise has been adversely affected by the general financial crisis.

In general, the function of the voluntary associations, great and small, has been a unifying one. They satisfy the various social and cultural needs specific to the exile community and promote group cohesion and continuity. They also fulfil a secondary function by providing leadership opportunities to a large number of energetic and capable people who would otherwise have found life in exile colourless and frustrating. While they have retarded assimilation (or denationalisation, from the Polish viewpoint), the exile associations have done much to help their members accommodate themselves to British life. As the years pass, however, it seems likely that the S.P.K. and the various 'grass root' organisations will assume more specifically *Polonia*-type functions, that is to say, they will promote the permanent integration of the Polish community in British society.

The Younger and Second Generations

Of particular interest are the associations that have attempted to perpetuate a sense of ethnic identity among the younger and second generations. In 1960, the Union of Sports Clubs catered to about 2,000 younger men and women of the 'half-generation' non-intelligentsia of that time, who might not otherwise have found much of interest in organised Polish social and cultural life. There were over 40 of these sports clubs, most of them connected more or less informally with the S.P.K. and covering soccer, volley ball, basketball, and table tennis. By 1975, substantial generational changes had occurred among organisers and participants (the latter now entirely from the second generation), and sporting activities which had declined in the intervening years were beginning to revive. Soccer, played all year round, remained the most popular sport, with 20 clubs divided into seven regional leagues. A special cup was introduced by the S.P.K. in 1975 for the team among the final six each year whose members were judged to speak the best Polish.

In the late 1950s a fair number of the small 'half-generation' received higher education in Britain. Many of these educated young people found the older exile organisations ineffectual, tedious, irrelevant, and resistant to their needs. A more intellectual minority set up students' groups, promoted specialised periodicals and opened up contacts with their counterparts in Poland. They looked to the Poland which they hardly knew rather than to the older exile generation which they knew all too well for the sources of their patriotic, though not usually their political, attachment. The less active majority of this 'half-generation' were preoccupied with establishing themselves economically. They would usually maintain their Polishness through the ties of family and friendship, by reading Polish literature and the exile press, and in some cases by participating in the activities of a Polish parish. The members of this half-generation are now in the 35–45 age bracket and it appears that not as many have moved away from contact with organised exile life as seemed likely in 1960. A small but important minority have established themselves in British academic, intellectual, and media circles.

Religious Organisation

After the war the Polish exiles in Britain inherited a religious as well as a lay organisational nucleus. The main nuclei for the Catholic majority were the original Polish Catholic Mission in London, set up in 1894 to minister to the 'Old Polish' emigrants, and the 1939 exile group of military chaplains under the jurisdiction of Bishop, later Archbishop, Gawlina. When the Polish armed forces were demobilised in 1947 this jurisdiction ceased and the chaplains were left without a superior. To remedy this the Holy See appointed Monsignor Michalski as Chief Chaplain to all the P.R.C. camps and 'closed' parishes in Britain, i.e. those with an exclusively Polish population.

As resettlement proceeded, however, arrangements had to be made to provide for the increasing number of Polish civilians in 'open' centres. During the war and afterwards, the authority or titles of the exile Catholic religious leaders came to be drawn in a rather complicated manner from three sources: the Holy See, the Polish Episcopate, and the British Episcopate. This situation still obtains (Zubrzycki 1976: chapter 9; Patterson 1961:88–90). By 1960 most of the original 'closed parishes' which functioned in Polish camps and hostels had ceased to exist. There were, however, 72 'open' or 'ethnic' parishes in England and Wales and another four in Scotland, served by some 80 Polish priests. A boys' secondary school and a boys' hostel served by eight Marian Fathers and a Polish girls' convent with its own chaplain also existed. The ethnic parishes were located in areas of substantial Polish settlement and the priests became formally responsible to the local British ecclesiastical authority. The relationship between priest and congregation was and is based on personal and voluntary ties, and the priest's stipend depends on voluntary offerings. This means that the latter's personality is much more important that it would be in an ordinary territorial parish.

In 1960 there was some reason for anxiety about the well-being and future prospects of the Polish ethnic parishes. Not only was the attitude of the British Catholic hierarchy rumoured to be not entirely favourable to the continuation of this exotic foreign-language appendage, but fewer than twenty students had at that time come forward to be trained for the Polish priesthood in the West, and most of the Polish priests in Britain were elderly (the average age being 55 years). Moreover the majority had endured considerable physical and psychological suffering during the war years, either as deportees in the Soviet Union or as prisoners in German concentration camps. The effects of such experiences were sometimes noticeable in the general factiousness and emotionality of Polish exile life at this period, to which the priests were not always immune. A further consideration which sometimes complicated relationships between priests and their exile congregations was the fact that a number of the former had been village priests before the war, and did not always find it easy to establish a satisfactory relationship with an urban professional or predominantly middle-class congregation. This led some Polish Catholics to attend English Catholic churches by preference.

Fifteen years later, anxiety over the present and future has moderated. While many of the oldest generation of priests have died or retired, an adequate supply of new priests, many from Poland but some trained in Rome or France, has become available. Up to a score of parishes now maintain their own churches and the divisions of the earlier post-war years have for the most part been overcome, as in most other spheres of exile life. Most recent reports of exile activities have stressed local as well as national cooperation between priests and lay ex-combatant and other organisations.

In 1976 there were 73 Polish parishes in England and Wales, four in Scotland, and 110 priests. Now, as in 1960, the more successful parishes depend mostly on the character, energy and organising ability of their priests. Writing in 1960, I cited as a particularly successful London parish that centred on St. Mary's Church, Clapham. This was a cohesive, prosperous, mainly artisan parish, with a large population of young men and women. About 30–40 marriages and 50 baptisms were being celebrated there each year and the annual Corpus Christi procession drew an attendance of up to 4,000. A number of similar parishes outside London could be cited, but for another London example (not necessarily typical) at the present time we may look to Ealing, the Polish settlement which has expanded so fast since 1960. This parish has five priests, 5–6,000 parishioners, a large and democratically run parish council of people in the 'middle generation', a highly organised social life, and well-run Saturday schooling.

Both in London and in the rest of Britain the parishes remain, as in 1960, in regular contact with at least the same number of exiles as all the lay voluntary associations put together. The association of Polish national values and identity with Catholicism (the Virgin Mary is called 'Our Lady, Queen of Poland') is profound. The Polish parishes have continued to function as a strong factor reinforcing social control and Polish culture, language and traditions, even for the younger generation. On the whole, they represent more of a *Polonia*-type organisation, as in the United States and Canada, rather than the first-generation 'political emigration' orientation, but the intensification in recent years of contacts with Poland and the militant patriotic stance taken by the Polish Episcopate have undoubtedly reinforced direct patriotic attitudes.

The future development of the ethnic parishes is difficult to predict. While the short-term threats which were noted in 1960 have not been realised, it is not clear whether all or some of the parishes will survive as specifically Polish institutions, identified with a traditional, highly nationalistic Catholicism linked with Polish culture and patriotic values, and preserving Polish language rites, hymns, carols and national saints' days. Recent events in Poland and the current climate of religious and ethnic pluralism in Britain seem favourable to such a survival, as does the conservatism of many parishioners. As a second-generation Polish student commented recently (Wilk 1970:14):

Priests administer all rites—masses, confessions, baptisms, marriages, funerals, and youth education, all in Polish. The quality of religious sentiment is very much tied to words used to evoke it, and the change from Polish/Latin to English/Latin is unsatisfactory. Like the taste of national cooking, English equivalents tend not to evoke the same response.

Other alternatives could include a gradual weakening of the Polish element in ethnic parishes, and a strengthening of British-style Catholicism. This has not yet happened among most ethnic communities of Catholics in the United States, despite some academic predictions, and the strong Irish affiliations of many English Catholic parishes seem unlikely to faciliate the process here. Furthermore, there is little or no evidence of Catholic Poles exchanging their faith for a Protestant one, which could be regarded as a positive effort at assimilation. There is, however, also a certain drift away from organised religion altogether, especially amongst working-class Poles and the younger intelligentsia.

Political Orientations

In other types of immigrant or minority communities, political associations may be considered as just another sector of social organisation. In political exile communities the entire associational network tends to be infused with this political orientation. One should, however, distinguish here between 'patriotic-political' and 'party-political', which is the sense more commonly used in British society. The Polish community, when describing itself as an *emigracja polityczna* (political exile community) is, on the other hand, using 'political' in the first and wider sense, to denote the fact that its members left Poland and remain in exile in order to reverse the imposition of totalitarian rule upon their country. In this sense the term 'political' is a unifying one. It is, however, characteristic of the Poles, as indeed of most other political exiles, that the most politically-active individuals differ as to the policies and the means whereby their agreed goal should be achieved. As the cherished goal recedes the differences frequently become greater than the unity, so that political exile communities can carry within them the seeds of their ultimate dissolution.

During the 1939–45 war the exile government and the underground civilian organisation in Poland itself were in the hands of a coalition formed mainly by pre-war opposition parties, ranging from the Polish Socialists on the left through the Peasant Party to the National Democrats on the right. The legal continuity and authority of this government derived from the constitutional act of the President of Poland who after 1939 nominated the late Mr. Raczkiewicz as his successor. In theory, at least, this legal continuity was not affected by the British Government's recognition of the Warsaw regime in July 1945. The broad-based unity of the exile wartime coalition was, however, partially destroyed as a result of the entry of the Soviet Union into the war, its subsequent advance into Poland and the imposition of a Communist political regime.

Meanwhile, after years of fighting, suffering, privation and loss, most rank-and-file Poles who decided to stay in Britain were preoccupied with the problems of resettling themselves and their families in civilian life. They were, relatively uninterested in the manoeuvres of politicians representing pre-war parties for which most of them had never had the occasion to vote, although there was a strong desire for unity. A process of fission nevertheless began in 1954, when August Zaleski, the appointed successor of the exile President

Raczkiewicz, refused to retire at the end of his seven-year presidential term of office. After some abortive attempts to achieve political unity a provisional Council of National Unity and a Council of Three, which included General Anders, were set up in opposition to the Zaleski group (known as the *Zamek*, or Castle).

The consequences of this move were far-reaching. It divided the politically-conscious minority in every Polish exile community and either split or forced all the lay associations to take one side or the other. It undermined the legalistic principle and indeed the whole 'political exile' idea, and diminished any outside political influence that the exiles still possessed in London and other Western capitals, or in Poland itself. Finally, as the sharp decline in exile contributions to the political fund called the Polish National Treasury showed, it alienated still further the rank-and-file ex-soldiers, the younger generation and the provincial communities from the ageing, increasingly self-appointed political leaders in London.

After the deaths of President Zaleski and General Anders, there was a return to exile legalism in 1972, under a new President, Stanislaw Ostrowski. With this development a new exile government was formed which was joined by a majority of political groupings. Another development in the 1970s was an informal cooperation between the 'opposition' Federation of Polish Democratic Parties and the younger post-1968 emigrants from Poland. By 1976, however, the political parties, lacking the normal mass support of a national electorate, and with no real prospect of a return to Poland, were down to a solid core of ageing activists, most of them in London.

Meanwhile, the primary patriotic aspect has once again come to the fore for the exile core community. This seems to be due to a combination of factors, including the economic, residential, and organisational consolidation of a substantial core of exiles. It is also due to the muting of party-political disputes and, perhaps most important, to increasing contacts with Poland and the arrival of new political exiles. Furthermore, there has been a refocusing of patriotic interest on the homeland as a result of events from 1956 onwards, following the student ferment of the late 1960s, the workers' revolt in

Szcecin and other cities in 1970, and the protests against mono-party abuses by workers, intellectuals, and the Catholic Church in 1976.

The Polish-Language Exile Press

After the withdrawal of exile government funds in 1945 the Polish-language press had to rely for its continued existence on the support of readers, voluntary organisations, and advertisers. As a result the 202 periodicals published in Britain between 1939 and 1949 (Zubrzycki 1956:135) had by 1960 shrunk to 33 titles, all published in London. By 1976 the number remained much the same: it comprised one daily, three weeklies, one fortnightly, several monthlies, two or three bi-monthlies, nine quarterlies, and eight annuals and bi-annuals.

With few exceptions, these publications have survived from the early years of exile, sometimes with a change of name or format, a shift of editorial coverage and policy, a reduction from fortnightly to monthly, monthly to quarterly or annual in response to a declining readership and inflated printing costs. For the most part, they meet the needs and interests of the exile core: political, religious, organisational, literary-cultural and, increasingly, historical. There were nine organs of exile political parties in 1959, but the dissensions of the 1960s took their toll and only six now remain. To these has lately been added the quarterly *Aneks*, published by younger left-wing dissidents recently arrived from Poland.

Only one paper has endeavoured to meet the needs of the exile community as a whole. This is the *Dziennik Polski* (*Polish Daily*) which, after it was forced to become self-supporting in 1945, became a greater link between Poles in Britain than all exile associations put together. It reached its peak circulation of about 31,560 in 1951, before the emigration of many readers to the United States, Australia, and elsewhere. Thereafter the circulation declined at the rate of nearly a thousand each year until 1959, although the process was checked by editorial innovations, many of them designed to hold the large number of younger 'middle-brow' and provincial readers who might otherwise have switched to the *Daily Telegraph* or *Express*.

Despite these innovations the *Polish Daily* remained a political exile paper in orientation, endeavouring to reflect the basic aims and feelings of the wartime army in exile but often criticising the incessant political factionalism. In mid-1959, however, the *Polish Daily* itself became a battlefield for this internecine strife, and fell entirely into the orbit of one of the two rival political factions in London. For some years the *Daily* remained virtually a political organ of this camp (Czaykowski and Sulik 1961:515). More recently it has shed this image and reverted to its pre-1959 coverage, combined with an increasing volume of political news from Poland. Its circulation of nearly 25,000 in 1959 had dropped to 15,000 in 1976. The major reason for this drop is illustrated graphically by the black-edged obituary notices on the back page of every issue.

The Evolution of the Polish Exile Community

Unlike most studies of immigrant and minority groups, this paper has been written from the inside out. It has been concerned with the internal organisation and the values of the Polish core-community, and with the major factors at work within the group—strengthening, weakening, or redefining community bonds and boundaries. As I have indicated, family and kinship ties span the exile world, and also link the exile generations to their homeland. Conflicts have arisen between the older generation and the 'half-generation' of younger adults. Yet for many of this 'half-generation' the idea of Poland still evokes emotional loyalties that the society in which they now live and work does not command. This is true even for many who 'pass' for English. How strongly, and in what form, such ethnic ascription will persist among the true second generation—the young adults and their children of the 1970s—is still unclear. It will depend increasingly on outside factors such as the attitudes and pressures of the majority society.

Social and economic class distinctions, whether pre-war or post-war, do not play a very strong part in exile organisation.

During the last war, most Polish exiles lost all of their material possessions, while service in the armed forces had a levelling up effect on the rank-and-file. The majority of the exiles in any case appear to be middle-class orientated in British terms and this tendency has become stronger with the settlement and consolidation of the community (Patterson 1968:29).

For the majority of exiles, the memory of the wartime community of aims, suffering and loss has remained the strongest bond. As noted earlier, it would be more apt to call this exile community a 'fighting' or 'wartime' *emigracja* rather than a 'political' *emigracja*. The wartime bonds are quite compatible with the moves towards *Polonia*-type communities in many provincial settlements, and towards a world-wide cooperation between *Polonia* communities overseas. Most older Polish exiles, in the provinces as well as in London, would still reject strenuously the idea that they are developing or may develop into a *Polonia*, even one with a strong political orientation. The increasing acceptance of naturalisation has, however, been a move in this direction. In the first years of civilian resettlement individuals applying for naturalisation met with exile community disapproval and often rejection (Zubrzycki 1956:164), but by 1960 it was recognised that exiles might become British without losing their Polish emotional loyalties. Most were doing so because non-British nationality affected their job security and chances of promotion, or put them last on local housing lists. Others applied for convenience in travelling or because they wished to visit their families in Poland. At the time of the 1961 Census 35,000 former citizens of Poland were naturalised, while 92,000 were not. Today about two-thirds of the resident population born in Poland are British nationals.

The post-1956 revival of patriotic-political orientations among Polish exiles has been focused directly on Poland and not on the exile government, thereby helping to move all but a dwindling 'political' nucleus further towards a *Polonia*-type community. The increasing number of visits from and to relatives or friends in Poland over the last twenty years has also had a considerable impact. While these visits to Poland have encouraged 'Polishness' in the second generation, they have made many of the first generation realise how far apart they are from those who remained in Poland and how much circumstances have changed there, quite apart from the Communist superstructure. One former air force officer said to me:

I would still leave everything and fight for Poland if she needed me. But I do not think I could settle down there again for good. Some things have changed too much to be reversed... And—do you know?—when I came back through customs and saw the bobbies and the smog and the bus queues, I almost felt as if I were coming home.

The Polish Exile Community and the British Receiving Society

Unlike more traditional countries of mass immigration (for example, the United States and Canada), Britain has not embarked on programmes aimed at the assimilation or even integration of first-generation immigrants (the Polish Resettlement programme was a rare though successful exercise in promoting initial group accommodation). Indeed, until large numbers of immigrants from diverse New Commonwealth countries began to arrive in the late 1950s, little official thought was given to the nature or mechanics of these processes, presumably because, in the case of earlier immigrants, absorption has usually been accomplished in the second or third generation as a result of strong social and educational pressures. First-generation immigrants might become British, but were not really expected to become 'English'.

Such attitudes augured well for the preservation of a separate national and cultural identity. Many Poles who did not wish to return to Poland after the war saw Britain as the best centre in which to spend the years of their exile, which they expected to be brief, and to maintain and build up a political exile organisation. The generous provisions of the Polish Resettlement Act also meant that the exiles would be ensured the means of material survival. British insularity and the wave of left-wing and trade union xenophobia directed against Poles on political and economic grounds for several years after the end of the war also reinforced exile group solidarity.

The passions and misunderstandings of the early post-war years have long been forgotten by both sides. By 1960 the Poles were no longer conceived of as potential scabs, fascists, or Casanovas. Instead they were seen as good workers, rate-payers, solid citizens and family men. Perhaps the best illustration of latter-day relationships between British and Poles is that, even in cities with a large Polish community, many local officials are barely aware of its existence. In Croydon, for instance, I was told: 'After all, they're one of us now. They don't have any problems or make any trouble.'

Despite the exile community's recent reconsolidation, and its continuing endeavours to keep 'Polishness' alive into the next generation, long-term pressures from the receiving society are working towards its ultimate integration and absorption. With their large proportion of urbanised, educated members, such exile groups are more adaptable and ultimately more acceptable to the receiving society in social and cultural spheres than are most groups of economic mass migrants. In Britain these pressures are now well under way. If there are no major changes in Eastern Europe, the usual processes of adaptation and acceptance, slowed perhaps by continuing contacts with Poland, or by the arrival of new refugees, will continue to the point of integration, assimilation and—ultimately—absorption. In a generation or so names like Kowalski and Maslak may seem as familiar in Britain as O'Brien, Lebrun, Levy, Freyberg, or Janson.

NOTE

This paper is an updated essay based on work first presented in 1961; it has now been substantially revised. The results presented here are a distillation of the experience of three decades of participant observation and honorary membership in the Polish community in Britain. Specific fieldwork was carried out in 1958–60 in Croydon for a comparative study of West Indian, Indian, Polish, and Irish immigrants in industry. Two years of field research among the Polish community in Canada in 1952–4 had earlier afforded useful comparative insights and contrasts.

I should like to express my sincere appreciation and gratitude to all those who helped in the research for this paper: in particular to Stefan Soboniewski, President of the Polish Ex-Combatants Association, World Federation; Karol Zbyszewski, Editor of the *Polish Daily*; Stanislaw Grocholski of *Veritas*; Bohdan Jezewski; the staff of the Polish Library; and my husband, Tadeusz Horko, former Editor of the *Polish Soldiers' Daily* and the *Polish Daily*.

REFERENCES CITED

Brodzinski, B., 1976, Mlode Pokolenie Polskict Imigrantow. *Kultura* 7/346. 8/347.

Czaykowski, A. and B. Sulik, 1961, *Polacy w Wielkiej Brytanii.* Paris: Instytut Literacki.

Jezewski, B., 1958, *Rocznik Polonii, 1958–9.* London: Taurus.

Jezewski, B., 1962–1976, *Polski Londyn* (Annual Polish Guide to London). London: Taurus.

Patterson, Sheila, 1961, The Polish Community in Britain. *Polish Review* 6(3):69–97.

Patterson, Sheila, 1964, Polish London. In *London, Aspects of Change* (eds.) R. Glass et al. London: MacGibbon and Kee.

Patterson, Sheila, 1968, *Immigrants in Industry.* London: Oxford University Press for the Institute of Race Relations.

Patterson, Sheila, 1971, Immigrants and Minority Groups in British Society. In *Prevention of Racial Discrimination in Britain* (ed.) S. Abbott. London: Oxford University Press.

Sterminski, Zygmunt, 1976, Emigracja w Liczbach. In *Kalendarz Dziennika Polskiego.* London: Dziennik Polski.

Tannahill, J. A., 1958, *European Volunteer Workers in Britain.* Manchester: Manchester University Press.

Wilk, A. M., 1970, The Polish Community in Great Britain. Paper presented for B.Sc. Social Sciences. University of Southampton.

Zubrzycki, J., 1956, *Polish Immigrants in Britain.* The Hague: Martinus Nijhoff.

Zweig, F., 1954, The Polish Worker in England. *Kultura* 3/77.

CHAPTER 9

ROBIN PALMER

The Italians: Patterns of Migration to London

The number of people in London of Italian birth is not large in relation to other minorities discussed in this volume. The last census records a mere 32,545. Adding persons of Italian parentage, the total 'within the circumscription of the Italian Consulate of London' is swelled to 140,000 (Problemi 1972). But the London collectivity remains small in comparison to the great centres of Italian expatriation—New York, Boston, Toronto, Montreal, Sao Paolo, Buenos Aires, and Sidney. The Italian ethnic minority in Britain numbers no more than a quarter of a million, even if one includes the third generation. Despite Britain's entry into the European Economic Community (to which Italy already belonged), Italian immigration has waned since 1967, and in the 1970s repatriation has greatly exceeded immigration. In 1972 Britain sustained a net loss of 5,000 Italian citizens (Problemi 1972, Pt. I:86).

When one compares the Italians in London with other immigrant groups in Britain, two characteristics stand out: the Italians have been classified as 'aliens' rather than British Commonwealth subjects, and they have specialised in the tertiary sector of the economy. As aliens, they have had to obtain labour permits, and then wait patiently for four years to elapse before becoming eligible for permanent residence. In the meantime, they have been able to enjoy the comforts of family life, a privilege not given to all Italian emigrants. Specialisation in catering over a long period has permitted Italians ample opportunity for socio-economic advancement. While most attain a satisfactory degree of prosperity, some have become wealthy entrepreneurs. There are an estimated 2,000 firms run by Italian businessmen in London (Marin 1969). The Italian collectivity in this country is more heterogeneous economically and socially than other Italian diaspora groups.

There is an additional distinction, perhaps an obvious one. All immigrant and diaspora groups have unique historical experiences. The Italians have had a long history in London, one that has been traumatic at times. These historical circumstances cannot be ignored when analysing such problems as the slow rate of assimilation, the intense involvement with associations, and the 'loyalty' to Italy felt by members of the second and even third generation.

Thus, in this essay historical analysis is combined with an ethnographic case study. In keeping with recent developments in anthropology (Dahya 1974; Philpott 1973; Watson 1975), this study focuses on both ends of the migration chain. Abbazzia (a pseudonym) is a parish in the Emilian Apennines in Northern Italy. Field research was conducted in this parish during 1973. The experience of the majority of parishioners who emigrated and the minority who stayed behind will be examined. In the last part of this essay the relevance of relationships between migrants and non-migrants for the decision making of the former is shown in the case of the Abbazzini. But the main task is to describe and account for the singularity of the Italians in London; hence, special emphasis will be placed on the migrants' adjustment abroad.

Emigration from Southern Europe often begins in response to economic necessity at home—and subsequently becomes a matter of routine. This is the inference of research among Southern European migrants in Australasia since the Second World War (Price 1969:210). 'Chain migration' is the term used to describe the process whereby a pioneer, or group of pioneers, becomes established in another region or country and later brings over relatives to share in the new opportunities. Emigration in this context thus takes on something of the character of a *rite de passage*, as young men become subject to the moral expectation that they will emigrate for a few years. 'America' or 'Germany' often acquires more meaning for them than Rome.

'Chain migration' is a central concept in this essay and I shall use Price's model (1969) adapted slightly, as a vehicle for describing the process of migration between Northern

Italy and London. This model does not, however, explain why people from a given region or a given country choose to migrate to a particular centre. Where chain migration occurs it becomes crucial to know what factors governed the decision of the pioneers to emigrate at all, why they chose their destination, and why they settled there. Such information is vital because historical causes of emigration may influence people for generations after the initial conditions have changed. This has been the case with the Abbazzini to a great extent. Although there are problems involved, the best approach to the study of the causes of migration is still the well-known 'push-pull' model. Pull factors are those which attract migrants to a particular area; push factors are conditions at home which compel workers to look for employment elsewhere. I will now examine these factors briefly, paying particular attention to the conditions under which the pioneers migrated from Italy to London over one hundred years ago.

The Migration Process: Historical Background

Italians have been drawn to the British Isles since the time of Julius Caesar. Nor was he the last whose motive was economic imperialism: agents of the Vatican monopolised the important British wool trade in the Middle Ages and Italian banks (the so-called 'Lombard' banks) controlled the Royal Exchequer during the reign of the Tudor monarchs. Trade was sufficiently lucrative to justify setting up a Venetian colony in London which minted its own currency (known as 'Galley Halfpence' by the natives). However, the 'imperialist' phase of the Italian presence in Britain did not outlast the Medieval period, and as the Italian Renaissance declined and the British mercantile expansion began, so Italians came to Britain in the new role of 'client'. Architects, sculptors, artists, musicians, and scholars came in search of patronage. An Italian church existed in London in 1581; it had a congregation of 66 (de Smith 1972:3). By the mid-seventeenth century a colony of some importance had been established in Clerkenwell, as Italian artisans began to settle in London. A century later Clerkenwell had become a thriving 'little Italy' and had acquired its own Italian parish church. The census of 1861 records about 4,500 Italians in Britain, nearly all of them in London. A large proportion of the immigrants were hawkers and street-entertainers.

The nineteenth-century Italian migration to Britain is of the greatest importance, for these early migrants were not only itinerants; they were, for the most part, peasant farmers from the mountainous parts of Northern Italy who had developed subsidiary trades to support themselves during the long Alpine winters. Frequently they came to London in the autumn, having pushed their barrows across Europe, and then returned to their fields in the spring. The knife-grinders of the Rendene Valley in the Trentino, who are now firmly established in London, had such origins. The seasonal migrants, as we shall see, were an important channel of communication in the chain of migration between Northern Italy and London.

By mid-century, then, London offered opportunities for an immigrant elite of professionals and craftsmen, and a seasonal proletariat of itinerants who rapidly became a regular feature of London's streets. This population was concentrated in the district of Clerkenwell. One important influence on the embryo community was the arrival of Mazzini, the Italian patriot and political activist, in the company of 1,000 Republican exiles. The significance of this accident of history I shall explain later. For the present it is sufficient to note the small number of Italians in London and the absence of a large-scale migrant proletariat. However, circumstances soon changed and more labourers began to arrive.

Before 1905, when the Aliens Order was passed, the immigration of Italians into Britain was not impeded by legislation. Between 1861 and 1891, the census reveals a steady increase in the numbers of immigrants born in Italy. Thus in the space of thirty years, the Italian community in Britain doubled from about 4,500 to nearly 10,000. Then, in the last decade of the century, there was a sudden increase from 10,000 to just over 20,000 (based on 1901 census data). Further immigration was reduced to a trickle as the Aliens Order was reinforced by the Aliens Act of 1919 (which introduced work permits). In addition the First World War disrupted emigration and a subsequent decree of Mussolini's government prohibited the emigration of any except those middle-class Italians who would enhance the prestige of Fascism abroad. For these reasons, the number of Italian-born residents in Britain remained static at 20,000 or less until after the Second World War.

What prompted the sudden influx at the end of the last century when immigration was unconstrained? The British did not encourage immigration during this period; the attitude of the Victorians towards the Irish and the Russian Jews who entered Britain in great numbers presaged the chauvinism later directed towards New Commonwealth immigrants. Yet, the Italians have remained largely unaffected by these reactions because of their small numbers and their concentration in an uncontested sector of the economy. It was towards the end of the nineteenth century that the Italians discovered the catering trade in London and they have exploited and expanded this niche ever since.

The census of 1911 records the presence of 1,600 waiters, 900 chefs, and 1,000 labourers employed in hotels—all of Italian nationality. In addition, Italy supplied 1,200 domestic servants and 1,400 bakers and confectioners. Already 500 Italians had saved enough capital to open cafes and restaurants of their own. Others were employed outside of catering, in asphalting or ice-hauling, occupations that native workers found unacceptable. While trades allied to the construction industry, such as the laying of mosaic and *terrazzo* flooring had long been recognised as Italian specialities, Italians were otherwise barred in Britain from sectors in which they had made important contributions elsewhere. In Switzerland and in the United States, Italians built roads and railways, but in Britain this was a prerogative of the Irish; in Belgium and France, Italians were mineworkers, but in Britain powerful unions have protected this industry. In an important sense, therefore, the Italian selection of catering before the First World War was a 'Hobson's choice'; but it proved a happy and profitable one.

Catering was wide open to immigrant labour in Victorian Britain for various reasons. At the present time, when the balance of economic power in Europe has shifted so radically, it is well to remember that at the turn of this century, London was the greatest capital in the world. Britain was not only the most powerful but also the earliest industrial economy, and rapid expansion had made Britain the centre of a vast mercantile empire. The new middle class had service needs of an enormous scale. At the time, British and Irish workers were employed in what amounted to the construction of London's West End. Three and four storey town houses were erected in large numbers for the wealthy classes, and enormous hotels were built for their entertainment. Colonial soldiers and administrators enjoyed 'long leave' on large salaries from their tropical outposts, and they too swelled the throng at the new hotels, restaurants, and provincial spas. The demand for domestic staff in these large households and for catering staff in the hotels and restaurants far exceeded the supply of indigenous workers willing to tolerate long hours, under bad conditions for low salaries.

Economic and Social Conditions in Italy

As has been mentioned, the peasant farmers of mountainous areas in Northern Italy have always had difficulties during the winter season. Bailey has discussed the importance of labour-intensive strategies for the success of 'a farming programme of fantastic subtlety, which made a harsh and apparently unpromising environment yield a living for what nowadays seems to be staggeringly large populations' (1971: 29). The problem with labour-intensive systems is that there are often too many mouths to feed during the winter. Fortunately, there is also little work to do, so the temporarily unemployed can either develop cottage industries (of which Swiss wood carving and watch making are prime examples), or migrate for a limited time, selling their skills or labour in the cities of the North Italian plain, or in neighbouring countries.

Associated with the seasonal factors affecting mountain peasantries is one which influences longer-term emigration. According to Bailey, the labour-intensive farming techniques can only be maintained within limited ratios of population to land (1971:31). This is certainly the case where the supply of agricultural land is limited and technology is unchanging.

These conditions pertained in rural Europe during the last century, at a time when the countryside was under considerable demographic pressure (Armengaud 1973). 'Natural' population growth, combined with certain improvements in medical care, made the limitation of population by any means but emigration unlikely. The experience of the Abbazzini may be illuminating here.

Abbazzia is a parish composed of 18 hamlets and a number of farmhouses scattered over one flank of Monte Ermano (also a pseudonym) in the Apennine range. The traditional economy was mixed farming at an altitude of between 500 and 1,000 metres. Bailey's generalisations therefore apply to Abbazzia. Because the parish has an ancient ecclesiastical history, parish records have been kept for many centuries (Abbazzia is located on the site of an important medieval abbey). From these it appears that the local population remained static at between 600 and 650 from the sixteenth through the nineteenth centuries (Jesini 1976). There is some evidence, from the turnover in surnames current from century to century, that emigration may always have been an important means of population limitation; but by the nineteenth century the parish experienced a crisis of major proportions. Over-population was a problem Abbazzia shared with all the mountain communities of the province. It persisted until the Second World War when the area began to suffer from depopulation.

The demographic problems in Abbazzia are paralleled by the change from seasonal and temporary migration to a more permanent expatriation. Towards the end of last century, Abbazzini heard of the opportunities in London. They also heard the myth of Boston's golden streets. The latter had already attracted Southern Italians in their hundreds of thousands. Besides the lure of promised wealth, there were many negative aspects that caused Italians to leave their own country. Throughout Italy, inheritance is based on equal shares to each child. During periods of population increase, this can lead to the fragmentation of land and to the reduction of agricultural efficiency. The process may be delayed through cousin-marriage, and there is evidence that Abbazzini frequently applied this solution in former generations. However, it would seem that a more drastic solution was sometimes necessary. The oldest inhabitants of the parish recall a practice (long extinct) that applied in cases where the property was largely disposed of at the heirs' marriage. Fragmentation of land could be prevented by permitting only one or two sons to marry formally. The other siblings were effectively disinherited, though they could remain in the parish. If this solution was applied as rigorously as elderly informants attest, it is easy to see how such a custom could act as an incentive to permanent emigration.

Because of adverse economic factors such as these, Abbazzini, and mountain peasants from all over Northern Italy found themselves excluded from the means of production at home. But information about opportunities in other countries was spreading through Europe via an earlier generation of seasonal migrants, many of whom had reached London in the course of their travels. The highland populations of Tuscany, Lombardy, and most particularly Emilia-Romagna were strongly attracted by the news of employment in London's catering establishments. Before proceeding to a more detailed examination of the process of chain migration, we should consider the reasons why Northern Italians (especially the Emilians), as opposed to Southern Italians, have predominated in the movement between Italy and London. Technically, the answer does not rest on 'push' factors as such; rather it is a matter of historical 'timing', and certain cultural predispositions.

Emilian Values and the London Catering Trade

The literature on migration from Southern Italy is so extensive that it is quite forgivable if people assume that Italian emigration is a regional rather than a national phenomenon. This assumption is fostered by the decrease in emigration from Northern Italy since the war, at the same time as Southerners have started to move into Western Europe in greater numbers. Yet no matter how many Southern Italians have migrated both overseas and within Continental Europe, it is nevertheless important to remember that in the history of migration from Italy, the Southern movement is the more recent development. Before the turn of the century, two-thirds of the seven million Italians who had emigrated were Northerners, and three-fifths of them were directed to countries within Continental Europe (Briani 1972:23). Only after 1901 did the ratios begin to reverse as the exodus from the South to America began to gather momentum. That date also corresponds to the restrictions on alien immigration in Britain. Only workers from areas which had representatives already established in London could expect to emigrate to Britain. Under these circumstances, chain migration from Northern Italy continued to be the dominant form of recruitment in London's catering trade.

Within the London Italian community, the Emilians have a particularly long record. They also have a high success rate as catering entrepreneurs. This may in part be due to cultural factors peculiar to the region of Emilia-Romagna. In discussing the characteristics of this region Nichols mentions tendencies which have remarkable adaptive value for immigrants in London's catering sector (1973:266ff). The Emilians are renowned throughout Italy for their capacity to produce and consume foodstuffs. Parmesan cheese, Parma ham, and various salamis are all made in this particular region. Nichols cites statistics which show that Emilians spend more on food than the average Italian. Abbazzini traditionally make their own wine and cure their own ham and salami; in the autumn the women gather mushrooms and the men are avid hunters. In London, Abbazzini also make their own wine with grapes bought in street markets; some purchase pigs in the countryside and form salami-making cooperatives; whole families go on mushrooming expeditions in the New Forest; and the men rent 'shoots' in Cambridgeshire or Surrey.

Another fact of Emilian life that is striking to the outside observer is the intense desire for economic independence. Although Emilia-Romagna is as prosperous as any other Northern Italian region, with most of its territory in the Po Valley, it has not realised its full economic potential. The agricultural sector is still fragmented into smallholdings and the industrial sector is dominated by small factories. Furthermore, the tertiary sector holds the record among all the regions for small shops and bars (Nichols 1973:269).

I would argue that Emilian values have proved adaptive in Britain. In a country which has never prevented aliens from becoming property-owners and businessmen, the Emilian petty-capitalist aspirations to independence and 'the good things in life' could be realised. The skills required in running a snack-bar in London are not dissimilar to those of successful peasant farming: in both cases economic rationality and the need to provide a living for the family are at odds. Production is only made possible by the mobilisation of family labour, with everyone working long hours. All that is required to make the transition is sufficient starting capital (saved during a period of employment), some catering experience, and a rudimentary knowledge of English. In this manner the Abbazzini emigrants made the transition from small-scale farming and sharecropping in the Italian Apennines to the successful management of small-businesses in London, which they owned outright or in partnerships.

In 1973, I traced 184 Abbazzini households in London; 93 of them were associated with a private business. All but eight of these were cafes, snack-bars, or restaurants; the others consisted of three greengrocers, two garages, a hairdressing shop, an antique shop, and a driving school that specialises in Italian clients. Six entrepreneurs have sold out since the recent British recession began. Abbazzini of the first generation who are neither in business nor in catering have entered trades which are in some measure Italian specialities. Mosaic flooring and tailoring occupy many men; frequently their wives are employed as waitresses in the restaurants of others. The Abbazzini are typical of Italian migrants to London in that they have been largely occupied in a niche within the ancient establishment—the 'Italian sector' of small-businesses, catering work, and specialised crafts. Likewise, the Abbazzini live in the 'Italian' districts of London. The 'Little Italy' of Clerkenwell may have disappeared, but the Italians remain in particular areas of North and South London. The choice of occupation and district of residence is, of course, a reflection of chain migration.

Chain Migration

The study of chain migration provides a framework in which one might profitably analyse the historical process which has shaped the Italian community in London. In the following discussion of Italian migration, I rely heavily on a model first used by Price (1969:210–11) to describe the process of migrant assimilation in Australasia. Price posits a sequence of five stages: (1) Pioneers emigrate and settle in a particular place. (2) The pioneers invite relatives and others from their village to join them. These are usually single men, so intermarriage with women of the host country is likely in some cases. (3) The emigrants become sufficiently established in employment and business and begin to think in terms of long-term settlement. Wives, children, and fiancées are brought over; property is purchased and voluntary associations are founded. The founding of family and community life at this stage is associated with a growth of ethnic consciousness, a demand for a vernacular church, schools, and a press. (4) The second generation grow up, having been socialised differently than their parents. They may have career aspirations beyond those occupations filled by the migrant generation. Succession in the trades and businesses founded by the pioneers is a problem sometimes only solved by the importation of further waves of kinsmen from the old country. (5) The third generation reaches maturity. Assimilation has not yet been achieved. Price suggests that 'where chain migration continues strongly, or where the group remains geographically distinct, or [traditional] institutions are well developed, many of the third generation live and marry within the ethnic group' (1969:211).

The conditions favouring non-assimilation in the third generation are all present in London, as far as Italians are concerned. Since the Second World War there have been sufficient numbers of second and third generation Italians to determine whether this minority will be absorbed. Observers generally agree that assimilation has been slow, but their explanations vary considerably. Compare the following:

(A) At the present time [1954] one main characteristic of the Italian community in London seems to be an emphasis on cultural differences between Italianates and other Londoners. Many Italianates are convinced that having an Italian name may be basis enough for some discrimination to be directed against them, even if they are of British nationality and speak English as their mother-tongue... Integration of Italians into

English society is very slow; it probably does not become fully effective before the third generation. (Garigue and Firth 1956:69)

(B) Such liberalism [as that of British immigration policy], while it favours and accelerates the adaptation of the immigrant to the new society, functions strangely to permit and legitimise his foreignness. Not being made to feel 'foreign' the immigrant does not need to shed his culture. This is something which does not often occur, even within the Common Market. Here one is not ashamed to be Italian. Even those who were born [in Britain] declare it—and they have to say it in English! (Marin 1969:17)

Two sets of commentators, writing fifteen years apart, thus differ in their interpretations of the manifest non-assimilation of 'Italianates', to use Garigue and Firth's term. The difference is a function of historical circumstance, as well as the relative value placed on Italian ethnicity. There is also a tendency on the part of British social scientists to interpret the reactions of immigrants in terms of 'discrimination', which Marin—as an internal observer—does not share (see also Dahya 1974). At the same time, it is important to note that Garigue and Firth conducted their fieldwork in the immediate aftermath of the Second World War, for Italians in London the greatest trauma ever experienced. Marin, on the other hand, was observing the community as a participating member (he is a missionary priest) at the zenith of post-war commercial affluence and community life. I give this example to underline the importance of historical explanation when applying the chain migration model, and to justify its extensive use in the following illustration.

Italian Emigration to London

In the first stage of Italian emigration to London, there were conditions that Price's model cannot accommodate: before the pioneer migrants expanded into the catering niche, seasonal migrants had already visited London—a process of perhaps two centuries' standing. Following Bailey (1971), these early seasonal travellers should be seen as vital in the dissemination of information about opportunities abroad to those Northern Italian villagers contemplating more permanent settlement elsewhere. In important ways, the existence of the seasonal migrants modified the experience of the pioneers.

Another influence at this time, a mere accident of history, was the arrival in the first half of the nineteenth century of nearly a thousand political exiles from Italy. The Republicans were an important presence in a community of less than 5,000 people and their leader, Mazzini, had a very special role in shaping the community. Mazzini was an intellectual, and much favoured by the Victorian establishment. An enthusiastic patriot, he advanced *'Italianita'* (Italianness) among his compatriots abroad as much as at home. The school he established in Clerkenwell did not endure, but his 'Society for the Advancement of Italian Workers in London' —the so-called 'Mazzini-Garibaldi Club'—is still one of the premier Italian institutions in London. Further research may reveal that Mazzini's charisma helped foster a 'climate' in which other enduring institutions, such as the Italian church of St. Peter's in Clerkenwell and the Italian Hospital in London, could flourish.

An infrastructure of impressive dimensions thus awaited the first large wave of true labour-migrants to London. It was the product of a unique set of circumstances in which Mazzini acted as a catalyst, unifying disparate elements among his expatriate conationals in a social climate of Victorian romantic 'Italophilia'. After the passing of the Aliens Order of 1905, however, further immigration was greatly reduced, and the unprecedented numbers of new entrants during the previous fifteen years were able to consolidate their positions in the Italian speciality occupations without competition from their own countrymen. Using the new work permit system, entrepreneurs could recruit from Italy such staff as they required. Thus their expansion was not unduly hampered. As noted earlier, cafes began to proliferate in London after 1911. By 1933 the 'Association of Italian Ice-Cream Vendors' had 4,200 members throughout the British Isles (Guida 1933).

Classified telephone directories of the period also give some indication of the spread of other types of small businesses run by Italians (the names of these concerns usually reflect the national origins of the proprietors). Consistent with the chain migration model, migrants of the first and second stages established themselves in small businesses, intermarried with British women in some cases, and became involved in association activities. Despite the hiatus of the First World War, when many patriots returned to Italy to fight, by the 1930s the third stage had been attained. But once again, external historical factors ensured that this third stage was in many ways uniquely successful.

The Great Depression may have hampered Italians in their economic aspirations, but in many ways they found themselves in a protected sector. During hard times in Britain people who can no longer afford extravagance may take comfort in minor pleasures. This could explain the great expansion of the Italian ice-cream trade during the period. Yet, a more important influence on Italian upward mobility was the sudden and unprecedented intervention of the Italian government on their behalf.

'Italians living abroad were wheedled, at great cost to the exchequer, into becoming [Mussolini's] greatest fans and propagandists' (Mack-Smith 1959:399). The London community was the greatest beneficiary of this largesse because it was the British that Mussolini most wanted to impress. Headed by Dino Grandi, Italy's ambassador and a 'first hour' Fascist, Italian professionals and businessmen went to London to reorganise the migrant community along Fascist lines. The pre-existing institutions received massive support; a branch of the 'Fascio' was built as a showpiece; and emigrants from all walks of life were invited to lavish receptions at the Embassy, an initiative that former ambassadors had not taken. One of the more winning aspects of the policy was that the children of every emigrant household received generous Christmas parcels from Mussolini, and they were also given free holidays at the English seaside and in Italy. The Fascist government also underwrote an Italian school at Hyde Park Gate, the first since Mazzini's in Clerkenwell. Published memoirs of two Italian entrepreneurs of this period reflect the sense of patriotic gratitude which caused the men to join the party and sport black shirts, and the women to give up their gold jewellery during the British boycotts of Italy beginning in 1935 (Cavalli 1972, Leone 1964). Between the wars, London offered perhaps the most favourable environment for Italian migrants anywhere in the world. At home, where millions of 'blocked' emigrants endured hardship, news of the British capital was being disseminated widely throughout rural Italy, among people who would not experience at first hand the traumatic disillusionment the immigrants were soon to suffer.

On June 10th, 1940, Mussolini declared war on Britain. The effect of such a *volte face* was stunning. Never, since the Roman invasion of Britain, had Britons and Italians found themselves on opposite sides in a conflict. The Victorians had regarded Mazzini and Garibaldi as heroes, and the immigrants had basked in the reflected glory. Lest it be forgotten, Churchill, Lloyd George, and Chamberlain initially favoured the 'cooperative system' in Italy (Mack-Smith 1959:399). Yet Mussolini was now to be ridiculed in Britain as a ludicrous megalomaniac, and the Italian immigrants who had realised so many of their bourgeois aspirations were to be persecuted as 'enemy aliens'. If the major source on the policy and practice of internment in Britain at this time is reliable—and the fact that it was banned soon after publication suggests that it may be—then 'persecution' is not too strong a term for what one informant called his 'calvary'. Lafitte (1940) describes in considerable detail the muddle which surrounded the classification of Italians into 'grades' of Fascism, their deportation to Canadian and Australian camps, and their detention on the Isle of Man. From Lafitte's accounts of the 'tribunals' and from the memoirs, it appears that patriotism and extreme fascism were consistently confused. This in itself would have been of little importance, were it not for the fact that only so-called 'grade A' fascists were sent abroad. Thus, when the *Arandora Star*, one of the liners transporting 'enemy aliens' to Canada was torpedoed, most of the political leaders of the London community were lost. Of 717 Italians on board, 470 died. There were few members of the small community in London who were not touched by the tragedy. The incompetence of those who administered internment meant it was months before relatives of the victims knew for sure whether their fathers, husbands, and sons had gone down with the liner or were reinterned on the Isle of Man. A monument in London's Italian church commemorates the disaster, but it is hardly necessary since the event is engraved in the memories of the older Italians, and it has become part of the oral tradition passed down to future generations and to successive waves of migrants.

If the third and fourth generation entrepreneurs and community leaders in London were unique among Italian emigrants in the favours they received from their home country, they were also unique in the degree of their negative experiences as 'enemy aliens'. Although Italians were interned in all allied countries, in no other place were so many Italians affected so heavily by the experience and for so long. That Garigue and Firth (1956) should find a community after the war in which individuals were deeply involved with their kinsmen at home and abroad, conscious of their Italianness and highly suspicious of the English, comes as no surprise when their immediate history is taken into account.

Post-War Immigration to Britain

The *paesani* (fellow-parishioners) of the internees, the youths growing up in mountain communities like Abbazzia, were not deterred by the news from London. Their own experience contradicted it in so many ways. Those entrepreneurs who could sell out and support themselves in Italy anticipated the war and retired prematurely. Non-emigrant Abbazzini were impressed by the returned emigrants who bought tracts of land to add to their patrimonies and built large villas in which to live. Having no direct experience of internment themselves, the returnees orientated their anecdotes towards the positive aspects of emigrant life in London. Furthermore, the Apennine farmers had no quarrel with the British. Emilians very readily espoused the partisan cause, epecially after Armistice in 1943, and even non-combatant civilians did what they could. Apart from supplying their husbands and fathers in the mountains, the women and old men risked their lives sheltering English prisoners-of-war released by the Badoglio government. Many Englishmen were looked after for months in Abbazzia. They were sincerely grateful, and some still keep in touch thirty years afterwards. Thus the first impressions that parish youth

gained of the English were very positive, and there are indications that this experience influenced their decisions to
migrate to London instead of America after 1947. The United
States had relaxed immigration restrictions as a gesture towards the worst afflicted nations of Europe, and the old
association with Boston could have been renewed by the
Abbazzini. But, instead, the youth of the parish chose to
become European Voluntary Workers and labour in the
heavy industries of provincial Britain, in the hope of being
reunited with their relatives in London after four years.

The long-standing 'push' factors operating in the Emilian
Apennines, exacerbated by wartime disruptions, caused more
Abbazzini to leave for Britain between 1945 and 1955 than
at any other time. Of the 163 Abbazzini migrants for whom
I have entry dates, only 18 arrived between 1909 and 1940,
whereas 83 arrived in the decade following the war. The
early experience of the men who became E.V.W.s was
traumatic in the extreme. Since they accepted jobs allocated
to them by the administrators of the scheme, and they were
required to remain there four years, they did not represent
'second stage' immigrants in the usual sense implied by
Price's model. Arriving with unrealistically positive notions
about the English and conditions generally pertaining in
Britain, the Abbazzini became rapidly disillusioned as they
endured heavy industrial labour in dismal environments.
The same young men who had taken food to fugitive
Englishmen in cellars and barns were now being showered
with xenophobic abuse by a population made truculent
through personal loss and discomfiture during the war itself,
and rationing during its aftermath. As a result very few
Abbazzini settled in provincial Britain when they were
granted permanent residence. Some returned to the parish
with their savings, but the majority migrated internally to
join their *paesani* who by this time had re-established themselves in London. They hoped to gain experience in catering
and expand their capital sufficiently to buy into partnerships
or lease cafes of their own.

The fact that the post-war wave of first and second stage
immigrants could realise quite rapidly their entrepreneurial
ambitions was due to the rapid recovery of the British
economy in the 1950s and 1960s. The 'restaurant boom' to

which Watson alludes benefited not only the Chinese, but Indians and Italians as well (1975:104). There is a common factor in the success of all three national groups in catering: the cuisine they purvey is attractive and, to the British, exotic; but the pasta, noodles, and rice which make up the bulk of the dishes are inexpensive ingredients, and the meat component in the cooking of all three nationalities is small. Thus, these restaurants could survive during periods of austerity as in the 1920s and 1940s, and they could prosper when the post-war affluence gave new sectors of the British public the incentive to 'eat out'. From the Italian point of view the fast-growing spending power of the young in Britain was of particular importance. Just at the time when large British ice-cream corporations were driving Italian entrepreneurs out of business, the 'Coffee-Bar' came of age and in London *cappucino* became the fashionable beverage during the 1950s. This innovation led to further innovations in that coffee-bar proprietors began to serve 'pasta' dishes as well, at prices young people could afford. The demand for this kind of informal catering was so strong that a new grade of restaurant specialising in less expensive dishes began to appear. These *trattorie* became so popular that chains were built up rapidly, public companies floated, and large fortunes made. The entrepreneurs concerned were nearly all from North Italy, especially the Emilian Apennines. Although few of the Abbazzini became involved in these innovations, preferring to remain in the accustomed snack-and-sandwich bars, they too were able to profit from the increased spending power of Londoners. The expansion of these enterprises was at least sufficient to inspire further immigration from Abbazzia up to 1970, a good fifteen years after the 'push' factors associated with Emilia-Romagna had been superseded by a powerful demand for labour on the nearby plain.

The hope of eventual independence and large profits continued to sustain the 'chain' of Northern Italians bound for London. They gained experience in the hotels and restaurants, and then invested in their own firms. Many stayed on, inviting wives and fiancées to join them, or selecting brides from among the daughters of the pre-war immigrants.

In previous generations, Abbazzini in Boston and London

had sent remittances and donations to the parish on an individual basis. When local ecclesiastical building projects required their support, the emigrants organised themselves into temporary action sets. Only in London were the Abbazzini present in sufficient numbers by the 1960s to justify the formation of a permanent, corporate Committee. There was ample precedent for such an organisation. Groups of *paesani* from other communities in Emilia-Romagna and other regions of Italy had formed similar overseas associations in the past. In the case of the Committee of Abbazzia, changes in the membership and scope of the organisation clearly reflect a sequence of stages: as the Abbazzini have become more settled and have acquired wives from the wider London community, so they have made 'affines' of other *paesani* groups. Those Apennine villagers who have few *paesani* of their own in London were incorporated in the larger associations. Thus the Committee of Abbazzia had increased its membership since its founding in 1965 by admitting non-Abbazzini members. The scope of the organisation has been expanded to include emigrants from the parishes and communes of the entire region surrounding Abbazzia. The second and third generations who have Abbazzine ancestry are now beginning to take an active part in the Committee.

The Abbazzini themselves have particular reasons for strong ties of sentiment with the parish. This is what Italians call *campanilismo*, identification with the church campanile (or bell tower)—the symbol of the natal community. In Italy, one's birthplace is next in importance to the family in the formation of character and outlook (Nichols 1973:58). *Paesani* who are from the countryside usually own property in their native *paese* (parish; literally place). Many of the emigrants, therefore, have vested interests in the parish. The Abbazzini, who are now nearly three times more numerous in London than in the parish, have a landed interest of considerable size. Their stake in Abbazzia is larger than mere numbers indicate because, several long-established landowning families now have emigrants in London. Some of these families have lived in the parish for over 300 years (Jesini 1976:63). Lopreato has presented comparable data from South Italy (1967). It appears that the truly destitute of a community, relatively speaking, rarely migrate; it is the agrarian middle-rank which responds to local emergencies by emigrating. In a sense, the Abbazzini agricultural entrepreneurs sent out sons to found branches of the family enterprise in London's catering sector; they were 'diversifying'. Later these same sons may inherit family property and may form an overseas Committee to advance their interests in their home parish.

But there are more specific reasons for the home-orientated association activities of the Abbazzini in London. Abbazzia is an ancient parish with a distinguished past; hence, *campanilismo* is more justifiable in this parish than in most places. And the people who feel the most pride of place are those whose families have had the longest association with the parish. But now the most vigorous representatives of these families reside in London. Thus the emigrants of the immediate post-war era, having reached their full maturity and having acquired financial security, feel the need to symbolise their success in the home parish by investing heavily in ecclesiastical monuments.

Twice or three times a year, the Committee calls all the expatriate parishioners together for a dance or a dinner, and the chairman gives a progress report. The priest of Abbazzia keeps all the emigrants informed of developments in the parish via a newsletter sent out at Christmas and Easter. The Committee also brings him to London once or twice a year to celebrate mass and visit families. In return, donations are solicited by the Committee, and money has been forthcoming in sufficient quantities over the years to pay for the renovation of the local church and a chapel, and the construction of a large new cemetery with its own chapel. Members of the Committee devote much of their free time to this work. Other *paesani* groups are similarly preoccupied in London. *Campanilismo* is not the sole explanation. The 'elders' among the Abbazzini, as in all the somewhat gerontocratic associations of the Italian community in London, are either men who migrated in the aftermath of the last war, or they are the sons of men who arrived before the war and experienced internment. This very influential generation has been deterred from making active efforts to become assimilated by the historical events described earlier. In this case, therefore, the fifth stage of Price's 'chain migration sequence' does not lead to assimilation in London, but rather to an intensification of associational activity oriented towards Italy.

The Repatriation Process

Social scientists who specialise in migration studies often neglect the return movement, and indeed most interaction with the community and country of origin. Typical of this tradition is Price's study of chain migration. While the sequence has great heuristic value, there is a dimension of migration which is not covered by the model. Historically, Southern European migrants have been motivated by short-term goals: by selling their labour abroad, they wish to acquire just enough capital to make the traditional way of life tenable at home. Although Italian repatriation statistics reveal a higher proportion of return for those migrants who work within Continental Europe, there has always been a return movement of at least fifty per cent for destinations overseas as well (Briani 1972: chapt. 2). What happens to the returnees? Do they always resettle in the village of origin? As in the emigration chain, does the experience of earlier repatriates condition the behaviour of later returnees? There is very little research undertaken in this area. Watson discusses the disillusionment of Chinese emigrant restaurant workers who return to find their home village much changed; bored and 'let down' by the realities of a depopulated, economically inactive community, many reemigrate (1975: 167). Lopreato studied a village where emigrants of the first two stages did resettle permanently after long sojourns in America: all subsequent beneficial social change is attributed to capital and 'standards' acquired abroad. Nevertheless, the returnees were not well received—they are called 'stupid Americans' (Lopreato 1967:175ff). Both tendencies may be noted among the Abbazzini. The returnees, few as they are, find themselves avoided or reviled in the parish. Much of the malicious gossip in circulation is attributed to the London-born wife of an old returnee from the pre-war period. Those who have not enriched themselves are regarded as failures, and do not command respect. Even the loyal and affluent members of the Committee who return regularly to Abbazzia with their families for long visits are called, ironically, *Inglesi*—and treated as a different category of *paesani* by the locals. The result has been not so much the reemigration which Watson describes, but rather the development of chain repatriation: retirement or resettlement in Italy, but not in the home parish.

There are many factors operating to differentiate the *Inglesi* and the non-emigrant Abbazzini into distinct 'moral communities', in the sense Bailey uses the term (1971). By 1973, the year I conducted fieldwork in the parish, the Italian-born *Inglesi* had lived in London for upwards of twenty years. Although they did not assimilate, their values were those of an earlier Italian generation. In addition, they felt their own behaviour and that of their families should be commensurate with an improved socio-economic position. The result was that the *Inglesi* behaved with considerable restraint during their summers in Abbazzia. They often arrived in new cars, dressed in new clothes, and made sure that their daughters (who have considerable freedom in London) behaved in conformity with obsolete ideals of modesty during their stay in the parish. The *Inglesi* behaved differently; and, as a consequence, different standards were applied to them. One young man, born in London, had inherited extensive landholdings from his late father. He fervently wished to return and rediscover the life of his forefathers; thus he attempted manual labour during his three months in the village. The locals were horrified, and eventually ostracised him, not because he was doing anything unusual by local standards, but because he was not fulfilling local expectations of the *Inglesi*.

Other resentments centre around the Committee's 'control' of the parish from London. Committee members respond that if they did not look after the upkeep of the buildings and road, using their influence where they could, the parish would sink into disrepair. The fact that parishioners have benefited not only from their stewardship of the property of emigrant relatives, the remittances they receive, and the rise of Italian welfarism (agricultural subsidies, credit, and the like) also gives rise to jealousy on the part of the *Inglesi*. If conditions in London had not favoured Italian immigrants, the Abbazzini might have returned and confronted these problems.

But as things stood until the onset of the British recession, the tensions between emigrants and non-emigrants on the occasions they met were sufficient disincentives to resettlement in the parish.

Inevitably, however, there are those who cling to their dreams and make plans for retirement in the village. The non-emigrants have a powerful sanction 'at their disposal which they may use against the returned emigrants. The emigrants may have extensive landholdings in the parish, but rarely do they own sites in the capital hamlet of Calotta or nearby hamlets which are the only suitable places for a 'civilised' retirement villa with all modern conveniences. (By no means do all the hamlets have reliable water supplies, drainage, and telephone service.) Non-emigrants who control suitable sites become extremely reluctant to sell them to *Inglesi*. Thus the emigrant's return may be too fraught with difficulties to contemplate seriously. Yet he does have one option other than settling in the parish or staying in London: he can retire to the towns on the plain, or on the coast.

Hence, a repatriation movement which does not involve resettlement in the natal village has developed. It is a form of migration and is therefore susceptible to analysis in terms of Price's 'chain' model. Once again, there is a first stage: a pioneer, or group of pioneers, who set the pattern. Among Abbazzini, the trend began before the war, when a man who had done well in 'ice' invested his savings in agricultural land on the plain, in the commune of Pratocane (a pseudonym). He considered the fertile land of the Po Valley a better alternative to investment in the landslide-prone fields of Abbazzia. Pratocane is close to Piacenza, the provincial capital. After the war industrialisation and urbanisation in the area proceeded rapidly, and Pratocane became a dormitory-suburb. Land prices soared as housing sites were developed. The pioneer was under considerable pressure to sell out. Eventually he sub-divided his large holding into housing plots, but rather than offer it to development corporations or Piacentine commuters, he advised his network of *paesani*, affines, and friends in London that villa sites were available in a prime investment area near the city, and they could have 'first refusal'. The response was enthusiastic from the start. The 'chain' has proceeded through second and third stages, and most recently a number of young rural-urban migrants from the parish itself have been gravitating towards the same area of 'greater' Piacenza. As more *Inglesi* retire the parish's centre of gravity will shift yet again.

Pratocane is the focus of but one of the 'repatriation chains': *Inglesi* have settled in Piacenza itself, and in the market town nearest the parish. As more and more young people move down to the plain, and the already aged population of Abbazzia continues to decrease, so *Inglesi* will be more inclined to choose between the plain, or permanency in London. Those entrepreneurs who have been most successful combine the best of both worlds. They live in Pratocane, an hour's fast drive from Milan airport, for some of the year, and spend the rest of their time with children in London. As the aged non-emigrant Abbazzini gradually fill the large cemetery built by the *Inglesi*, and the young people eschew agriculture and settle on the plain, so the wisdom of the Committee's policy becomes apparent. Investment in monuments rather than agricultural technology makes good sense under such circumstances. Lobbying in the provincial council for the resurfacing of the parish road is a better suggestion than that made by younger Committee members to build a football field. The urbanites who already frequent the park on Monte Ermano will have need for a good road to the monuments long after the last football-playing youth has emigrated. Furthermore, there are no longer enough young men resident in the parish to raise a team. With the local labour shortage this implies, investment in agriculture is pointless. Many returnees feel that it is better to let the land revert to scrub and thus make good cover for game. In the autumn Abbazzia already attracts hunters to its *pensione*, and their numbers would probably increase if more accommodation becomes available.

In London, the *Inglesi* of second and third generations have been watching these developments. They discuss the possibilities of turning their ancient parish into a year-round resort. Should the British recession outlast the economic troubles in Italy, Abbazzini in London may take such fantasies more seriously. Another chain migration movement might ensue. This time the pioneers would be British-born entrepreneurs who would emigrate, rather than repatriate, to

Abbazzia with the object of exploiting the growing tertiary sector in a local economy once given over exclusively to agriculture. On land tilled by their grandfathers, these 'Italianate' British subjects would find ample scope for hotel and restaurant developments to attract the leisured classes from the industrialised plain. These tertiary activities could be profitably combined with intensive dairy-farming, as has been demonstrated in more developed regions of Alpine Europe. Already the farmers of Abbazzia have applied their agricultural subsidies to good effect in this area, and a milk cooperative collects their produce every morning. Such a future is predicted for a comparable community in the same latitude and altitude in Spain (Brandes 1975).

Conclusion

The concept of chain migration has proved useful in understanding the process of Italian emigration to and repatriation from London. As formulated by Price, the model is more specific than it need be. However a concept which draws attention to the priority of interpersonal communication in determining the direction of migration is universally applicable. In Europe, particularly, the centuries-old tradition of seasonal migration is a complicating factor, for these temporary migrants are the true pioneers as far as the dissemination of information is concerned. In addition, as I have shown, the history of migration between Italy and London is characterised by capricious reversals. The foundation of an overseas community was greatly accelerated by the presence of Mazzini, and the Victorian spirit of Italophilia; at a later stage a euphoric patriotism was engendered as the expressed policy of the Italian Fascist government. Both external sources of favour were suddenly withdrawn after Mussolini declared war on Britain, with the disastrous consequences I have described. All three factors are quite external to the inner dynamic of chain migration. Thus, Price's model has been modified considerably in its application here. But its greatest vindication has been in the actions of the Abbazzini themselves. They have frequently ignored these external factors—often to their own detriment—in their desire to follow their *paesani* and so perpetuate the chain. In this case, migration has to be seen in all of its complexity, as a multidirectional movement incorporating repatriation. The concept of chain migration should not be restricted to the analysis of that assimilation which the chain process itself most impedes.

NOTE

This chapter is based on fieldwork undertaken in London and Italy between November 1972 and April 1974. The project would not have been possible without the financial support of the Social Science Research Council, the Italian Government, and my parents. I am deeply grateful to those who financed the project, but thanks must also go to the people of the parish I call Abbazzia, at home and in London, who allowed me to invade their privacy. It is impossible to thank all who helped me individually, but for their moral and intellectual support I would single out two priests: Father Umberto Marin, in London, and the *Parrocco* of Abbazzia, in Italy. My supervisor at Sussex, Ralph Grillo, has been particularly supportive through a prolonged association.

REFERENCES CITED

Armengaud, André, 1973, Population in Europe 1700–1914. In *The Industrial Revolution* (ed.) C. M. Cipolla. London: Fontana.

Bailey, F. G., 1971, Changing Communities. In *Gifts and Poison* (ed.) F. G. Bailey. Oxford: Basil Blackwell.

Brandes, Stanley H., 1975, *Migration, Kinship and Community: Tradition and Transition in a Spanish Village*. New York: Academic Press.

Briani, Vittorio, 1972, *Il Lavoro Italiano in Europa Ieri e Oggi*. Rome: Ministry of Foreign Affairs.

Cavalli, Carlo, 1972, *Ricordi di un Emigrato*. London: La Voce degli Italiani.

Compendio Statistico della Provincia di Piacenza, n.d., Camera di Commercio Industria e Agricoltura. Piacenza.

Dahya, Badr, 1974, The Nature of Pakistani Ethnicity in Industrial Cities in Britain. In *Urban Ethnicity* (ed.) Abner Cohen. London: Tavistock.

de Smith, M. J., 1972, Italians in London: A Demographic and Socio-Economic Analysis. B.Sc. dissertation, Department of Geography, University of Southampton.

Foerster, Robert F., 1919, *The Italian Emigration of our Times.* Cambridge: Harvard University Press.

Garigue, Philip and Raymond Firth, 1956, Kinship Organization of Italianates in London. In *Two Studies of Kinship in London* (ed.) Raymond Firth. London: Athlone Press.

Guida Generale degli Italiani in Londra, 1933, London: Ercoli & Sons.

Jesini, Agostino, 1976, *Monastero di Val Tolla e Alta Val d'Arda: Notizie di Storia e di Cronaca.* Milan: Private Edition.

Lafitte, F., 1940, *The Interment of Aliens.* Penguin.

Leone, Peppino, 1964, *I Shall Die on the Carpet.* London: Frewin.

Lopreato, Joseph, 1967, *Peasants No More.* San Francisco: Chandler.

Mack-Smith, Dennis, 1959, *Italy: A Modern History.* Ann Arbor: University of Michigan Press.

Marin, Father Umberto, 1969, *Emigrazione Italiana in Gran Bretagna. Parts I and II.* Rome: Centro Studi Emigrazione.

Nichols, Peter, 1973, *Italia, Italia.* London: Macmillan.

Philpott, Stuart B., 1973, *West Indian Migration: The Montserrat Case.* London: Athlone Press.

Price, Charles A., 1963, *Southern Europeans in Australia.* Melbourne.

Price, Charles A., 1969, The Study of Assimilation. In *Migration* (ed.) J. A. Jackson. Cambridge: Cambridge University Press.

Problemi del Lavoro Italiano all'Estero, 1972, Rome: Ministry of Foreign Affairs.

Watson, James L., 1975, *Emigration and the Chinese Lineage: The Mans in Hong Kong and London.* Berkeley: University of California Press.

CHAPTER 10

PAMELA CONSTANTINIDES

The Greek Cypriots: Factors in the Maintenance of Ethnic Identity

In 1974, while the research on which this essay is largely based was still taking place, the situation in Cyprus was suddenly and disastrously altered by the coup against President Makarios and the subsequent invasion of the island by Turkey. The two villages in which the Cyprus end of my fieldwork took place are now behind Turkish military lines, and their inhabitants are refugees, homeless in their own land.

The effects of this invasion, emotional and practical, on Greek Cypriots abroad, and especially the Greek Cypriots from the occupied areas, has been immense. Night after night they watched on their television screens the military advancement on their former homes, and the death, injury and misery endured by Cypriots of all ethnic groups. London Cypriots found many key political events taking place on their own doorstep; the pre-invasion arrival in Britain of Ecevit, the then Turkish Prime Minister, to discuss the situation with the British Government; the arrival of the temporarily ousted President Makarios for top-level talks, and his personal appeal to thousands of British Cypriots from the pulpit of the Orthodox Church in Camden Town.

Wherever individual interests may have lain before these events, everyone, including the second generation of immigrants, became acutely conscious of their origins and of the emotional and kinship ties which still bound them to Cyprus. After the first desperate concern for the physical safety of relatives had passed, Cyprus aid and refugee relief groups sprang up in large numbers throughout the Greek Cypriot community. Especially among the second generation, political lobby and pressure groups formed to try and prod the British Government over what was seen as its failure to act as a guarantor of Cyprus' independence.

And yet at the same time as consciousness of specifically Greek Cypriot identity was at its highest point, so too was the awareness that the realities of the future lay in this country. Many had thought of returning to Cyprus to set up in business or to retire and while this was often little more than a daydream, since the actual return rate to Cyprus has been quite low, it now became for those whose villages were in the occupied areas, a physical impossibility. Before them also was the spectre of the small proportion of Cypriots who had gone back. Several had sold up all they had here and settled in one of the developing tourist areas of Cyprus, only to lose everything in the 1974 invasion and to have to return and try and start again in vastly more difficult economic times than those prevailing when they had first arrived.

Material losses were high even for many who never intended to return permanently to Cyprus. The investment of British Cypriots in holiday plots, flats, and villas in Cyprus was substantial. Even should there be ultimately some form of compensation, many will gain nothing, since they did not hold the deeds to their property, but were paying it off on a type of hire-purchase system.

Thus the paradox is that while ethnic consciousness has probably never been more acute, the immigrants, forced by events to think out the realities of their situation, now accept that they are in Britain to stay. And while the second generation has, in many cases, been shocked into awareness of its origins, so too this has led to greater social and political participation within the framework of the politics of this country.

It must be stressed that much of what follows, especially regarding relations between Londoners from the now-occupied areas of Cyprus and their villages of origin, refers to the period before the 1974 invasion. The fieldwork on which it is based took place over three years between 1972 and 1975. Research was carried out both in London and Cyprus but the main emphasis of the enquiry was in London. A period of about a year was spent becoming acquainted with the history and patterns of settlement in London, with the occupations of the immigrants, and with the more formal aspects of their association. Then followed two brief periods of research in Cyprus, about four months being spent in each of two selected villages. The emigrants from these villages who now live in London were traced. Many aspects of their lives here and their links with their home villages were recorded, both by informal interview and the standard anthropological technique of participant observation.

The History and Patterns of Immigration from Cyprus

Historically, emigration has formed one of the solutions to scarcity in the Mediterranean—scarcity of land, scarcity of jobs, scarcity of opportunity. We do not know if any Cypriots were numbered among the community of Greeks who established an Orthodox church in London in the seventeenth century (Dowling and Fletcher 1915) but it is certain that a handful of seamen and merchants of Cypriot origin settled in Britain during the next two centuries. The emigration of Cypriots to Britain on a significant scale only took place, however, well after Cyprus had come under British colonial rule, and the vast majority of Cypriots in this country have arrived during the last twenty to twenty-five years, during the 1950s and early 1960s.

Any study of Cypriot immigration into Britain must of necessity use as a starting point the thorough demographic analysis of Oakley (Oakley 1970 and 1971). The population census for 1931 gives a figure of only 1,075 Cyprus-born people in Britain, of whom nearly 74 per cent lived in Greater London. In 1951 the figure had reached 10,343 of whom approximately 77 per cent lived in Greater London. Then followed the peak years of Cypriot immigration, with most of the newcomers, well over 80 per cent, settling in a small cluster of boroughs near London's West End. The 1971 census gives a figure of 72,665 Cyprus-born people living in this country. Cypriots are not distinguished in the census by ethnic origin, and the figure includes Greek, Turkish, and Armenian Cypriots, as well as a small number of people born to British parents in Cyprus. The figure does not include children born here to Cypriot parents. If one does include the second generation, then taking Oakley's 1966 calculations in conjunction with the estimates provided by the Cypriots themselves, a more likely figure would be about 140,000. Although the recent war in Cyprus may have altered the ratio somewhat, Greek and Turkish Cypriots seem to be in about the same proportions here as they are in the homeland, namely about five to one.

My own research tends to confirm Oakley's conclusion that the decline in the rate of Cypriot immigration from the early 1960s was due less to the 1962 Commonwealth Immigrants Act and subsequent legislation than to the decline in economic opportunity here. The 'never-had-it-so-good' years were over, and if Britain was no longer eager to welcome foreign labour, neither were those seeking economic betterment so eager to come.

Though the Cypriot population in this country may not seem particularly large in relation to other minorities, considered in relation to the overall population of Cyprus, which in 1972 was only some 645,000, the exodus from the island was substantial. If one considers that about one Cypriot in six is a resident of Britain, the significance of this to the society of origin can be appreciated. If one considers that the majority of these British Cypriots live in London, the question of how these people of mainly village origin have succeeded in establishing themselves in an alien city becomes of great interest.

The Cyprus Background

Later in this chapter I shall go into greater detail about the circumstances of the two Cypriot villages in which I worked. However it would be useful at this point to make a few observations about the background of these immigrants.

It is many decades now since Cyprus was an island of peasant farmers. The population has increased and, particularly since the last World War, the economy has diversified. Towns have grown enormously and an educated elite fill business and government posts (see Loizos 1975, for greater detail on economic and political change in Cyprus). At the time the majority of British Cypriots left the island, this process of economic expansion, although well under way, was not providing enough opportunities to meet with the growing expectations of the islanders. Much has changed in Cyprus since 1950, but most of the emigrants grew up in villages communities which demanded of their members fairly rigid adherence to a set of social practices and associated values.

The literature on both Greece and Cyprus (see for example Campbell 1964; Peristiany 1965, 1968; Loizos 1975) stresses the importance of the nuclear family in the Greek-speaking world. A nuclear family expects to have its own household and its own property, and this is usually established on marriage. The pre-mortem system of inheritance ensures that the groom receives his share of the parental estate and the bride her's, in the form of a dowry. Far from dying out as a custom, the dowry in Cyprus is now often quite substantial, consisting of a house as well as other property.

Kinship is traced bilaterally to the degree of third cousin, and first and second cousins may not marry, though some second cousins seek Church dispensation to do so. The institution of fictive-kinship (marriage sponsorship and god-parenthood) is also important. A man or woman may not marry the children of their godparents.

Marriages in the village were traditionally arranged by the parents of the couple concerned, often with the help of a matchmaker or go-between. This still remains largely true. The only difference is the degree of initiative now left to the children themselves, who often choose whom they wish to marry and then pressure their parents into initiating formal proceedings. A vow to marry is pledged at a betrothal ceremony officiated over by a priest, and at which the dowry and other property agreements relevant to the marriage are spelled out. To break this engagement is tantamount to divorce, and brings severe dishonour on both participants, but especially upon the girl. Girls are expected to be virgins at the betrothal, though after that it is conceded, though not necessarily approved, that sexual relations may take place if the opportunity presents itself. This is what makes a broken engagement so dishonouring for the girl, and substantially reduces her further marriage chances. Whatever the facts it is assumed that sexual relations have occurred, or worse, that to take such a drastic course of action the fiancé must have found that she has had sexual relations with another. Once a marriage is finalised and blessed by the Church it is virtually indissoluble. The Orthodox Church recognises very few grounds for divorce.

Traditionally spouses were most often sought from within the village, or from geographically proximate villages. Land thus settled on the couple at marriage from both parental estates could then be conveniently worked. Furthermore, fellow villagers whose reputations were known, and with whom one already had working relationships, were considered better marriage propositions than 'strangers'. The Greek word with the double meaning stranger/guest is in fact still used in referring to those of other villages. Great pains are taken in arranging a union to ensure that economic circumstances and family honour are evenly matched.

The Maintenance of Ethnic Identity

In many ways a study of the Cypriots in Britain provides even greater theoretical possibilities than does that of African, West Indian, or Asian immigrants. These latter groups inevitably carry their colour as a distinguishing feature and may have markedly different religious and cultural backgrounds. The interesting point about the Greek Cypriots, as with other white European immigrants, is their potential invisibility within the British majority population. How far they are differentiated depends upon which of their physical and cultural features both the Cypriots and those who come into contact with them wish to stress. Greek Cypriots are white, though often olive in skin tone; they are Christians, though members of the Eastern Orthodox Church. Furthermore, most Greek Cypriot names have an English equivalent and could easily be Anglicised should their owners wish to do so. While it is difficult for a native speaker of Greek to acquire totally accent-free English, the language of the second generation is, by and large, broad London dialect. Yet in spite of this, those who have written about the Greek Cypriots in Britain have commented upon their strong sense of ethnic identity (see e.g.; George and Millerson 1967; Oakley 1970). Greek Cypriot social customs and institutions thrive here, and it is interesting to see how they have been modified by the new environment. I will suggest that three factors are of prime importance here: one is the strength of certain basic values which the immigrants brought with them; another is the fact that so many Cypriots arrived together over such a short period of time; and a third is the balanced sex ratio among the immigrants. Over the decade from early 1950 to early 1960 nearly as many women as men arrived, and a great many came as nuclear families, young parents with one or more children.

The observation that Peristiany (1965) made several years ago, namely that village-born Cypriots see themselves first as members of their family, second as members of their natal village, and only third as natives of their island remains true. In defining their ethnic identity, Greek Cypriots in this country see themselves in relation to a number of other ethnic, cultural, or national groups: Turkish Cypriots, Greeks from the mainland of Greece, other immigrant groups, and perhaps last of all to the native British.

Although Cypriot immigrants have clear, if sometimes conflicting, stereotypes of the indigenous British, based both on their colonial experience and upon contact through work and business, one of the surprises of my research was to discover that they had little intimate knowledge of individual Britons and that they were often unaware of British social conventions. This was because they had first moved into urban areas already occupied by other immigrant groups. Often they felt that friendly overtures made to English neighbours had been rebuffed and were reluctant to try again. While, as far as I was able to ascertain, some of these supposed rebuffs were due to cultural misunderstanding, one must not forget the often prejudiced and hostile feelings which many British held towards Cypriots during the EOKA period in Cyprus. Frequently the Cypriot immigrants were appalled at what they saw as the low moral standards of the run-down areas in which they first sought accommodation. The very fact that Cypriots were forced, for economic reasons, to seek cheap accommodation in so-called 'twilight zones' near their places of work, meant that they often found themselves co-resident with other groups to whom they felt both morally and culturally superior.

This initial sense of social and cultural distance is beginning to break down as Cypriots move outwards and northwards from the centre of London to areas offering better housing and better schooling for their children. Not only has increasing fluency in English made better communication possible but, more importantly, Greek Cypriots are now moving into neighbourhoods where their own essentially middle-class aspirations are shared by the other residents.

The Greek Cypriots' relationships both with Turkish Cypriots and with mainland Greeks tend to be more intimate and complex than with other categories of people in Britain. On the whole Greek Cypriots identify themselves as such and as distinct both from Turkish Cypriots and mainland Greeks. With the Turkish Cypriots they have in common birthplace, local history, appearance, and many common customs and attitudes. They differ principally in kinship, language, and religious practice. Though the Greek Cypriots share a common language, religion, and kinship system with mainland Greeks, they differ in dialect and in many details of custom. Political ideology has some part to play in the degree to which distinctions are felt or stressed. This is no place to examine in detail the complex politics of Cyprus. Suffice it to say that those on the left of the political spectrum would, at least intellectually, wish to place being *Cypriot* before questions of ethnic differentiation, while those on the right would wish to consider themselves as *Greeks* who come from Cyprus. In practice the majority, whatever their political views, interact largely with other Greek Cypriots.

Before 1974, relations between Greek and Turkish Cypriots in London were very good (at least at the unofficial level). Many Cypriots of both backgrounds had arrived here and established their working relationships before the intercommunal hostilities of 1963 and the withdrawal of large numbers of Turkish Cypriots into enclaves. Also, many of the Greek Cypriot immigrants held views to the left of the political spectrum in Cyprus. While they earnestly wished for Cyprus' independence from Britain, and supported the EOKA movement insofar as it was achieving that, they were less than enthusiastic about the notion of union with Greece, which was ultimately opposed by Turkish Cypriots.

Common origin and common working conditions in

Britain gave Greek and Turkish Cypriots a greater unity of outlook than prevailed in Cyprus after 1963. Large numbers of Greek and Turkish Cypriot men and women worked together in the same factories and businesses, and indeed still do. Relations between the British Cypriots of both ethnic groups were often held up as an example to be emulated in Cyprus. Though the Turkish invasion of Cyprus and its tragic aftermath have inevitably imposed a real strain on relationships—a strain quickly exploited by the extremists on the political right in both groups—individual and working relationships still remain good.

Intermarriage or co-habitation between Greek and Turkish Cypriots does exist, more commonly in this country than in Cyprus, but it tends to be frowned upon by both ethnic groups. This is principally because of religious differences and also, in more recent history, because of the political differences between them. There is some degree of intermarriage between Greek Cypriots and mainland Greeks in this country, though this is outnumbered by intermarriage with British and other national groups (Irish, Spanish, Italian, and others). Unions outside ethnic boundaries, however, still form a relatively small proportion of all marriages, and Greek Cypriots tend largely to marry Greek Cypriots.

Greek Cypriot Settlement in London

The Greek Cypriots who are living in this country and who make up what they themselves refer to as 'the Greek Cypriot community' do not necessarily see themselves as falling into the same social category. They distinguish among themselves by education, status, and reason for being in this country. According to their own criteria they can be placed into three rough, but overlapping, categories:

(1) Officials of the Cyprus High Commission and other banking, trade and tourist offices: senior posts usually go to people appointed from Cyprus, while more junior posts are recruited from among Greek Cypriots already living here. Senior appointments are often of such duration that officials are resident for many years and their children are educated here. Some became permanent residents, but the notion in

principle is that there is a home and a post waiting for them back in Cyprus.

(2) Academics and professionals: occasionally these are people on secondment from the Cyprus Government to government offices here, working, for example, in welfare departments of boroughs with a large Cypriot population. Most of the people in this category came here to receive further education or wish to receive additional qualifications. Some stay several years, receive their qualifications or practical experience and depart. Others become permanent residents and part of the academic and professional establishment here.

(3) The 'ordinary immigrant': these are people who came seeking work opportunities and, as they say 'a better life' than they felt they had in Cyprus. They are largely from villages and often have little formal education. Immigrants in this category vary considerably as to whether they originally envisaged short-term or long-term residence in Britain.

Although individual Cypriots like to make the above distinctions, the lines are in fact very blurred and the categories very fluid. The villager may become highly successful in business and choose to associate socially with officials and professionals; his or her children may become junior officials, academics, or professionals. Many professionals are themselves of village origin. Whatever the original intention to return home, only time in fact determines who does and who does not become permanently established in Britain.

During the 1950s, newly arrived Cypriot immigrants tended to cluster mainly, as I have indicated, in three boroughs—the present Islington, Camden, and Hackney—with smaller numbers south of the river. Though Islington contained the most Cypriots it was Camden Town which became, and has remained for many years, the 'heartland' of Greek Cypriot settlement, as its numerous Greek Cypriot restaurants, cafes, and clubs attest. In more recent years there has been a steady movement northwards to adjacent boroughs offering better housing. Haringey now has the largest number of Cyprus-born citizens, but already families are moving into Enfield, Barnet, Brent, and Waltham Forest.

It is a firm tradition in Cyprus that each nuclear family should have its own household, and one of the strongest motivations of the new settlers was to own their own home. This they began to achieve quite rapidly and there is now a very high proportion of owner-occupiers among the Cypriot population.

During the early stage of settlement parts of larger houses purchased in the inner boroughs were rented out, often to other Greek Cypriots. But as their financial security increases, families generally move to the privacy of smaller but better quality homes. Only a small percentage of Cypriots are in public housing, and that more often than not by virtue of the local authority having compulsorily purchased the property in which they were living. In fact, having a council house or flat carries something of a stigma, since it implies that one has not succeeded in achieving the commonly agreed goals of emigration.

Employment and Occupation

Before leaving Cyprus, most male immigrants were employed as craftsmen, labourers, and general service personnel (Oakley 1971). Only a small proportion of female immigrants were economically active in Cyprus, the majority being largely engaged in household duties.

It is perhaps the economic role of women which has changed most in the immigration process. Once in this country they began to work in large numbers, either for wages in the factory or home, or as an active part of a small family business enterprise. George and Millerson (1967) estimate that, up to 1958, well over 80 per cent of Cypriot women were involved in the clothes making industry here, and the percentage is still undoubtedly high.

Women contribute substantially to the income of their families. The norm among those who have pre-school children is to do dress-making outwork at home, and in most Cypriot households the ubiquitous sewing machine will be found in a convenient corner, surrounded by bundles of finished and half-finished dresses. The sewing is done on piece-work rates for Cypriot dressmaking manufacturers who deliver the fabric in ready-cut bundles. The part-sewn dresses are then finished off on special machines in the factory.

Though the piece-rates are rather low, women can earn large sums each week by working long hours day and night. Out-workers are the first to be laid off during the seasonal slack periods in dress-manufacturing, but they can also pull out easily to tend sick children, go on holiday to Cyprus, or attend to other family commitments. In general the flexibility of the system suits both manufacturers and women workers with young children. Moreover, these women consider it their right and duty to further the financial welfare of their family and they resent attempts, official or otherwise, to persuade them that they are being exploited. They equally resent attempts by some local councils to put a stop to out-working by imposing fines on these activities (up to £200 in some cases). Where the council investigation is prompted by the complaints of neighbours about noisy machines, women tend to feel that they have been victims of the prejudice or envy of their non-Cypriot neighbours.

For many years men remained overwhelmingly concentrated in the service and recreation occupations, and as craftsmen, production process workers and labourers (Oakley 1970). This meant to a large extent catering and hotel work along with clothing and shoe manufacture, hairdressing and grocery retailing. Increasingly the trend has been towards setting oneself up in business within these occupations, usually on a very small scale as a family concern. A substantial proportion of Cypriot immigrants are now self-employed.

The occupational mobility of Cypriots is one of the things that stands out most strongly in my investigation. Most were willing to try a wide range and variety of jobs, and to experiment with several types of small business enterprise before finding the one that worked best for them. Thus while the number of restaurants and clothing manufacture businesses has increased, so also have cake shops, travel agencies, dress shops, furniture stores, television and radio repair shops, butchers, builders, hairdressers, grocers and greengrocers, fish and chip shops, bakeries, dry-cleaners, mini-cab offices and estate agents. As the pattern of Cypriot housing settlement has moved outwards from the original 'heartland' of Islington and Camden Town, so has the proliferation of small businesses.

While the range of goods and services supplied by the Cypriots diffuses their economic role ever more widely in the overall economy, and makes them less and less occupiers of anything that could be described as an 'ethnic economic niche', at the same time it strengthens what has been called the Cypriot 'internal economy'. It is even truer today than it was in 1970 that 'almost anything one Cypriot needs can be bought from another' and that it is possible for most Cypriots 'to meet their needs without leaving the bounds of their own community' (Oakley 1970:101).

Whether in fact Greek Cypriots do confine themselves to an ethnic economy in their purchase of goods and services is however open to question. Evidence from my own investigation suggests that, while this is still largely true, the system is being eroded from two directions. The majority of Greek Cypriots have lived in this country for nearly twenty years. Proficiency in English is now common-place, even among women who, because of their confinement to home or Cypriot-owned factory, had greater problems in learning the language. The second generation, in spite of parental efforts, often speak very little Greek. While it may still be considered desirable it is no longer necessary, in terms of communication, for Cypriots to buy from each other. The Cypriot grocery provides a good example. Nearly all the couples I interviewed said that they did the bulk of their weekly shopping in supermarkets, buying only the ingredients needed for favourite island dishes from Cypriot groceries. However almost everyone used a Cypriot grocer or butcher from time to time for other than strictly economic reasons. One is the personalised services provided: a telephoned order has the bonus of an exchange of courtesies and a renewal of contacts, as does the home delivery service. Cypriot shops continue to play an important role in the exchange of news and gossip, the passing of value judgments, and therefore to some extent the upholding of values—as a visit to any such store on a busy Saturday will affirm.

At the same time, however, the wider British public has developed a taste for Greek food, and now frequents Greek Cypriot shops in increasing numbers. This is especially true of Greek Cypriot restaurants. Restaurants which served Cypriot workers in the early fifties were 'discovered' by the

British in the sixties. Nowadays new eating houses are often established specifically to capture a largely British clientèle.

Leisure Activities

Perhaps the first point that should be made is that Greek Cypriots are, on the whole, extremely hard-working. They came here for economic advancement and material betterment and most work single-mindedly towards these goals. This often means a six and sometimes seven-day week, especially for those running restaurants, fish and chip shops and cafes. Any leisure time that is available is spent largely in relaxing with the immediate family or visiting relatives. This being said, there nonetheless exists a range of Greek-language activities to attract them should they so wish.

Several Greek-language newspapers or newsheets are produced here, both for the mainland Greek and the Greek Cypriot communities. Newspapers have a definite political orientation. The most widely circulated is undoubtedly the left-wing *Veema* which carries, apart from reports on communist countries, news from Cyprus and news of events among Greek Cypriots here. Wider British and overseas news tends to be dealt with either as it illustrates a particular ideological point, or as it touches on Cypriot politics or the welfare of immigrants.

Cypriot bookshops, coffee shops, and groceries carry a regular supply of newspapers and magazines, both those imported from Cyprus and those produced here. In all areas containing significant numbers of Greek Cypriots, local cinemas are hired by entrepreneurs to provide weekend showings of Greek films. These usually have good audiences, as do visiting troupes of actors or comedians from Cyprus. A London-based Cypriot theatre workshop, which has been struggling for years to attract audiences in substantial numbers, has had mixed success. Its main role seems to have been in marshalling a small but dedicated group of second generation Cypriots into a theatre and arts experimental group. It also played a leading role in expanding the participation of various Greek Cypriot organisations in the annual Camden Festival to the point where an independent 'Cyprus

Week' was established. This event, in which other residents are invited to partake of Cypriot food and admire Cypriot handicraft, folk dancing, and arts has now been taken up by several other boroughs containing Cypriot minority groups as an exercise in community goodwill.

When Greek Cypriots are questioned about their leisure hours, almost all maintain that their most important and constant activity is visiting relatives and friends—which usually mean close kin, affines and fictive kin, one's wedding sponsors (best men and women) and the godparents of one's children. Another is attending wedding parties, principally of kin, of fictive kin, of former co-villagers and of workmates or business colleagues and their families. In fact for many this is the principal, or even only, type of family outing in which they take part. Greek Cypriot weddings are large and jolly affairs with a great deal of conspicuous consumption and ostentatious display. They are probably the most important social functions among the immigrants. All relatives and affines should be invited, and an attempt is made to deliver invitations to all those originating from the same village (at least all those with whom one's family is on speaking terms). Invitations are delivered by hand or passed on personally by a mutual connection. This involves a considerable amount of searching at 'last known' addresses and serves as a periodic reinforcement of old village ties. At the same time new contacts established in this country are reinforced by extending invitations, and often by the establishment of 'best men' and 'best women' links, since the bride and groom can have several best men and women. People with whom one does business, or with whom one wishes to start a business relationship, are invited. Most large weddings have their small contingent of amazed and interested English guests—workmates, business associates, or neighbours of the bride or groom's family. Guests may number from one hundred to a thousand or more. Large halls are hired for the event along with bands of Greek Cypriot musicians.

The brunt of the expense is borne by the bride's parents. The scale of the reception is taken as an indication of their status and the value they place both upon their daughter and upon the match they have made for her. In this sense it has taken on some of the significance of the dowry in Cyprus, though not one of its main functions, which is to provide for the future of the newly-created family. Relatives of both the bride and groom contribute to the couple's start in life through the custom of pinning money on them during and after the wedding dance.

Wedding parties are not only fertile grounds for the reinforcement of old ties and the establishment of new ones, but are also used by both parents and marriageable children as occasions for seeking out prospective marriage partners.

Education

The children of Greek Cypriot immigrants are involved in two types of formal education. Besides their local school, attendance at which is compulsory under the laws of this country, they may also attend evening and weekend classes in Greek language and culture. These latter classes are organised both by the Greek Orthodox Church and by certain independent and left-wing voluntary associations. They are organised locally at the request of the parents, and their specific intention is to keep alive a consciousness of belonging to a Greek-speaking ethnic group. The left-wing and independent groups have been set up to countermand what is seen as the excessive stress on Greek nationalism present in the church schools. There are now over fifty of these schools in Britain with some 4,000 children attending.

The Ministry of Education of the Government of Cyprus has taken an interest in the schools through the Cyprus High Commission, and a special Educational Mission has set itself the task of overseeing and standardising the level of teaching. All the bodies mentioned above have also put pressure on secondary schools in areas heavily populated by Greek Cypriots to include the teaching of Modern Greek in their curricula.

Prolonged participation in the British education system is thought by parents to cause a loss of 'Greek identity' as individual children conform to the values and behaviour of their school peers. Participation in the Greek-language schools is quite specifically designed to counteract some of the effects of State schooling. The Church-run schools have begun to organise supervised summer holidays in Greece as part of their cultural programme, and some individual parents were using holidays with relatives in Cyprus as a reward for satisfactory progress in learning Greek.

Following is what one of the officers of the Educational Mission has to say about Greek language schools (Adamantos 1972):

What is the purpose of these schools? The Cypriot parent is very contented living in Britain. He has found here a hospitable environment, a civilised society, good working conditions. Nevertheless he is scared. He is scared of the influence of the environment on his children. He has his identity, he is a Cypriot living in Britain. But what about his children? They are neither Cypriot nor British. They are not Cypriot because the English environment has affected them; their ways, aspects, beliefs, are those of English boys and girls. They are not English, they have peculiar long names, their parents are foreigners, they are not always accepted by their peers and society. Parents want an identity for their children. They have been stubborn in this respect. They will never accept assimilation.

It seems however that not all Greek Cypriot parents are as worried as this observer suggests, because he goes on to say:

Unfortunately, not all parents showed enough interest. There still exist parents who do not send their children to the Greek school. It has been one of the duties of the Educational Mission to convince these parents that it is their duty to see that their children attend the Greek school.

One of the problems for the children is that Greek language classes are extra-curricular, and this means extra time spent at lessons when their peers are at play. The children often develop fierce resistance to the classes and, if the parents insist, they may attend but be unruly and disruptive. Some attend for a short period and then drop out. If they are also having other difficulties reconciling their parents' point of view with the life-style they and their contemporaries aspire to, then this may lead to a general resentment about being seen as Cypriot or 'foreign'. This reaction is not irreversible, however, and children who desperately wanted not to be different when they were younger, often regain an interest in their parents' culture and language in later years. They often express regret that they did not seize the chance to learn the Greek language properly.

For many, a type of identity crisis seems to occur in the period after they have left school and sought employment. Those who have received their education in overcrowded and poorly staffed schools in the inner city find themselves poor candidates for the more glamorous jobs they have dreamt about. In the case of girls, parental concern for their moral welfare may place restrictions on how far away from home they are allowed to work. However, the ethnic economy is ready and willing to absorb them, particularly when there are family businesses to be maintained. For quite a few rebellious adolescents, this period marks their 're-entry' into their ethnic group.

The Church

One of the problems for many Cypriots here has been that their churches are not under the authority of the independent and autocephalous church of Cyprus, but under that of mainland Greece. Greek Orthodoxy has a long history in Britain, organised worship for Greeks going back to the 1600s, if not earlier. In 1922 the chief place of worship for followers of Greek Orthodox Christianity in Britain, St. Sophia's in Bayswater, was made a Cathedral by the Ecumenical Patriarch of Constantinople, who has spiritual jurisdiction over the Greek Christians of the *diasphora*—the scattering or emigration. The new diocese was named the Metropolitan of Thyateira. In 1964 this became the Metropolitan of Thyateira and Great Britain under the leadership of the present Archbishop Athenagoras. The clergy are principally from mainland Greece, with some Cypriot priests.

The influx of Greek Cypriot immigrants led to the fairly rapid establishment of a large number of centres of Greek Orthodox worship in London and in other parts of the country. This in time led to ongoing friction between mainland and Cypriot Greeks over representation and control of the lay aspects of the Church. Early differences of cultural background and opinion at St. Sophia caused the Cypriots to form their own church of All Saints in Camden Town in 1948. Continuing disputes within the Church have strong political overtones, and before the 1974 crisis in Cyprus the Church hierarchy had come under strong attack from the Greek Cypriot left-wing press for its allegedly anti-Makarios stance.

The Church carries out regular weekly services, always well attended, and the major rituals of the Greek Orthodox calendar. It plays a central role in the life-cycle ritual of the immigrants, officiating at engagements, weddings, baptisms and funerals. The welfare arm of the Church is less well developed, and its principal activities are Sunday-school and Greek-language classes for the immigrants' children.

Whatever their political feelings, Greek Cypriots in Britain continue to feel a need for the services of their religion, and one of the first forms of voluntary association in areas newly inhabited by Greek Cypriots is the formation of a group to petition for the use of a church and the services of a priest. Sometimes, by mutual agreement, existing protestant churches are 'shared' by Orthodox Greeks with their regular flocks. The Orthodox church calendar bears witness to the growing number and spreading distribution of small Orthodox communities. The calendar for 1974 lists 22 churches and congregations in Greater London, with a further 29 scattered throughout the cities and towns of Great Britain. There is also an Orthodox monastery in Essex and an Orthodox convent in Buckinghamshire.

Politics

I have no intention in this essay of pursuing in any detail the intricate and often turbulent nature of Cypriot politics. It is however impossible to talk about Greek Cypriot social organisation anywhere without discussing politics. And, it is impossible to discuss Greek Cypriot politics without reference to Turkish Cypriot politics, the politics of Greece, of Turkey, of Britain, both in her colonial days and now as a putative guarantor of Cyprus' independence, and of the Great Powers' interests in the Eastern Mediterranean. All these have played their role in the sad fate of Cyprus, and all find their reflection in the activities and attitudes of Greek Cypriots living in Britain.

Several American studies of immigrant groups have pointed to the sustained involvement that immigrants tend to retain in the politics of their country of origin, and this is generally true of Greek Cypriots here. The fact that the bulk of Cypriots largely support the British Labour Party has perhaps less to do with Labour's domestic policies than with the political stances adopted by the immigrants before they left Cyprus, and with the respective positions of the two major British parties at the time of the EOKA struggle, and Independence, in Cyprus.

The majority of Greek Cypriots in this country would categorise themselves as of the Left, a fact which might seem surprising in ideological terms, given the evidently bourgeois aspirations of the settlers. 'Left' and 'Right' are terms very loosely used to describe the political polarities which exist in Cyprus. In fact 'Left' constitutes a very broad category indeed and includes social democrats and socialists as well as adherents of AKEL, the Cypriot Communist Party. The Left has always stood for Greek and Turkish co-operation in a Cyprus independent of both Greece and Turkey. Since the years of the junta in Greece, the abortive junta-inspired coup against Makarios, and the subsequent invasion of Cyprus by Turkey, the latter goal is now that of most political parties in Cyprus. The goal of Enosis (union with Greece) has been abandoned by nearly all except those on the extreme right.

Greek Cypriots have conscientiously used their voting rights in this country, largely to the benefit of the Labour Party. Their disillusion at the Labour Government's attitude during and after the recent Cyprus crisis has led to a considerable dilemma for many, and it remains to be seen whether or not the Labour Party can still hope to command their support. Following 1974, there were signs of a dawning realisation of their voting power in the constituencies where they are most numerous. In at least one case known to me a Conservative candidate may well owe his narrow majority to his active support in Parliament for the Greek Cypriots both during and after the Cyprus crisis.

Voluntary Associations

A wide variety of Greek Cypriot voluntary associations exist
in Britain. Some, such as the Cypriot Brotherhood and the
Cyprus Communist Party pre-date the main influx of Cypriot
immigrants. Others have sprung up in large numbers since
then, many of them village clubs, often based on a cafe or
restaurant owned by a member of their former village. The
ideal of most of these village-based associations is to assist
the residents left behind in Cyprus. Though this does not
always happen in practice, some have made substantial
contributions—churches, youth centres, sports fields—to their
home villages.

A wide variety of sports clubs, youth clubs, parents associations, social and cultural clubs and student associations
also exist. Some aim to be free of overt political alliance but
most are associated with the politics of the 'Left' or the
'Right'—just as most Cypriot villages have their Left-wing
and Right-wing coffee shops.

It is evident that members often use office in these associations as a 'training ground' for active participation in the
institutions of the wider society, especially those members
who have political ambitions. Some leaders, through education, status, and language fluency, move easily within both
an ethnic environment and the wider society. These people
tend to act as 'brokers' for other members, for example in
dealing with the complexities of the welfare state or with
Local Authority bureaucracy. The reward of leadership in
such ethnically specific groups seems to rest largely in being,
as it were, a big fish in a small pond.

Emigration and the Home Community

While a knowledge of the more formal institutions and
associations established in Britain is important for understanding the nature of Greek Cypriot settlement, the fact
remains that the majority of immigrants do not in fact involve
themselves in political or in other community activities.
Instead they order their lives within the boundaries of family

and work ties. Many are little interested in building a 'British Cypriot community'. They see themselves rather as trans-planted members of their Cyprus village, and as individual family units struggling to achieve an acceptable standard of material comfort. Their view of the immigration process is highly personalised, and their occupational, living, and social experiences depend less on any community structure than upon the personal networks they have both here and in Cyprus among relatives and co-villagers.

Let us turn then to the other end of the migration to under-stand more of their social background. I refer here particularly to the two Cypriot villages in which I carried out fieldwork, villages which I shall call by the pseudonyms of Agraia and Thalassia. In 1973 Agraia had a population of 1,250 divided among 264 households; Thalassia's population was 807 in 241 households. These are average-sized villages in Cyprus.

Agraia had experienced only a moderate amount of emigra-tion. The village was made up predominantly of agricultural small-holders, landless workers, labourers and craftsmen, the sort of groups that normally figure heavily among the immigrants to this country. However, Agraia was near both a British base and a large, rapidly developing urban complex. Thus villagers were able to find jobs within a reasonable distance of home. Nevertheless, of the total population, 46 had adult emigrant children and 116 had siblings living abroad, mostly in England.

Thalassia was more typical of Cypriot villages with high rates of emigration. It was a poorer village in agricultural terms and also distant from any developing urban area. Proportionately more of its children had left the village to seek work either in the towns of Cyprus or abroad. It had a long history of emigration, to America, to Britain and more recently to Australia and Canada. Few of its 241 households did not have close relations abroad and, again, most of these are in Britain.

For both villages, farming had long since ceased to be the major occupation of the majority of its economically active inhabitants. Most men worked outside the village, leaving by bus in the morning and returning in the evening. As is quite widespread now in Cyprus, those who owned a little land, or an orchard, worked it on a part-time basis.

However, possession of quantities of land continued to be important in terms of village wealth and status. While the emigrants were not found to come entirely from landless families or families with small, non-viable holdings, this was largely the case. In Agraia village I recorded the genealogies over four adult generations of five family groups classified by the villages as 'poor', and five family groups classified as 'rich'. From the 'poor' genealogies thirty individuals and their families had left the village and gone to live abroad. Only five individuals had farming as their main occupation. From the five 'rich' genealogies only ten individuals and their families had emigrated abroad. Sixty had farming as their main occupation.

Although people emigrated for a wide variety of reasons—political, personal and idiosyncratic as well as economic—a fairly standard picture of the most usual type of emigrant of the 1950s and early 1960s began to emerge. This was a young man, often already married and with the beginnings of a young family. He had only elementary school education and no formal training. He had little or no land, certainly not enough from which to make a full-time living, nor was his wife able to contribute a substantial dowry. Aspiring to a better standard of living, he felt frustrated and restricted by the lack of opportunity in Cyprus. News of job opportunities in Britain reached home from relatives already abroad, many of whom promised to help prospective emigrants get established. Some young men arrived as bachelors, some brought their young families with them, many others set out to establish themselves in accommodation and employment before sending for their wives and children.

The Emigrants' Links with their Home Villages

A few emigrants, especially single men who had left in the early years, before large-scale emigration, and those who had left in the wake of political or sexual scandal, were completely lost to the village. In some cases nobody, not even their parents, have heard from them in years. However, most emigrants maintained close links with their families. News of their exploits was passed regularly to other villagers, particularly if they were thought to be doing well abroad and were therefore a source of pride to their parents. Several came back to the village after a false start abroad, only to be overcome by the same frustrations which caused them to leave in the first place. Second-time emigrants usually stay abroad permanently.

Cash remittances are usually sent back on a fairly regular basis to assist ageing parents. These are rarely large sums, averaging £5 to £10 a month, but this is enough to supplement the local income. Often during the course of my fieldwork, when I enquired as to the exact whereabouts of children abroad, the latest address would be shown to me from the back of a registered envelope in which the most recent cash remittance had arrived. In earlier years relatives would often send parcels of Cypriot foodstuffs abroad though this is less common now that a variety of groceries exist in Britain to supply such needs. Any villager that travels to England is armed with a list of addresses of relatives and neighbours' relatives to be visited, and laden with a variety of presents and messages to be distributed.

Especially in recent years, with the growing prosperity of Cypriots here and the increase in air travel, the volume of traffic between Britain and Cyprus has been growing steadily. Parents and siblings coming to visit those of their family established here; Cypriots from London returning on holiday to their villages in Cyprus. A host of small-scale Cypriot travel agents in London offer special 'ethnic fares' for Cypriots returning by air for a limited holiday period to Cyprus. The population of some small villages with heavy out-migration may be doubled during the holiday period. I witnessed a telling example of this in Thalassia village where the influx of holiday visitors from Britain, America, and Canada was so great at one point that it was almost impossible to find a place to stay.

Many emigrants have invested financially in Cyprus, most often by buying a plot of land or a holiday house, not necessarily in their own villages but more often in a rapidly developing tourist area near the sea. Before the 1974 invasion of Cyprus, Cypriot papers in Britain were full of advertisements for land, flats, or houses which could be purchased by instalments.

Accurate statistics on temporary visits of Cypriot emigres, and of investment by emigrants in Cyprus, are almost impossible to gather. However the Cyprus Report for 1972 indicates that, of 178,598 visitors to Cyprus, at least 15 per cent were visiting Cypriots who had originally emigrated to other countries. For the same period 67,598 Cypriots travelled abroad, 17.2 per cent of them to the United Kingdom. While many of these visits were undoubtedly for professional, government, or business reasons, it is fair to assume that a good proportion were made by people visiting kin in Britain. Similarly private remittances from abroad, *excluding* capital investment, are estimated by the Bank of Cyprus to have grown steadily from £2.5 million in 1958 to £6.8 million in 1972, though this of course includes all countries in which there are Cypriot expatriots.

Thus letters, food parcels, remittances and, more recently, visits and capital investment, have served to maintain links between the emigrants and their home country. Visits to Cyprus with their family often have a profound effect, positive or negative, on British-born Cypriots. Many feel moved to identify with the beautiful island and the relatives they find there, and are inspired to achieve a better standard of spoken Greek. Others are alienated by language difficulties and the restrictions on their freedom of action required by the relatively strict moral codes of village life.

The Villagers in London

Relations between immigrants in Britain reflect, in many ways, the social conditions that prevailed in the village at the time of their departure. Thalassia had fewer discrepancies in the size of land-holding and a higher rate of village endogamy. It had also managed to contain its political factionalism rather better. It showed more marked patterns of chain migration and a closer contact between co-villagers in Britain. Agraia, on the other hand, had considerable discrepancies in wealth, a higher rate of out-marriage, and was riven by political factionalism. The links in Britain between former members of Agraia village were looser, with the main interaction being betwen those already related through kinship, marriage, or fictive kinship. There was no special attempt to employ or work with fellow villagers on that principle alone, nor to marry one's children to co-villagers.

A loose but effective gossip network is the primary means by which former villagers keep in touch, even over a period of twenty years. Before 1974, holiday trips back to the village also yielded a great deal of knowledge about contemporaries, from the relatives left behind.

In the case of both villages, the reactions of the second generation are harder to understand. Most seem preoccupied with the question of Cypriot versus English identity rather than with maintaining ties to any particular village in Cyprus. How they react to parental tales of village life depends largely on whether the parents' view of the village was positive or negative, and on the general atmosphere in the family. Again, a holiday trip back to the village puts 'flesh' on the old stories and often has a dramatic effect on attitudes. Yet on the whole, the tourist spots of the island have more appeal for second generation visitors than out-of-the-way villages.

Social Change and the Second Generation

Although the second generation of Greek Cypriots retain, on the whole, their sense of ethnic identity, there have been, as I have already indicated, considerable modifications in their practices and values. Perhaps the most significant changes taking place are those relating to engagement, marriage, and the dowry.

On the question of marriage, nearly all the second generation Greek Cypriots of marriageable age that I spoke to said that they would prefer to marry another Cypriot. All said that they would have 'more in common'. This seemed to mean not only that they shared the same sort of background and problems, but also that they had a common set of values surrounding marriage and the family which they felt to be different from those of their British contemporaries. Although young people speak out against arranged marriages, when it comes to their own courtship many are prepared to accept the tradition as long as they feel their opinions on the matter are given adequate representation. It is often felt that a mistaken choice will have time to reveal itself during the engagement period. There is a growing tendency here for engagements not to be blessed by the Church, as in Cyprus, but simply to be agreed upon by the two families concerned and celebrated by a secular engagement party. This of course makes them much easier to break and, of necessity, less shame and dishonour comes to be attached to the broken engagement. It is not at all unknown now for the system to be completely abused, to the distress of older Cypriots, and be used by the young simply as a means to go out freely with a member of the opposite sex. Because of the high value placed on virginity and 'good reputation', Cypriot girls are very restricted in activities outside the home. Some see an engagement arranged by their parents as the only hope of leading a life similar in its freedom to their British contemporaries.

Registry Office marriage is also becoming more common in Britain, and has the character of a half-way marriage. Not only is it not a 'true' marriage in Cypriot terms, but it is also considered less stable. The commitment is felt to be less binding and the possibility of easy civil divorce is felt to leave the door open to retreat and remarriage. 'They have only gone to the Register' is a phrase of disapprobation in the Greek Cypriot community. If the match is felt to be sound, or there are children involved, then a great deal of pressure may be brought by relatives to have the marriage solemnised in Church.

In marked contrast to what is happening in Cyprus, the system of a formal dowry is beginning to disappear in Britain. This may be partly contingent on the changes in engagement and marriage ritual outlined above, but more probably it has roots in the social background of the immigrants themselves. Most came from the poor sections of Cypriot society. They may themselves have received very little in the way of dowry on marriage. Some of the early male immigrants who returned to Cyprus to find wives were more than willing to take a wife without a dowry. Property in a remote village was of little practical use to them with their new economic interests in Britain. It was the ongoing earning power of women here that became of overwhelming importance. It is through their work, rather than their dowry, that Greek Cypriot wives in Britain provide the foundations of their families' economic success.

But while most Greek Cypriots in this country display a rather negative attitude towards the custom of dowry, all believe that it is a parent's duty to help the child get established at marriage. All also believe that this help is probably more important for a daughter. As long as it is not formalised as a condition of marriage, most parents are prepared to help quite substantially in setting up a new couple's independent household. Though this could in effect be seen as constituting an informal dowry system, there is little of the attitude, prevalent in Cyprus, that the parents ultimate status rests on how well they have provided for their children. The feeling is, rather, that once the foundations are established the children should take care of themselves.

Conclusion

Why do Greek Cypriots in Britain maintain such a strong sense of ethnic identity? Studies of ethnic groups in the New World and in Africa (see e.g., Cohen 1969; Glazer and Moynihan 1975; Hannerz 1974) have suggested a wide variety of factors which may be involved. Two which are frequently mentioned are physical proximity or boundedness, the ghetto being the extreme form of this, and the monopolisation by the ethnic group of a particular niche in the overall economy.

While it is true that Cypriots have tended to cluster in certain boroughs of London, and that some streets are dominated by Cypriot shops and restaurants, nevertheless they are still a very scattered minority. Moreover, evidence from other, smaller, towns suggests that proximity has little to do with identity and interaction. Some small British seaside resorts have only a handful of Cypriots as permanent residents running cafes and restaurants. For a large part of the year these Cypriots mix with the indigenous residents and cater for British tourists. Yet, in the winter season when the restaurants are closed, these families interact largely with each other, though most spend a great deal of time in London or other centres where they visit kin, attend weddings, and catch up on news and events.

Again, while it is true that Cypriots have tended to specialise in catering and dressmaking, they by no means monopolise these trades. Greek Cypriots constitute just one of many ethnic categories engaged in the same area of endeavour. This is not to say that working in a Cypriot enterprise has no effect on one's sense of ethnic identity. Obviously the Greek Cypriot woman who leaves her home each day to work as a machinist in a Cypriot dress-making factory, who sews and gossips alongside other Greek Cypriot women, who listens to the non-stop Greek music piped through the factory, and who stops at the nearby Greek Cypriot shop on her way home, has little reason to feel that she is other than a Cypriot working in a foreign country. But this cannot be used as support for an argument which reasons that the exclusive occupation of an economic niche is what gives a people the motive power to maintain their ethnic identity.

The social norms and values which are so important in any people's sense of identity, may reinforce the distinctiveness of that identity if, as with the Greek Cypriot immigrants, they are felt to be superior to values current in the host society. As I have already indicated, Greek Cypriot social values focus principally on the nuclear family and the way individuals carry out their allotted roles within it. The notions of what constitutes a good husband or wife, father or mother, son or daughter, are fairly clear to all. People judge each other according to strict moral and economic criteria. A commonly heard reason for not carrying through some planned but untypical act is: 'I was embarrassed' or, more properly, 'I was ashamed'. The use of this verb, derived from *ntrope* 'shame', a key Greek concept, carries with it the weight of judgment of one's fellows. Greek Cypriots in Britain form, in the anthropological sense, a 'moral community'. This is not of course to say that everybody lives up to the ideal standards, for many do not. Even high status (which for the immigrant is based largely on wealth, education of one's children, and general 'success') does not protect an individual from communal criticism.

But I believe that two main factors emerge out of many as central to the maintenance of Greek Cypriot ethnic identity:

One is the large proportion of married couples and nuclear families who emigrated as a group. Another is the fact that the bulk of immigrants arrived over a limited period between 1955 and 1962. The presence of whole families kept the young men under a certain degree of moral control. Married relatives were almost always on the spot ready to provide, even if only occasionally, a Cypriot home background, and to help in finding suitable brides when the time came. This contrasts with the London Maltese, described by Dench (1975) as a case in which 'ethnic consciousness' was rapidly eroded. Significantly, the Maltese immigrants were predominantly single young men.

As the Greek Cypriots arrived in large numbers, an ethnic service industry developed simultaneously. A cluster of Cypriot restaurants and groceries were established to serve their needs, and the small family businesses expanded rapidly to employ them. The development of the dressmaking industry, which absorbed the majority of the economically active women, also meant that single girls began to arrive here to work under the care of relatives, thus making an ethnic marriage market even more feasible. Moreover, the ethnic economy is still strong enough to absorb a substantial proportion of the second generation school leavers.

Evidence from my research suggests that before Greek Cypriots began to arrive in substantial numbers, two disparate trends were developing. One was the 'ethnic disappearance' of young men due to marriage or co-habitation with English women and the Anglicisation of names. The other was an opposite trend, the reinforcement of ties with home villages as men returned or sent for suitable brides. However, as the Cypriot population grew in size, and as the sex ratio became more balanced, greater opportunities for ethnic marriage developed in Britain. Young men are no longer so frequently 'lost' to non-Cypriot women. Where they do marry foreign brides, the tendency is often, in fact, for the wives to be absorbed by the Cypriot culture. The marriage network for the second generation of Greek Cypriots is very largely based in this country. Since the original immigrants came from many different parts of Cyprus, patterns of marriage are increasingly pan-Cypriot.

The practices and values of the second generation rest, in

effect, somewhere between the two cultural systems—Greek Cypriot and British—to which they have been exposed. Cypriots in London often speak to each other in a creolised language, a mixture of colloquial English and Cypriot Greek liberally sprinkled with the Hellenised terms invented by the first generation to describe aspects of the dressmaking and restaurant trades.

The second generation are now marrying and raising their own children. It remains to be seen how these children are socialised and whether, in fact, the third generation will continue to maintain a sense of distinctiveness like their parents.

ACKNOWLEDGEMENTS

The research described in this chapter was financed by the Social Science Research Council through the London School of Economics and Political Science. Thanks are due to my colleague at the L.S.E., Dr. Peter Loizos, who was joint applicant for the research funds and who provided advice and assistance throughout. Thanks are also due to Dr. Robin Oakley for useful initial discussions and for making available to me his own valuable unpublished work on Cypriot migration and settlement. The facilities and help provided for me by the Director and staff of the Statistics and Research Department of the Ministry of Finance in Cyprus are gratefully acknowledged, as are those provided by Dr. John Peristiany and the Social Science Research Centre in Nicosia. And finally thanks are due to the very many Cypriots, both in Britain and in Cyprus, who treated me with courtesy and hospitality and who gave many hours of their time to help me.

REFERENCES CITED

Adamantos, Adamos, 1972, The Work of the Cyprus Educational Mission. In *Cyprus Week in Camden 1972*. London.

Cohen, Abner, 1969, *Custom and Politics in Urban Africa*. London: Routledge and Kegan Paul.

Dench, Geoff, 1975, *Maltese in London: A Case Study in the Erosion of Ethnic Consciousness*. London: Routledge and Kegan Paul.

Desai, Rashmi, 1963, *Indian Immigrants in Britain*. London: Oxford University Press.

Dowling, Theodore and Edwin Fletcher, 1915, *Hellenism in England*. London: The Faith Press.

George, Vic and Geoff Millerson, 1967, 'The Cypriot Community in London'. *Race* 8:277–92.

Glazer, Nathan and Daniel P. Moynihan, 1975, 'Introduction'. In *Ethnicity: Theory and Experience* (ed.) N. Glazer and D. Moynihan. Cambridge: Harvard University Press.

Hannerz, Ulf, 1974, 'Ethnicity and Opportunity in Urban America'. In *Urban Ethnicity* (ed.) A Cohen. London: Tavistock Publications.

Loizos, Peter, 1975, *The Greek Gift: Politics in a Cypriot Village*. Oxford: Basil Blackwell.

Oakley, Robin, 1970, 'The Cypriots in Britain'. *Race Today* 2: 99–102.

Oakley, Robin, 1971, 'Cypriot Migration and Settlement in Britain'. Unpublished D.Phil. Thesis. University of Oxford.

Peristiany, John, 1965, 'Honour and Shame in a Cypriot Highland Village'. In *Honour and Shame: The Values of Mediterranean Society* (ed.) J. Peristiany. London: Weidenfeld and Nicholson.

CHAPTER 11

SARAH LADBURY

The Turkish Cypriots: Ethnic Relations in London and Cyprus

The nature of the relationship between an immigrant group and its home society is a theme which has only recently become the focus of immigrant studies undertaken in Britain. Attention has been paid either to the ethnic organisation of the immigrant group in Britain or to the nature of contact between immigrant and 'host' society. These latter 'race relations' studies tend to share certain characteristics: the sample of immigrant groups chosen by the researcher (they are usually 'coloured'); a subjective 'problem solving' approach; and the consequent delineation of practical policies which aim to bring about what are considered to be ideal race contact situations. 'Integration', 'assimilation', 'absorption' are accordingly concepts frequently met with in such studies (e.g. Allen 1971; Banton 1966; Krausz 1971; Patterson 1969; Rose 1969). Indeed, given that ethnicity is a relatively new concept in the social sciences, and particularly in its application to this context, the race relations approach has undoubtedly been the main influence, and a rather restricting one, on the *types* of problems explored with reference to immigrant groups. Usually fieldwork is only carried out in Britain, and the nature of the relationship through time between the migrant and his home society is only deemed relevant to the degree that it continues to influence the rate of migration, or else affects settlement patterns and the type of residential unit set up by the migrant in Britain.

Yet an equal acquaintance with the home society and the immigrant population in Britain presents the researcher with a much greater range of problems for investigation than those explored by the majority of studies referred to above.

One can, for example, imagine a continuum of migrant/home relations. At one extreme the relationship will be characterised by complete interdependence: the home society will be financially dependent on the migrants' remittances, and the migrants will conversely be dependent on the home society for women, status and prestige, and perhaps also for continued acceptance in terms of native moral standards, such as might be necessary for their reintegration when they return. Watson's work with the Chinese in Britain (1975) would seem to suggest that they most nearly exemplify this extreme; not unnaturally his study attempts to explain why and how this encapsulation of traditions is being brought about.

At the other extreme of the continuum one can imagine a relationship between immigrant and home society of complete independence: with no financial ties and an eradication, however gradual, of emotional ones, so that eventually the two become distinct. The migrant group either assumes an identity of its own or gradually merges into the majority population. Dench (1975) describes how this process of absorption is occurring among the Maltese in Britain and his study consequently focuses on the factors which appear to be responsible for what is, in effect, the gradual loss of ethnic distinctiveness.

But for most immigrant groups in Britain, the closeness of the tie with the home society falls somewhere between these two extremes. Thus the immigrant group, while not losing its ties with the homeland, may still develop a dynamism of its own. The emerging norms and values will constitute an identity which might be described as 'ethnic' since they will have developed in opposition to those held by the majority. At the same time they will cease to be an exact replica of those held by the home society, for they represent an adaptation of traditional patterns to the new environment. In such a situation the relationship between migrant and home society becomes more complex, the tie more diffuse. Migrant and home society norms no longer back each other up, thereby reinforcing tradition; the ways in which each continues to influence the other are harder to delineate.

The relationship between Turks in London—the term 'Turk' will be used to refer to Turkish Cypriots unless otherwise stated—and Turks in Cyprus typifies the complexity of this in-between pattern. The two groups are autonomous in a way that the Chinese of London and rural Hong Kong are not, yet the Turkish Cypriot population in London is in no way losing its identity as a distinct ethnic group as are the Maltese. Perhaps the most significant point of difference between Turks in London and the Chinese (or even the West Indian Montserratian migrants of Philpott's study, 1973) is that Turks in Cyprus are not financially dependent on migrant remittances for their livelihood. Indeed, migration is not an economic necessity for the majority but a matter of personal choice for the individual. Perhaps in the early days of migration during the 1950s, and particularly in times of drought or other economic crisis in Cyprus, remittances may have been sent on a regular basis. But now, although gifts of money may be sent to relatives in Cyprus from time to time, the society as a whole does not depend on them; nor do individuals expect their relatives in London to support them financially. The only exceptions are the very old who may expect support if all their children have migrated. How and why this has come about will be discussed in more detail presently; for now it is enough to state that Turkish Cypriots see London as an alternative place to live and, more importantly, a good place to make money.

In these circumstances, where the migrant population is established as an independent and self-sustaining community, different influences may affect both the migrants and the home society so that considerable differences develop between them. This paper will discuss one sphere in which such differences are noticeable. Here I want to concentrate on intergroup, and specifically interethnic, relations and on the attitudes that Turkish Cypriots have towards certain other groups with whom they come into contact. It should be possible to illustrate how the 'environment'—political, economic, social, and ideological—influences ethnic relations. Thus Turkish attitudes to one group in London are not necessarily identical to those held towards the same group in Cyprus. The purpose of this paper is to analyse and account for these differences.

The Concept of Ethnicity

In this essay the Turkish Cypriot population in both London and Cyprus are referred to as an 'ethnic group'. Since the term 'ethnicity' is variously defined in both popular and academic speech, its connotations in this particular ethnographic context will be briefly summarised. Although no attempt will be made to review the literature on ethnicity more generally, it should be noted that Abner Cohen's work in this field (1969, 1971, 1974a, 1974b) has been a major influence on my own research.

The label 'ethnic group' is here applied to a population whose members interact on the basis of shared values and a common culture, aspects of which they stress in order to differentiate themselves from others who do not share them. This emphasis on a distinctive and shared culture—which may include language, religious beliefs, myths, rituals, a moral code and so on—is important here because, lacking the bureaucratic structures of statehood, it is the only way in which group members may be recognised. But, although aspects of group culture are the signs or expressions of group distinctiveness, they are not themselves the cause of it. In other words, an emphasis on certain cultural features explains how, but not why, individuals continue to stress their ethnic status. To understand this one must look for the advantages, or disadvantages as the case may be, which accrue to the individual if he emphasises his ethnic identity. For example, we learn from Dench (1975) that it is in the interests of the average Maltese man in Britain *not* to stress the fact that he is Maltese when in the company of Britons, since the latter, he feels, associate all Maltese men with vice and corruption. This belief also makes him unwilling to fraternise openly with other Maltese, or to adhere to the traditions which could, in another situation, have become distinguishing marks of Malteseness. The result is that the Maltese population in London might, within a short time, no longer be distinguishable as an ethnic category. On the other hand, numerous examples could be cited of ethnic groups whose political or economic monopoly of a scarce resource means that a continued stress on those traits which are seen to characterise their distinctiveness is essential if their ethnic monopoly, and consequently the status and/or livelihood of individual members, is to be maintained (e.g., Cohen 1969, 1971; Moerman 1965; Parkin 1974; Orans 1965).

Thus, implicit in the use of the ethnic label to describe the Turkish Cypriot population in London and Cyprus—and, it follows, to distinguish Greek Cypriots and mainland Turks in the two countries—is the recognition that (a) the group is informally organised, (b) its members share, or think they share, a common cultural heritage and value system, and (c) individuals are continuing to stress or to play down their ethnic identity for a reason. They may, in fact, have no understanding that they are actually maintaining or diminishing the distinctiveness of the group in the process.

Cyprus and England: The Migrant and his Migration

The field research on which this paper is based was largely carried out in London between April 1975 and October 1976. Two months were spent in northern (Turkish) Cyprus in 1976 for the specific purpose of research although the author was familiar with the area before this date, extended visits having been made every year since 1970 to either mainland Turkey or Cyprus.

Cypriot Turks in London are a well-established minority of approximately 40,000. According to Oakley, whose detailed statistical research into Cypriot migration and settlement in Britain is the only thorough study of this kind so far made, fluctuations in the rate of migration since 1950 can be related to a number of factors. Thus in 1960–61, the economic aspirations of Cypriots, raised as a result of their newly won independence, were not fulfilled when the British withdrew, taking with them many well paid jobs on the sovereign bases. Disappointment at the lack of opportunities provided the stimulus for migration. The magnitude of this movement was a direct result of the favourable economic conditions in Britain at that time, where there were good business prospects for the small-scale entrepreneur (Oakley 1971: 124ff, 206). These migrants of the 1950s and early 1960s have now been living in Britain for at least 15 years; consequently many of those who came as children are now married and starting families of their own.

Most emigration from Cyprus has been to Britain and specifically to London. Indeed there are very few Turks outside Greater London and most of these live in the Home Counties, though there are small settlements in some other towns, notably Birmingham and Manchester. Census figures have not distinguished between Greek and Turkish Cypriots, but by considering other sources Oakley estimated that by 1966 the Turkish Cypriot population of Greater London was fairly evenly distributed north and south of the river, to the east of the main areas of Greek settlement, Camden and Islington (1971:261ff). The 1971 Census indicates that settlement since 1966 has progressed further north of these two areas. The borough of Haringey has now become the largest centre of Cypriot settlement (Kohler 1974:10). Indeed it was largely in this area that the author's fieldwork was carried out. But despite this northward expansion, the Turkish population remains relatively scattered, a fact which has important implications for group organisation and communication. In some boroughs, especially those in South London with very few Greek Cypriots, five or six Turkish households may live close together but be cut off from the main areas of Cypriot settlement north of the river and other Turkish enclaves in the south. However, even in Haringey, where there is a considerable Turkish population, it is unusual to find more than three Turkish families in one street. Moreover there is no residential or business district, nor even a cultural or social centre in the form of a hall or central meeting place. One North London street (in Newington Green) boasts a Turkish coffee shop, a Victorian terraced house converted into a mosque specifically for Turks, and two shops selling Turkish pop records and paperbacks. Several windows advertise forthcoming Turkish films which are shown at two North London cinemas at weekends. Younger people come here to buy the latest records imported from Turkey or posters of Turkish singers, for example.

The small mosque is only full on Fridays, the Moslem religious day, though prayers are held there every evening. This is indicative of a more general phenomenon: only a tiny minority of Turkish Cypriots in London, men or women, make any concession to formal religion, either by attending a mosque or by making *namaz* (prayers) in their homes. A small, influential group, the Turkish Islamic Association, does have plans to convert a larger building or a church into a Turkish mosque and money has been promised by another Moslem country for this purpose. But there are problems with choosing an accessible site for the mosque, and coming to an agreement with the leaders of other Turkish Cypriot organisations who would prefer the money to be used for an all-purpose community centre.

Thus, neither organised religion nor other forms of organisational activity (about which more will be said presently) provide a centralising focus for Turkish Cypriots in London. If one is to find such a focus one must turn to the ties of kinship and affinity and to the interdependence of neighbours, all of which link individuals and provide the means whereby Turks in London retain, as far as possible, their self-sufficiency as an ethnic group.

While a detailed discussion of the social organisation of Turkish Cypriots in Britain is not possible in this essay, one point is worthy of note as it provides an example of the independent nature of Turkish settlement here. In some rural-urban migration studies (Suzuki 1966; Little 1970) the continuity of village ties in the town is discussed. Special attention is paid to the mutual aid associations set up by rural migrants in the town for the benefit of their co-villagers. There are no comparable associations for Turks in London, though it seems that there were in the early days of migration when an individual was not assured of finding some of his kin already resident here. Now, however, marriages are not arranged between members of families who originally migrated from the same village in Cyprus, nor do non-kin based ties seem to have been maintained long after the move to London. Rather, certain kin relationships have been strengthened and completely new relationships formed between individuals who now relate, not on the basis of where they once lived in Cyprus, but on the basis of their present status. Thus, a Turkish Cypriot family will quickly come to know and depend on other Turkish families when it moves into a neighbourhood and the most relevant kin become those who live nearest and who visit most frequently.

Family life too persists in both London and Cyprus without any assistance from relatives abroad. Indeed, it seems that even in the early days of migration, young Turkish men were able to find wives in Britain. Since there were many more Turkish men than women here at that time, this apparently resulted in a greater incidence of out-marriage, most of which was to British girls, than is usual today. Nowadays, however, there is a balanced sex ratio and in London both sexes agree that it is preferable to marry someone who has also been brought up in Britain, as there is a better chance of mutual understanding. This is not to say that marriages are never arranged between London and Cyprus. Indeed a family will not hesitate to send a son or daughter to relatives in Cyprus if there is some difficulty in finding him or her a spouse here. The mother country thus acts as a safety valve and is especially useful when there are problems of marriageability. In the case of a daughter this may mean that her reputation has suffered. Sons may have difficulty if they are not especially good looking, in which case the fact that he lives in London might be enough to ensure him success in the Cypriot marriage stakes. Similarly young girls in Cyprus will not refuse an invitation to stay with relatives in London if they are unmarried, in order to 'have a look around'. For the most part though, marriages are arranged in the country of residence.

The self-sustaining nature of the Turkish family in Cyprus and London is connected with the financial independence of the two populations. Since in London it is the nuclear family and not the unattached working male who constitutes the normal, or at least desirable, residential unit, wages are spent and capital is invested for the benefit of the immediate family. Money is not remitted for the benefit of more distant relatives. The justification for this practical attitude is that anyone can migrate if he wants to, and that therefore, if one's relatives have chosen to stay in Cyprus and are not now rich, they have only themselves to blame. It is indeed true that those who have come to London represent a cross section of the Cypriot Turkish population. Although Oakley notes that the original migrants tended to be service and white collar workers rather than farmers (1971:79), it now seems that everyone from government officials to the poorest of villagers has relations in London. Indeed approximately one in six

Cypriots is now in Britain (Oakley 1970:99) and every adult individual has probably at some time weighed the pros and cons of migration. The movement itself has been relatively simple, since it can be accomplished by plane or overland by car and boat. In either case, arrangements could be made through one of the many Turkish travel agents in London. Formerly employers would arrange travel for prospective employees. Immigration controls have greatly increased the complexities involved and it is now difficult to arrange passage *in absentia*.

Thus there has been an element of choice in who has migrated and when, together with a tendency of most migrants to be joined by their wives and children or to establish a family in Britain. Moreover it seems unlikely that now, despite considerable contact between Turks in London and Cyprus, the majority of those who have migrated will return permanently to Cyprus. Many long-term settlers actually admit that they do not mind if they never return to Cyprus to live. Similarly, there are numerous reasons why the second generation may not want to 'return', or may find it difficult to do so. To them Cyprus is a foreign country which they might have visited only once or twice. Those who return normally do so to retire or to invest their savings in a small business once the children have married and become independent. Usually, however, ties and responsibilities continue into old age: parents become grandparents and, as such, they continue to play an important functional role in family affairs. Similarly, despite the comings and goings of individuals for holidays and business, the vast majority of Turks in Cyprus will now almost certainly never emigrate. The rate of migration has been declining since 1962 according to Oakley (1971:28) and one would expect the events of 1974 and the stricter enforcement of the British Immigration Acts to stem any further movement.

The separateness that each population has attained can be illustrated in a number of ways. My main concern is with ethnicity, though the institution of marriage could, if dealt with in depth, equally well exemplify the sort of adaptations that are being made by Turks in London and Cyprus. The word 'adaptation' is particularly appropriate here. For example, the differences discernible in the form of marriage in London do not represent changes in attitudes towards marriage itself or attempts to copy English customs so much as practical compromises in the face of certain environmental factors. Thus, although it is customary in Cyprus to have a lapse of nearly a year between becoming officially registered as married (*nikâh*) and becoming man and wife on the occasion of the wedding feast (*dügün*), in London the two occasions are often held close together, sometimes on the same day or within a month of each other. This is because it is impractical for a young man in London to attempt to save up and buy a house before he marries. Furthermore it is not always necessary because council housing is usually obtainable, even if this means staying with in-laws initially. Thus, the gap between the civil and public ceremonies, which is traditionally a time of saving and preparation in Cyprus, tends to be considerably shortened in London—if not dispensed with altogether. And it follows that although the two events are still thought of as being quite distinct, the celebrations connected with the first are modified and it often becomes a small family affair. This is largely for financial reasons, as few families can afford to hold two large-scale events, each involving several hundred invited guests, within a short period.

Of course, all this is not to suggest that the marriage ceremony in Cyprus has remained static. But here change is more obviously an attempt by an urban educated minority to become more 'Western'. And, as such, this represents a conscious desire to implement new forms rather than to readapt old ones.

Internal Divisions in Turkish Cypriot Society

Before we go on to consider relations between Turkish and Greek Cypriots in London and in Cyprus it is important to make clear the *level* of Turkish Cypriot society involved. For, although the dichotomy between townsman and villager is much less obvious in Cyprus than it is in Turkey, there nonetheless exists an urban educated elite. Members of this elite run the Turkish Cypriot administration in Cyprus and the various ethnic associations in London. These associations are not only run by, but also tend to cater for, this educated middle class. Some came over from Cyprus especially for the purpose of setting up such organisations. But, with a few notable exceptions, this group has very little influence on the vast majority of ordinary working class families in London. Although the main Turkish Cypriot movement here (the *Cemiyet*—the 'Association') claims to be the voice of Turkish Cypriots in London, it only represents the Turkish Cypriot population insofar as it receives foreign visitors on their behalf. Its publications (in English and Turkish) also represent the views of those who take the official government line on political issues, including the Cyprus problem itself and the question of settlement. Most Turks in London have heard of the association and may have benefited from its activities (e.g., Turkish lessons for children, dinner and dance functions on national holidays), but they almost certainly have had no more contact with it than this. Moreover, they are unlikely to be aware of other such organisations, like the Turkish Islamic Association, the Ladies Association, the Turkish Arts Society as well as several overtly political organisations run largely by students.

These student organisations are exclusive in a different way, due to their political philosophies which tend to be extremely Left—so much so that some organisations have to meet in secret for fear of recriminations from Cyprus or from right-wing factions of the Turkish community in London. Although nucleated and well organised (here we might mention the small but cohesive Turkish Communist Party), their overt politicisation makes them somewhat irrelevant to the older, more conservative settlers as well as to the majority of second generation London Turks. Most of the British-born are now out of touch with the complexities of the Cyprus situation and the internal wranglings of Turkish and Cypriot politics. Moreover, the continual disagreements between the individual organisers of these associations and their apparent inability to provide a unified and stable organisation which can represent group interests as a whole means that the majority remain unaware of their respective aims and activities, and in some cases of their actual existence.

This internal division makes generalisations about Turkish 'attitudes' or 'interests' especially difficult. For this reason I will restrict my discussion to the majority of ordinary working class Turkish Cypriots in London, thereby excluding the educated and politically active groups mentioned above. Indeed most people probably have very little objective awareness of the Turkish Cypriot population in London. For the majority, interaction with other Turks is frequent but fairly limited in its scope. Apart from weddings, visits to the Turkish cinema, and other extraordinary activities, the individual's day-to-day relations with other Turks are restricted to his kin, his Turkish neighbours and work mates. From these people every service can usually be obtained, be it a case of finding a job, a husband, or someone to mend the roof. They constitute the individual's social universe in the context of which his behaviour as a Turk is judged, and his attitudes to non-Turks are formed.

Interethnic Relations: Turkish and Greek Cypriots

As has already been stated, the peak years of Cypriot migration to Britain for both Turks and Greeks were 1960 and 1961. Oakley estimates that in these two years just over 25,000 Cypriots migrated to the United Kingdom (1971:28). However by 1962, numbers had already dropped to pre-1960 levels (4.000 p.a. maximum), and they continued to decline steadily through the 1960s. Even by 1963 then, when intercommunal fighting broke out in Cyprus, the majority of would-be emigrants were already settled in Britain. Thus the vast majority of Turks now resident here did not personally experience the hostility and conflict which characterised the period between 1963 and 1974 in Cyprus, either because they had migrated to Britain before that date, or because they were subsequently born, or at least brought up, in Britain. Cyprus 1963 also saw the beginning of a physical separation between the two communities: the Turks moved into enclaves in order to better protect themselves and more adequately obstruct Greek desires for *enosis* (union with Greece). This separation, together with the economic restrictions placed on Turks between 1963 and 1967, increased feelings of insecurity and allowed resentment to build.

But the emigrant of the 1950s and early 1960s experienced

none of this first hand. He had not migrated from a Turkish enclave, but from a village which may have been ethnically mixed; in any case, as a member of a minority population, he would normally speak Greek as a second language. It was this state of affairs which allowed and encouraged the first Turkish migrants in Britain to turn to Greeks, some of whom were well established in business by that time, for employment and for essential services when there were no Turks available. At the time then, this initial interdependence of the two communities might be seen as the result of a tendency for early settlers to build on pre-existing patterns of relationships in an otherwise alien environment. But why, one might ask, has it continued to the present? For, despite the sensitisation of group feeling at times of particular crisis in Cyprus—during the fighting of 1967 and the war of 1974 for example—Turks have maintained firm work and business relations with Greeks in London.

It may help clarify the problem if we consider the present situation in Cyprus. Since the July 1974 war and particularly since the adoption, in September 1975, of the agreement for an official population exchange, relations between Greeks and Turks on an individual level have been almost non-existent. Though there are reported to be 5,800 Greek Cypriots still in the north (*The Economist*, 4 September 1976:43), the vast majority of these are living in the Karpaz region (the 'panhandle' in the north-east of the island), and entry to this area is strictly controlled by the Turkish military. In a few other villages a handful of Greeks have remained in their homes and live alongside the Turks. Cut off from their kin and the Greek Cypriot majority, their numbers are decreasing as they too move south. There are, therefore, very few Turks in present day Cyprus who have any direct contact with Greeks, and it could be argued that relations are no longer based on ethnic criteria at all since they are conducted through the formal bureaucratic structures of *de facto* statehood. Of primary importance, however, is the fact that there has been *a war*, and this has resulted in an almost complete termination of personal relations between Greeks and Turks on Cyprus.

But it appears that the fluctuating nature of Greek-Turkish relations on Cyprus since 1963 has not had any profound consequences for interethnic relations in Britain. Here Turks have maintained work and business ties with Greeks for several practical reasons. To begin with, there are still not enough Turks in sufficiently varied occupations for them to be ethnically self-reliant, and Greeks continue to be chosen as work mates and business partners. This is partly because the type of relationship established by the early settlers has continued to be economically viable for both groups. It would have been detrimental to their combined interests if, for example, the recent war and consequent partition of the island had caused them to terminate relations in London.

This is not to suggest, however, that Greeks and Turks are interdependent at the group level. Greeks have to turn to Turks much less often than Turks do to Greeks. There are approximately four times as many Greeks in London as Turks. Not only do their greater numbers make them more self-sufficient occupationally, but also the fact that a higher percentage of Greeks own their own businesses means that they are more likely to be employers of Turks, and not their employees. Moreover, the extent of interdependence and the form this takes will vary according to a number of other factors: for example, the percentage of Greeks to Turks in a neighbourhood; the number of years they have lived as neighbours in Britain; the situation in Cyprus at the time— all these will influence the nature of Turkish-Greek relations in London.

Nonetheless interdependence, even if often unequal, does exist between Turks and Greeks as Cypriots and is based in part on shared roles in the work context, which makes discrimination on ethnic grounds untenable. One type of work in which both groups are well established is the clothing industry or rag trade. Here patron-client type relationships are built up between employer and employee, but they develop independently of ethnic status. Indeed, were a factory owner who employed both Greeks and Turks to begin to openly patronise his workers on the basis of their respective ethnic identities rather than according to their skill and efficiency, he could jeopardise his business. Not only would others of the same ethnic identity leave but his reputation as an employer, and his economic viability as a contractor, would suffer. The same arrangement exists in a number of other occupations where one group depends on the other for its patronage or for providing an essential service. Thus one might find a Greek wholesale greengrocer visiting a Turkish family during the evenings and selling on credit; or another calling on Sunday afternoon with carpet catalogues. It is this flexibility in hours and the lack of distinction made on ethnic grounds that ensures these small entrepreneurs a faithful clientèle, Greek and Turk.

On a business level then, and especially in areas inhabited by Greeks and Turks, it would be economically inexpedient for both parties if Turks did not patronise Greek businesses as customers or employees. I would argue that the implicit recognition of this has stopped the various political crises in Cyprus from causing serious conflict between individuals in Britain. (Here we must confine ourselves to individuals; for conflict does exist on the group level as represented by political organisations.) Cultural differences which could have been used to activate political divisions have not been appealed to, at least not by Turks. Instead, cultural familiarity has allowed and encouraged the continuation of interethnic ties. Thus Turks maintain that they shop at the nearest Greek corner store because they eat the same food as Greeks, though in fact most vegetables could just as easily be bought from a West Indian shop, while the staples could be purchased more cheaply at an English supermarket. This element of choice, positively exercised by Turks *for* continued contact, is also partly responsible for the tendency of both groups to remain concentrated in the same types of employment. Shared experience of tailoring and dressmaking in Cyprus encouraged the early settlers to move into the clothing industry in Britain, a niche they have continued to exploit successfully. A preference for self employment has also encouraged Turk and Greek to move into the service industries—catering in particular, but also wholesaling, retailing, hairdressing, shoemaking, minicabbing,—and these occupations have the additional advantage of catering for, and in turn being patronised by, the entire Cypriot population.

However, it is not merely a question of playing down differences so that the basic task of earning a living can continue without interruption. Rather, it is a case of drawing a line which allows for contact and co-operation in one sphere while tabooing contact in another; and thus maintaining ethnic distinctiveness without evoking xenophobic sentiments. For, given the constant interaction of individuals, friendships inevitably develop across the ethnic boundary at school, at work, and between neighbours. In most cases these remain 'public', confined to the classroom, factory, or street. It is rare indeed to find Greek Cypriots visiting Turkish Cypriots in their homes on a purely social basis, even if the families concerned have been acquainted for years. But occasionally, often due to unusual circumstances, relationships do go further than this and it is then that the lines delineating respective ethnic boundaries are drawn with renewed vigour. Not that social condemnation necessarily serves as a corrective to the individuals concerned, but like other forms of punishment, it acts as an example to would-be transgressors.

The effectiveness of such sanctions is attested by the fact that in 18 months of research I have only learned of three marriages between a Greek and a Turkish Cypriot, though I know of several cases where English girls have been successfully incorporated into a Turkish Cypriot family by marrying a son. One of the Turkish-Greek marriages is particularly interesting as it occurred very recently (in September 1976— the other two both took place over fifteen years ago), and the bizarre nature of this event illustrated its uniqueness. The couple, a Turkish girl and a Greek boy, were both in their early twenties. They had both come to London as children and had known each other for eight years prior to marriage. Although both families knew about the friendship, only the girl's parents were informed of the wedding, as it was feared that the groom's family might attempt to disrupt the proceedings if they were to be told. Indeed, when they heard that the wedding had taken place, all relations with their son and his wife were severed. Due partly to the expected communal and familial opposition, the marriage ceremony itself was not held according to either Greek or Turkish tradition, but took place in an English church, neutral ground and the only place where the respective ethnic identities of the couple would not be an issue. Nonetheless, only the bride's kin attended the reception, though several of the groom's Greek friends were present. Apart from these Turks and Greeks, the guests included English, Irish, Scottish, Pakistani, and West Indian friends; while the bride's kin included her Armenian and English in-laws. A Greek band played Greek, Turkish, English and even Spanish songs, though English was the *lingua franca*, at least for all the young people present.

To explain how and why the marriage occurred is beyond the scope of this essay. My aim is merely to stress that it was an occasion for which there were no rules prescribing the form it should take, and that includes the ethnic identity of the guests invited, simply because there were no precedents. It was only due to the independent nature of the girl herself, and her own family's understanding, that the marriage was even conceivable in the first place. Most relationships of this kind are never allowed to get so far, and the problem of marriage to any non-Turk, let alone to a Greek, never arises.

There is no doubt that interethnic association in the wider social environment means that boundaries have to be rigidly drawn at the familial level. The individual Englishwoman can be incorporated into the family as a Turk, but the incorporation of a Greek into a Turkish family, or vice versa, with all the implications this would have for the in-law relationship, is seen as neither socially possible nor ethnically desirable. Group sanctions correspond accordingly, their severity proportional to the extent to which the liaison is perceived as threatening to ethnic distinctiveness.

Ethnicity, as the above example indicates, is a relative and a dynamic phenomenon. That is to say, the nature of the relationship between any two ethnic groups can, over time and in different environments, alter gradually or even be changed suddenly and consciously by the people themselves. Cultural differences which exist, or are perceived to exist, may be played down, emphasised, even created, depending on the nature of the relationship that each is trying to establish with the other. Of course it may happen that a relationship which is ideal for one group is not at all ideal for the other. This is a point which I will return to. For now it should merely be noted that the Greeks with whom I am personally acquainted in London tend to be those with Turkish neighbours, work mates or business associates, and may for this reason be unrepresentative of the majority who come into contact with Turks less often. Nonetheless, by comparing the nature of Turkish Greek relations in London and Cyprus, the dynamic aspect of ethnicity, overlooked in many ethnic studies, can be illustrated.

Interethnic Relations: Cypriot and Mainland Turks

Interestingly, present day Cyprus presents us with another example, complementary in form, of this ethnic dynamism. Here the cultural differences between Cypriot Turk and mainland Turk, non-existent to the unitiated observer, are emphasised and exaggerated by Turkish Cypriots in order to justify their exclusive claim to certain resources which seem to be both scarce and, at present, unjustly distributed. A comparison of Cypriot/mainland Turkish relations in London, though difficult to assess because of their unobtrusive character, nonetheless confirms the importance of local environmental conditions in determining the nature of ethnic relations.

Following the intervention of mainland Turkish forces on behalf of the Turkish Cypriot minority in July 1974, and the finalisation of the boundary which now divides Turkish and Greek Cyprus, there followed a period of population movement. In ones and twos and often with considerable difficulty, those Turks previously resident in the south, about 65,000 in all, moved to the security of the Turkish held north, and the 200,000 or so Greeks who were living north of the new border moved to the south. This migration was eventually completed, at least for the majority, in September 1975 when the official population exchange took place. But whereas Turkish Cypriots had previously constituted less than 20 per cent of the population, they now controlled 40 per cent of the land. It was therefore imperative to increase the population, so that apart from any political objectives, there would be enough labour, both skilled and unskilled, to set the economy on its feet. To this end Turkish Cypriots who had migrated to London, Turkey, Australia, and even Canada were formally invited to return to settle, and were given certain economic incentives to do so (including rent free accommodation for two years and the assurance of a job). Although the Turkish population of Cyprus is now 160,000—an increase of 40,000 on the pre-1974 figure—it is difficult to determine what percentage of this number is made up by these returnees. Certainly the exodus from Britain was not very large, and although the British press (*Sunday Telegraph*, 5 October 1975) reported that, by October 1975, 4,000 Turks had already left Britain for Cyprus, and another 6,000 were expected to follow, it is impossible to know how many of the first group have since returned and how many of the second ever really left. Such figures were not, to my knowledge, based on any actual statistical survey made by Turkish Cypriot officials and the number quoted probably included many holiday makers. Turkish Cypriots in Britain successfully exploit an economic niche that gives them considerable security—security which could not easily be assured in Cyprus, then or now, despite the economic inducements and the promise of opportunities to rebuild businesses left by Greeks.

The vast majority of these migrants are likely to have come from the Turkish mainland. Officially classed as 'returnees' they may, nevertheless, have migrated from Cyprus many generations ago, and in historical perspective their return represents one more phase in an exchange of populations between Turkey and Cyprus which has been going on since the first influx of Turks to the island after the Ottoman conquest in 1571. In consequence, they are no longer distinguishable as Cypriots by their accent or dress. A Cypriot can usually tell a mainlander by his 'clean' pronunciation—which is much admired—whatever part of Turkey he is from. Mainlanders on Cyprus are also conspicuous by their dress: traditional village wear, which the Cypriots have now put aside in preference for more westernised styles. The women wear brightly coloured floral dresses over *shalvar* (long baggy pants) and a headscarf; the men can also usually be identified as mainlanders, if only by their old fashioned suits and cloth caps which replaced the fez in Turkey when the latter was banned by Ataturk in 1925.

But, for the ordinary Turkish Cypriot, neither historical processes nor official terminology justify differentiating between this group of mainland 'returnees' and those who have come ostensibly as a work force and who are officially termed 'seasonal migrant workers'. Just as the so-called 'returnees' do not look or sound like Cypriots, the migrant workers are not seen as being seasonal and their stay, as far as local Cypriots are concerned, is permanent. And this opinion is what matters. It is the actor's interpretation of a situation which determines attitudes and influences behaviour.

Whatever the official justification for their presence in Cyprus, the point to emphasise is that mainland Turks are particularly noticeable, whereas other returnees are not. Thus, when the London Turk returns to Cyprus, or even visits for a holiday, he is immediately absorbed into the society at the level of kinship. He returns to his relatives as brother, son, or cousin. Sometimes young men on holiday continue to relate to each other on the basis of their 'London-ness' and can be found congregating on certain beaches; otherwise London Turks in Cyprus never come together to form a group of any kind. Similarly they do not differ in appearance from Turkish Cypriots in Cyprus. Even though they try to look like rich tourists, this is merely part of the London image and is one way of *showing* their relatives that they are making the right decision by remaining in England. Not so with the mainlanders. Unabsorbed into Cypriot society on a kinship basis, they are allocated houses in specific areas of a town, or even whole villages. This means that they are marked out merely in terms of their settlement patterns so that certain streets and villages are known by Turkish Cypriots as being *Turkiyeli* (mainland Turkish). The fact that practically all these people are villagers from Anatolia and the Black Sea region, uneducated and poor, also differentiates them from Cypriots and provides the latter with grounds for prejudice and discrimination.

An irony exists here. On the one hand the Turkish Cypriot will tell of the bravery and hardiness of the Turkish soldiers who intervened on his behalf in 1974, whose success was due to their tough training in Turkey, living in the mountains, 'eating frogs and snakes'. On the other hand he makes it quite clear that this is not at all the sort of person he wants living next door. The mainlander is respected for his fighting ability, but not for his cultural ingenuity ('they saw the legs off tables'), commonsense ('after two years they still ride their bicycles on the right'), or Western ways ('they wear shalvar'). This dichotomy is all pervasive. The civilised/ Western category he uses for himself is constantly contrasted to the uncivilised/Oriental category that is the lot of the Turkiyeli. Even the religiosity of the mainlander is used in the process of ethnic delineation ('they build mosques before schools'). This classification is strictly relative, and Turkish Cypriots do not think of all mainlanders as being uncivilised or overreligious. It is also reciprocated in this particular context as the mainlanders think the Cypriots are sinfully irreligious and not 'pure' Turks at all, having been exposed to the corrupting influence of the Greeks and the West generally. But the fact remains that there exist these cultural differences between Turkiyelis and Turkish Cypriots in present day Cyprus, and these are exaggerated and extended by Cypriots beyond the sphere of reality into the realm of myth.

The reasons for this are fairly obvious. They relate to perceived inequalities and ironies caused by the war and to the indiscriminate way that rewards and punishments seem to have been handed out. Thus the Turkiyeli is, for the most part, thought of as an economic parasite; as having come with the intent not to work but to cash in on the economic potential of post-war Cyprus. Since most things of value, from businesses to the most productive land and classier houses, tended to be in Greek hands prior to 1974, this economic potential is considerable. Those Turkish Cypriots from the south who have benefited economically, perhaps by being allocated a larger house or more land than they originally owned, have had to pay for it in other ways. They have left their villages, their homes, often their neighbours and friends, and for the older people especially, no amount of additional land is recompense for the loss of these. The Turkiyeli on the other hand is not seen as having lost or suffered in any way at all. Even though there was some loss of life among the mainland soldiers during the initial phase of the war, the fact that mainlanders now receive benefits for which many of the Turkish Cypriots themselves are not eligible (subsidies on certain foods, for example) makes them an object of considerable resentment.

I would also suggest that mainland Turks in present day Cyprus fulfil an important social role for the Turkish Cypriots hitherto played by the Greeks: namely that of scapegoat. As scapegoats, both Turkiyeli and Greek have, by representing the outside-in-opposition, facilitated the maintenance of ethnic distinctiveness. The fact that Turkish Cypriots and mainlanders are not naturally separated by language or religion has meant that the cultural differences which do exist have had to be greatly exaggerated for them to serve as efficient boundary-maintaining mechanisms. Conversely, Turkish Cypriots have not had to invent differences with Greek Cypriots to explain or justify their antagonism to them, as differences have always existed. But it is ironic nowadays to hear the occasional remark which indicates that the speaker is actually identifying himself first as a Cypriot and only secondly as a Turk, something he would probably never have done prior to July 1974. As one man said after considering the relative merits of his ethnic neighbours, past and present: 'At least the Greeks were human beings. . . .'

But the significance of this much emphasised cultural disparity, used in the ethnic demarcation process by Turkish Cypriots against their mainland neighbours, can only be grasped when the relationship between the two groups is considered in another environment. In fact, and perhaps unfortunately for our purposes, there are relatively few mainland Turks in London, and many of these are students. The thousand or so students, some of whom help swell the ranks of the various political organisations referred to earlier, are not those with whom the ordinary Turkish Cypriot comes into contact. They have usually come straight from Turkey to complete their education and have little prior experience in Britain. Neither is there contact with the 300 or so government and administrative personnel who staff the Turkish Embassy and Consulate, and the Anglo-Turkish Association. Rather it is the working population, concentrated in the same type of employment (especially catering) and living in the same areas, which typifies the Turkiyeli for the Turkish Cypriot in London. This category of mainlanders, which numbers over 4,000 not including dependants (Turkish Consulate General statistics), is merely a tiny proportion of the 850,000 Turkish mainlanders who are working in Europe at the present time (Paine 1974:122). This means that a Cypriot family in Britain is likely to have only occasional contact with a very few mainlanders. This is not to imply that frequency of contact between two groups is necessary for the formation of ethnic attitudes. Once an ethnic stereotype has been established it takes very little for the attitudes which underlie the stereotype to become self-sustaining, and they can be reinforced merely by the infrequent interaction of individuals. Incidents which are interrupted as typifying group characteristics—as defined by the stereotype—are easily relayed to the group by selective gossip.

In London, however, this ethnic stereotype is not employed very often. That is to say, although Cypriot Turks will in conversation distinguish a mainlander terminologically (by referring to him or her as a Turkiyeli), this need not have derogatory overtones, though it may, depending on the context. Thus, in normal circumstances visiting will occur and occasion marriages will be arranged between Cypriots and mainlanders. It is only if things go wrong that ethnic differences are used to justify a breakdown in relationships. To give an example: a Cypriot girl and a Turkiyeli boy were registered as married (*nikâh*) within two weeks of meeting each other in 1975. This hurried arrangement was necessary because the boy's visa had expired and only by marrying a British citizen, which the girl was, could stay in Britain. This also suited the girl who had wanted to get married for some time; at 23 she was aware that she had passed the age when most Turkish girls get married—between 17 and 19. Besides, she thought she would get on well with her husband once they became better acquainted. Unfortunately, however, the couple soon found they were not at all suited; the boy's visits became less frequent and then ceased altogether. (True to Turkish custom the couple were not yet living together as there had been no *düğün*, or marriage feast.) Realising that there was to be no future in her marriage the girl eventually started proceedings for an annulment. The reaction of her Cypriot family, who had been instrumental in arranging the marriage in the first place, was predictable. Not only was their daughter's husband immediately characterised as untrustworthy and deceitful, but this stereotype was extended to cover *all* mainlanders. What initially began as a quarrel between two individuals became explained by their families as a basic difference in attitudes and standards obtaining between Cypriots and mainlanders.

Thus ethnic identity is made relevant by the actors themselves in situations of conflict or disagreement. The reason why an ethnic stereotype is not used at other times and on a group level is, I suggest, because Turkish Cypriots do not see the existence of mainland Turks in Britain as a threat to their own interests as individuals. Economically, they are not regarded as competitors; ideologically they are of the same mould and are seen as, if anything, more traditional and certainly more religious. However, these characteristics are not reinterpreted as they are in Cyprus to mean 'backward' and 'uncivilised'; there is no reason to delineate the ethnic boundary with such fervour. Besides, the religiosity of the Turkiyelis is positively utilised by Turkish Cypriots in London when it comes to finding someone to conduct a *mevlit*. This is a religious meeting, held usually in memory of someone who has died. In London it is usually performed at the house of a close relative and it will be attended by as many female kin and friends of the deceased as possible. Special poems (*the* mevlit) depicting the birth of the prophet Mohammed are read in the original Arabic. It is more likely that the poems will be known to the old Turkiyeli women than to the Cypriots (who in Cyprus rely on their *hoca*—religious teachers). Thus in London, Turkish Cypriots invariably turn to a nearby Turkiyeli family on these occasions. The Turkiyeli women will come to the house, often bringing a score of her female relatives who are accorded a great deal of hospitality by their Cypriot hosts. Sometimes the family will hold a *mevlit* once a year in memory of a very near relative; sometimes they will be held purely as thanksgiving occasions, for a new-born child or a new house, for example. Thus a Turkish Cypriot family might come to know the Turkiyeli woman and her kin quite well over time, and become dependent on her for this service.

We have so far discussed the relations between Turkish Cypriots and two other ethnic populations, Greek Cypriots and mainland Turks, in different environments, London and Cyprus. The larger issue has been the separate development undergone by a migrant population and its home society. Up to this point however, only those ethnic relationships that Turks in London and Cyprus have *in common* have been considered. But in order to fully appreciate the complexity of the interethnic situation in London this comparative aspect must now be set aside so that the relations Turkish Cypriots have with other groups can be briefly considered.

Interethnic Relations: Turkish Cypriots in London

Turkish Cypriots in Cyprus have had little sustained contact with minority populations other than Greeks and, of late, Turkish mainlanders, though it might be argued that over a century of contact with the British has helped develop the 'superior culture' complex which currently plays an important part in the delineation of Cypriot-mainlander boundaries. On the whole, however, contact with people of other nationalities is minimal and has not taken place on a group level. Apart from the British on sovereign bases and the contingent of Ancient Brits (the self-defined colony of 200 or so Britons who still live in the north), the only minority population of which I am aware is a small group of Pakistanis who have settled since the 1974 war, and who now live and work among Turks quite unobtrusively.

There is certainly nothing here to compare with the ethnic mosaic facing the Turkish Cypriot in London. For although Greek Cypriots and, to a much lesser extent, mainland Turks are the paramount reference groups, the mere fact that the majority of the society is neither Greek nor Turkish means that everyday contact with others is inevitable. However, because most Turks in Britain live in London, and the majority of these in boroughs with a considerable immigrant population (Haringey, Islington, Lewisham, and Southwark for example), it is not a simple matter of interacting with the English majority. Indeed, attitudes toward the English seem to be rather vague and ambivalent. On occasions they are seen to epitomise everything that is 'modern' and therefore commendable; at other times this same modernity becomes reinterpreted as immorality, which of course is not commendable and must be guarded against. Neither of these two reactions persist as a result of knowing English people personally, however. Even those friendships that develop at school and which are not hindered by a language barrier (as relations between an Englishwoman and an older Turkish migrant would be), are not usually continued when the individuals concerned leave school and start working. In the case of girls this is because of the pressures that operate to draw them back into the all-Turkish milieu once they become marriageable. Initially the boys have much more freedom to continue associating with their non-Turkish friends, as their activities in this pre-marital period are not circumscribed by their parents or kin. But after marriage, they too are usually drawn back into the ethnic environment, to which their wives, by this time, are already accustomed.

Yet, despite this uncertainty about who the English are and what they represent, Turks have adopted many English racist attitudes toward members of other groups, particularly West Indians and Africans. Pakistanis incite less prejudice, partly because their settlement patterns do not coincide with those of Cypriots and they are therefore less visible, partly because they are Moslem, and partly because they are perceived as being 'less black'. That this prejudice has evolved in Britain is almost beyond doubt. It is unlikely that the original migrants would have had contact with black people before they came to England as there are *very* few black Moslems in either Turkey or Cyprus; moreover the phraseology used to express these attitudes is the same as that used by the English themselves. Significantly, racial attitudes are often expressed in my presence as if to say, 'We're like you (English and white), not like them (foreign and black).' But this sort of ethnic stereotype used by Turks in London is of a very different order from that which is used for Greek Cypriots and mainland Turks. It is not that Turkish Cypriots see West Indians or Africans (between whom in any case they do not distinguish) as threatening to their own individual interests. They do not occupy the same economic niches and they are not even seen as constituting a moral threat, as are the English on other occasions. Rather it is that in certain situations, notably when working with or simply getting to know English people, it is expedient for Turks to identify with the English majority and the colour difference is the most obvious criterion for creating a common outgroup. Most Turks are also aware of the associations that the term 'immigrant' has for the English. This follows from their reading of the British press, which is mostly confined to the popular dailies—just those which are apt to sensationalise·stories concerning immigrants and the Englishman's attitude to them.

It is not therefore surprising that the Turkish family, surrounded as it usually is by non-Turkish neighbours, does not like to think it is being classed as 'immigrant'. And again, the most obvious means of getting into the non-immigrant category is to stress that they are white. All the associations that 'black' has for the English working class are then advanced to justify this prejudice and support the ideological and cultural 'Englishness' that they ascribe to themselves. What is interesting here is not so much that group stereotypes are invoked for outsiders who have no particular relevance to Turkish Cypriots as an ethnic group. Rather it is that Turkish Cypriots themselves have adopted those stereotypes already in use by the English majority and, in doing so, differentiate themselves from other minority groups—a status which, for that moment in time, they cease to ascribe to themselves.

Conclusion

My main concern in this essay has been to consider the nature of the relationship between the migrant group and its home society. The ethnic relations of Turkish Cypriot migrants in London have been compared to those of the Turkish Cypriot population of present day Cyprus. This focus provided an example of a phenomenon which I suggested could have been exemplified in a number of ways—for the financial and familial independence of migrant and home societies has enabled the two groups to develop fairly independently of each other. Thus, even though Turks in Cyprus still tend to think of their relatives in London as mere sojourners who are working abroad for a while, and despite the fact that family disputes are still maintained between individuals in the two countries, it is true that many basic institutions of Turkish Cypriot life have been transformed in the move to London. They have also undergone changes in Cyprus since the original migrants left. This is important because it is usually assumed that the home society remains static and that it is the migrant population which, on its return, introduces new ideas and so influences the otherwise unchanging country of origin. But with Turkish Cypriots there have been influences at work in London and Cyprus so that both populations have adapted, and for the most part differently. In terms of ethnic relations this adaptation has taken some paradoxical turns: for example, relations between, say, Turkish Cypriots and mainlanders in London are not only dissimilar to those between the same groups in Cyprus, but emphatically contrast with them.

Ethnicity is not, as noted earlier, a static phenomenon. Thus in Cyprus, Turkish Cypriot attitudes to Turkiyelis might change considerably in the next few years: if, for example, 'returnees' from the mainland settle permanently and inter-marry with local Turkish Cypriots. But it is possible that relations between the two communities might get much worse, especially if a further influx of mainlanders settle in the still underpopulated north. However, a plan to transport another 45,000 Turkiyelis to Cyprus has now apparently been abandoned due to the antagonism of the Turkish Cypriots towards the 18,000 who have already settled (*Sunday Times*, 26 September 1976).

A settlement of the Cyprus problem might also be expected to change not so much the nature of ethnic relations currently observable in the north, but the intensity of xenophobic attitudes toward outsiders. For, despite the relative stability of the current political arrangement, there are still feelings of great uncertainty—an awareness that war might be resumed one day, and worse, that a permanent peace might never be achieved. Moreover, the fact that the Turkish Cypriots are having difficulty finding international markets for citrus fruits and other exportable goods has produced a siege mentality, a feeling that all of the non-Turkish world is against them. This includes the British who, as former guarantors of the constitution, it is felt have especially let them down. This feeling of isolation, together with the political uncertainty, perpetuates for the individual the relevance of identifying himself in ethnic terms. It will only be when, or rather if, Turkish Cyprus is recognised as legitimate that ethnic status will cease to be so relevant in day-to-day affairs.

As for the London side, predictions however tentative are more difficult to make, partly because we are faced here with a more complex pattern of interethnic relations and interdependence. In Cyprus at the present time, relations between Cypriot and mainland Turks are quite straightforward: mutual resentment. In London, however, it is economically advantageous for Turks to play down their differences with Greek Cypriots, although there is no reason to suppose that it is equally advantageous for any but a minority of Greeks—those whose businesses depend on Turkish patronage, for example—to do the same. Note that it was the Greek bridegroom who could not afford to tell his parents that he was getting married to a Turkish girl, rather than vice versa; her family accepted the match much more readily and, in the end, turned up at the wedding in force. Indeed, on the whole Greek Cypriots in London have less need and perhaps also less desire to be understanding in such a situation. Not only are they more self-sufficient, but it is the Greeks in Cyprus who have suffered most as a result of the 1974 war. Economically they have been the biggest losers because they were once the dominant group. Psychologically there is no doubt that they have 'lost' and the Turks have 'won', especially as it becomes obvious that the Turks will make few concessions territorially, and that the *de facto* arrangement on Cyprus is, for them, a completely satisfactory one. It might therefore be expected that the bitterness will be on the Greek side, though how this has affected the attitudes of the Greek Cypriot majority in London to their Turkish neighbours is beyond the scope of this research. The current political climate makes it impossible for the fieldworker to fraternise equally with Greeks and Turks.

All that can be said regarding Turkish-Greek relations in London, therefore, is that individuals will continue to act rationally in terms of their own perspectives: they will make compromises which, while not overstepping the norms of social distance, will allow them to attain their own personal economic goals. Meanwhile a generation is growing up which knows the beaches of Cyprus better than its politics and, in many cases, does not care very much about either. The future rests with these people and their children.

NOTE

The research on which this paper is based was made possible by grants from the Social Science Research Council (1974–6) and by an award from the Governing Body of the School of Oriental and African Studies (1976–7). The author is also grateful to the Central Research Fund, University of London, for photographic equipment and for a grant to cover expenses (1975–6). Thanks are also extended to Dr. Robin Oakley for the use of his statistical data on the Cypriot population in Britain and to Dr. Richard Tapper for his helpful criticisms of preliminary drafts. Finally, the author would like to thank Edward Condon for his assistance, encouragement, and invaluable criticisms both during the course of fieldwork and in the writing of this paper.

REFERENCES CITED

Allen, Sheila, 1971, *New Minorities, Old Conflicts: Asian and West Indian Migrants in Britain*. New York: Random House.

Banton, Michael, 1967, *Race Relations*. London: Tavistock.

Barth, Frederik, 1969a, 'Introduction'. In *Ethnic Groups and Boundaries: The Social Organization of Culture Difference*. London: George Allen and Unwin.

Barth, Frederik, 1969b, 'Pathan Identity and its Maintenance'. In Ibid.

Cohen, Abner, 1969, *Custom and Politics in Urban Africa*. London: Routledge and Kegan Paul.

Cohen, Abner, 1971, 'The Politics of Ritual Secrecy'. *Man* (n.s.) 6: 427–48.

Cohen, Abner, 1974a, *Two-Dimensional Man*. London: Routledge and Kegan Paul.

Cohen, Abner, 1974b, 'The Lesson of Ethnicity'. In *Urban Ethnicity* (ed.) Abner Cohen. London: Tavistock.

Dench, Geoff, 1975, *The Maltese in London*. London: Routledge and Kegan Paul.

George, Vic and Geoffrey Millerson, 1966–67, 'The Cypriot Community in London'. *Race* 8:277–92.

Kohler, David (ed.), 1974, *Ethnic Minorities in Britain: Statistical Data*. London: Community Relations Commission.

Krausz, Ernest, 1971, *Ethnic Minorities in Britain*. London: MacGibbon and Kee.

Little, Kenneth, 1970, *West African Urbanization: A Study of Voluntary Associations in Social Change*. London: Cambridge University Press.

Moerman, Michael, 1965, 'Ethnic Identification in a Complex Civilization: Who are the Lue?' *American Anthropologist* 67: 1215–30.

Oakley, Robin, 1970, 'The Cypriots in Britain'. *Race Today* 2: 99–102.

Oakley, Robin, 1971, 'Cypriot Migration and Settlement in Britain'. Unpublished D.Phil. Thesis, University of Oxford.

Orans, Martin, 1965, *The Santal: A Tribe in Search of a Great Tradition*. Detroit: Wayne State University Press.

Paine, Suzanne, 1974, *Exporting Workers: The Turkish Case*. London: Cambridge University Press.

Parkin, David, 1974, 'Congregational and Interpersonal Ideologies in Political Ethnicity'. In Abner Cohen (ed.), *Urban Ethnicity*. London: Tavistock Publications.

Philpott, Stuart B., 1973, *West Indian Migration: The Montserrat Case*. London: Athlone Press.

Patterson, Sheila, 1969, *Immigration and Race Relations in Britain*. London: Oxford University Press for the Institute of Race Relations.

Rose, Eliot J. B. and Associates, 1969, *Colour and Citizenship*. London: Oxford University Press for the Institute of Race Relations.

Shibutani, Tamotsu and Kian M. Kwan, 1965, *Ethnic Stratification*. New York: Macmillan.

Suzuki, Peter, 1966, 'Peasants Without Ploughs: Some Anatolians in Istanbul'. *Rural Sociology* 31:428–38.

Watson, James L., 1975, *Emigration and the Chinese Lineage: The Mans in Hong Kong and London*. Berkeley: University of California Press.

CONTRIBUTORS

CATHERINE BALLARD was born in Steyning, Sussex (1945) and read Anglo-Saxon and Norse at the University of Cambridge. Later she worked in India and from 1971 to 1975 was a Research Associate at the SSRC Research Unit on Ethnic Relations at the University of Bristol. She is currently lecturing on Indian and Pakistani minorities in Britain.

ROGER BALLARD was born in York, England (1943) and read Social Anthropology at the University of Cambridge. From 1966 until 1968 he carried out fieldwork in a village near Simla in the foothills of the Himalayas, and gained his Ph.D. from the University of Delhi in 1969. From 1970 to 1975 he was a Research Associate at the SSRC Research Unit on Ethnic Relations at the University of Bristol. During this period he carried out a second field project in the Punjab and in Leeds. In 1975 he was appointed Research Lecturer in Race Relations at the University of Leeds.

PAMELA CONSTANTINIDES was born in England and brought up in Australia. She attended University College London where, in 1968, she graduated with a B.A. honours degree in Social Anthropology. A period of research into women's spirit possession cults followed with fieldwork in the Northern Sudan (1969–1971). She was awarded a Ph.D. from the London School of Economics and Political Science (University of London) in 1972. From then until the birth of her son in 1975, she was first Research Officer and subsequently a Lecturer in Social Anthropology at the L.S.E.

NANCY FONER is an Associate Professor of Anthropology at the State University of New York (Purchase). Born in New York City in 1945, she graduated from Brandeis University and received her Ph.D. from the University of Chicago. She has done fieldwork in rural Jamaica (1968–69) and among Jamaican migrants in London (1973). Her publications include *Status and Power in Rural Jamaica* (1973) and *Jamaica Farewell*, a book now in press.

ESTHER N. GOODY was born in Ohio, USA, in 1932 and educated at Antioch College (B.A. in Sociology). She received her Ph.D. in Social Anthropology from the University of Cambridge. She has done fieldwork among the Gonja of northern Ghana in 1956–57, 1964, and 1965. Her research has focused on problems of family life, marriage, and fostering of children. Her publications include *Contexts of Kinship* (1973) and numerous articles on African ethnology. Since 1966 Dr. Goody has been a Fellow and Lecturer in Social Anthropology at New Hall, Cambridge.

CHRISTINE MUIR GROOTHUES was born in Blackpool, England, in 1944 and received her B.A. in Social Anthropology from the University of Cambridge. She went on to do a Diploma in Social Administration at the London School of Economics and later worked as a Child Care Officer in London from 1967 to 1969. She spent two years (1972-73) in Ghana doing research on child development. Since her return she has worked as a social worker for the Commonwealth Students' Children Society. Christine Groothues is co-author of two reports and an article in *Race*.

SARAH LADBURY was born in Leicestershire in 1951. She has a B.A. honours degree in Anthropology from the University of Durham (1972) and an M.A. in Near and Middle East Area Studies from the School of Oriental and African Studies, University of London (1973). She is currently completing her Ph.D. thesis at SOAS on research carried out in London and Cyprus on Turkish Cypriots. Future plans include field research in Eastern Turkey.

ROBIN PALMER was born in Newcastle-upon-Tyne in 1947 and received his B.A. honours at the University of Durham and an M.A. in Anthropology from the University of Sussex in 1973. He is currently Lecturer in Social Anthropology at the University of Cape Town. He has conducted field research in Italy and in London, and is completing his D.Phil. thesis for the University of Sussex.

SHEILA PATTERSON was born in Maidstone, Kent, and holds a B.A. honours in Classics from the University of Oxford and a Ph.D. in Anthropology from the London School of Economics. She has worked as a translator for the Polish Ministry of Information, London, 1941–50, and has served as editor of *New Community* (Journal of the Community

Relations Commission, London) since 1971. She is also an Honorary Research Fellow in Anthropology at University College London. Dr. Patterson's publications include *Colour and Culture in South Africa* (1953), *Dark Strangers* (1963), *Immigrants in Industry* (1968), *Immigration and Race Relations in Britain* (1969), and (editor with Meyer Fortes) *Studies in African Social Anthropology* (1975).

STUART B. PHILPOTT was born in Toronto, Canada, in 1933 and educated at the University of British Columbia (M.A. 1963) and the London School of Economics (Ph.D. 1971). He is now an Associate Professor of Anthropology at the University of Toronto and has also taught at the University of British Columbia and Memorial University of Newfoundland. Dr. Philpott has researched and written articles on British Columbia native workers, Canadian industrial anthropology, and sign language. He is author of *West Indian Migration* (1973) and numerous papers dealing with the island of Montserrat.

VERITY SAIFULLAH KHAN was born in Windsor, England, in 1949 and educated at the University of Sussex (B.A. Social Anthropology) and at the University of Bradford (Ph.D. Anthropology). She is currently a Research Associate at the SSRC Research Unit on Ethnic Relations at the University of Bristol; she has also worked for the Runnymede Trust on problems of bilingual education. She spent a year in the Punjab (1970–71) as a teacher and later conducted field research in Bradford and in Mirpur, Pakistan (1971–74). She is currently directing a project on ethnicity and work among Asian women in London. Her publications include numerous articles on the Asian minority in Britain.

JAMES L. WATSON was born in Iowa, USA, in 1943 and educated at the University of Iowa (B.A. Chinese Studies) and at the University of California, Berkeley (Ph.D. Anthropology, 1972). He is currently Lecturer in Asian Anthropology at the School of Oriental and African Studies, University of London and has previously taught at the University of Hawaii, Honolulu. Dr. Watson is author of *Emigration and the Chinese Lineage* (1975) and several articles on traditional Chinese ethnography. He has conducted field research in Hong Kong, London, and Honolulu.

Index

Greek Cypriot, 273–4, 277, 283–4, 294–6; Turkish Cypriot, 308–10, 323; Greek-Turkish, 316–17

Marxist analysis, 11–14

Middle class: among minorities, 6, 16; Pakistani, 74; West Indian, 97–100; Chinese 195, 198

Migrants: as change agents, 4, 210; recruitment of, 12–13, 27, 72, 190–191; ideology of, 98–100; disillusionment on return, 146, 263; ties to home, 207–9, 223–5, 260–1, 291–3

Migration: research on, 2; effects on home villages, 3–4, 100, 209–10; types of, 4; causes of, 6–7; rural-urban, 6, 63ff, 210; Marxist analyses of, 11–14; chain, 31, 66, 189–190, 243–4, 251ff; of families, 33–35, 201; return, 41, 83, 100, 137–138, 146, 262–6; organisation of, 188–91; exile versus economic, 214–15; seasonal, 247–9; chain repatriation, 264–6; *See also* Myth of return, Push-pull

Medical problems, 203

Moslems. *See* Religion

Myth of return, 5, 40–1, 138

Naipaul, V. S., 120

Naturalisation, 238

Networks (social): West African, 173–4; West Indian, 114–15

Newspapers: and Chinese public image, 207; Polish, 236–7; Greek, 282

Ng Kwee-choo, 193

Nursing, 167, 203

Oakley, Robin, 271–2, 305, 308, 312

Pakistanis, in Britain, 57ff

Partnerships (business), 192

Patterson, Sheila, 11

Peach, Ceri, 7, 123

Pedlars, 21, 28–9

Peristiany, John, 275

Philpott, Stuart, 303

Poles, in Britain, 214ff

Powell, Enoch, 43, 133

Press. *See* Newspapers

Price, Charles, 126, 243, 252–3, 266

Professional class: among migrants, 15–16; South Asian, 51–2; West African, 164–8; Chinese, 195, 198;

Polish, 219–20; Greek Cypriot, 278. *See also* Leaders, Middle class

Punjab, 24ff, 59–60

Push-pull, models of migration, 6–7, 123–4, 244, 249

Race, concept of, 8

Race relations, research on, 11–12, 58, 301

Racial discrimination: against South Asians, 2, 46–7, 52–5; against West Indians, 2, 129ff, 145; against Chinese, 206–7; among Turkish Cypriots, 326–7. *See also* Xenophobia

Reggae music, 17, 145

Religion: Sikh, 37; Pakistani, 62, 81; West Indian in Britain, 110–11; in West Africa, 160–1; Polish, 219, 230–3; Italian, 244; Greek Orthodox, 286–7; Turkish Cypriot, 306–307, 324

Remittances: dependence on, 4, 13; South Asian, 31; West Indian, 95, 100–2, 106–7, 112–16; Chinese, 207–8; Polish, 224; Italian, 260; Greek Cypriot, 292; Turkish Cypriot, 303

Repatriation. *See* Migration

Resettlement camps, 226

Restaurants: Indian, 24; Chinese, 181ff; take away trade, 191–2; restaurant niche, 193–5; Italian, 246ff; Greek Cypriot, 281–2

Return migration. *See* Migration, Myth of return

Return trips, 70–1, 209, 262–3, 292–293

Rex, J. and R. Moore, 52

Rural-urban migration. *See* Migration

Schools: South Asians in British, 46; Pakistanis in British, 83–5; Pakistani mosque school, 85; in West Indies, 97–8, 134ff; West Indians in British, 135–8; West Africans in British, 153ff; in West Africa, 155–62; Chinese in British, 182, 198, 201–2; Poles in British, 220; Polish language, 228–30; Greek school, 284–6

Seamen: South Asian, 21–3, 65–6; Chinese, 189; Cypriot, 271